THE COMPLETE
OCEAN SKIPPER

ADLARD COLES
Bloomsbury Publishing Plc
50 Bedford Square, London, WC1B 3DP, UK
29 Earlsfort Terrace, Dublin 2, Ireland

BLOOMSBURY, ADLARD COLES and the Adlard Coles logo are trademarks of
Bloomsbury Publishing Plc

First published in Great Britain 2016
This edition published 2022

A catalogue record for this book is available from the British Library
Library of Congress Cataloguing-in-Publication data has been applied for

ISBN: HB: 978-1-3994-0052-7
ePub: 978-1-3994-0051-0
ePDF: 978-1-3994-0050-3

2 4 6 8 10 9 7 5 3 1

Designed and typeset in 10/13pt Myriad Pro Light by Susan McIntyre
Printed and bound in China by Toppan Leefung Printing

FSC
www.fsc.org
MIX
Paper from
responsible sources
FSC® C104723

All photography © Cunliffe Images with the exception of the following:
Gregor Schuster/Getty Images © 4–5; EJ Lovell © 8; Jeff Rotman/Getty Images © 113;
Leon Schulz © 114, 216; Lorna Geraghty © 188; MSOS © 244, 246, 247, 248;
Planet Observer/Getty Images © 99; Yachting Monthly © 204

This product has been derived in part from material obtained from the UK Hydrographic Office with the
permission of the UK Hydrographic Office, Her Majesty's Stationery Office. Figures 10.4, 10.5, 10.14, 10.27,
10.28 and 11.2 © British Crown Copyright, 2022. All rights reserved.

THIS PRODUCT IS NOT TO BE USED FOR NAVIGATION
Notice: The UK Hydrographic Office (UKHO) and its licensors make no warranties or representations, express
or implied, with respect to this product. The UKHO and its licensors have not verified the information within
this product or quality assured it.

Note: Every effort has been made to find the copyright holders of any material used in this book that is not
the author's own.

To find out more about our authors and books visit www.bloomsbury.com
and sign up for our newsletters

THE COMPLETE
OCEAN SKIPPER

DEEP-WATER VOYAGING, NAVIGATION AND YACHT MANAGEMENT

2nd Edition

TOM CUNLIFFE

ADLARD COLES

LONDON · OXFORD · NEW YORK · NEW DELHI · SYDNEY

CONTENTS

Acknowledgements

Leon Schulz, of Regina-Sailing, the modern ocean sailor, for help with photographs. John and Margaret Hart for their continuing encouragement and expert input. Nick Skeates, Annie Hill, Andrew Shortland, the late Harold Hudson, Ian MacGillivray, James Wharram, and all those other skippers and wanderers who have been my friends and my counsellors. My shipmates John Lovell, Chris Stewart, Pol Bergius and Martin Smith; in particular the memory of the longshoreman-sailor-philosopher Robert Riddle, along with many more trusted friends who have sailed the seas with me and put up with my behaviour. Doctor Spike Briggs of MSOS for all the medical help he supplies to sailors worldwide and for his invaluable assistance to me. To Hannah and Dan, my family, who have continued to ship out in fair weather and mainly foul when most would have long since given up. And Roz, without whom none of this would have come to pass.

Further reading

For heavy weather, study *Storm Tactics* by Lin and Larry Pardey, *Heavy Weather Sailing* by Peter Bruce, and *Surviving the Storm* by Steve and Linda Dashew. For big, fast boats read Steve Dashew in general. For surviving on very little money, read Annie Hill's *Voyaging on a Small Income*. To secure a successful one-year family sabbatical you can't beat Leon Schulz's *The Missing Centimetre*. If you want inspiration about adventuring in the modern world try *Brave or Stupid* by Tracey Christiansen.

All manner of useful books are available today. The books are generally far better than relatively sketchy internet content. To read the final word on taking a hard look at yourself, buying the right boat, understanding your motivations and sailing away on the sort of money that wouldn't even buy a family car, don't miss *The Boat They Laughed At* by Max Liberson. This may not suit the dream image of your perfect yacht, but to achieve happiness we all must define our objectives. Not only is Max an entertaining read, he shows us that even when times are hard there is more than one way to skin the proverbial cat.

I know nearly all these people and have corresponded with those I haven't met. You couldn't have better mentors.

INTRODUCTION

The Ocean Skipper

My first real deep-sea experience came in the form of a 90-ton trading ketch, bought out of commerce in the Baltic in 1968. She was fully crewed but a long way from her first blush of youth. We made the masts and spars ourselves. Five years later I sailed from England bound for Brazil with just my wife in our ancient 32ft Norwegian pilot cutter designed by the great Colin Archer, a vessel whose engine failed more often than it ran. So wretched was this machine that for over a year of intense cruising we managed without power of any sort. Neither of these boats had any electronics whatsoever. Navigation was by the sun, planets and stars – a situation that continued into the early 1990s in subsequent boats. Steering on our boat was by windvane. The ketch didn't even have electric lighting and I spent many an evening trimming and filling the sidelights, then hanging them in the rigging. It really does seem like a different world.

Since then, although I have favoured traditional boats, my approach to seafaring has moved with the times. After the Colin Archer came family and a 51ft Bristol Channel Pilot Cutter built in 1911. In her we voyaged to the Arctic, the Caribbean and the US and were, I understand, only the third Western yacht to visit Soviet Russia after the 1917 revolution. With this fine vessel, I cut my teeth on GPS navigation. She was followed by *Westernman*, a 41ft replica pilot cutter designed by my good friend Nigel Irens, better known for his record-breaking multihulls. With *Westernman*, chart plotters grew up and I embraced long-range radio reception, giving me more idea of the weather than I could gain from looking at the sky and the sea and assessing the movements of the barometer. *Westernman* was built in eastern North America and her first trip was a romp home across the North Atlantic from Cape Cod to the Bishop Rock.

During all this time, I had been plying my trade as a skipper for hire. This led to a number of interesting voyages, including a 'transat' with an unstayed carbon Aerorig, which impressed me mightily. My present boat is a Mason 44 cutter, heavily built in GRP with a long keel, a powerful diesel, big tanks, metal spars and stainless rigging. Although not what you'd call a high-speed 'cruising sled', she is a thoroughly modern yacht equipped with a generator, a freezer, cabin heating, a fine autopilot, two computers, internet access and all the navigational electronics available.

To have lived through such a dramatic period of development has placed my generation of sailors in a privileged position, with what I believe to be a sound perspective on ocean sailing today. I, for one, have wholeheartedly embraced the new, but have sufficient experience of what went before to understand where some of the latest ideas fall short when tested in the courtroom of reality. I love my cold beer, my warm, dry feet, my bright lights and the complete

The author's first ocean cruiser, Colin Archer pilot cutter, **Saari**, *built by Archer himself in 1903. Note the Gunning pendulum-servo wind vane.*

lack of deck leaks. I especially enjoy knowing more or less where I am all the time, although more on that subject in Chapter 9. Today I can carry on my work as a journalist wherever I may be by virtue of modern communications. Rather than waiting months to receive mail at a poste restante, I can be in contact with my family and friends, knowing they'll receive my missives the same day, unless I'm lurking somewhere around the Date Line, in which case they might even get it before I send it. The ability to communicate easily and the general proliferation of yachts on the oceans have transformed medical planning for the far-flung sailor. The list goes on.

The result of all this progress is that there's a lot more to ocean sailing than ever there was back in the 1970s. Then, it was a matter of applying common sense to issues of victualling for the ship and her people, learning astro navigation, finding out about tropical revolving storms and how to manage a yacht caught out in one. Ocean passage planning hasn't changed much, except that we are now far better served with publications and data culled from thousands of yachts who've been actually doing it. Everything else has undergone a revolution and much of this book is about the results of that revolution, understanding them and considering how we can best use them to our advantage.

I have included a chapter on basic astro navigation and I do this without apology. It isn't much of an ocean skipper who can't deliver a position from a sun-run-sun celestial fix. It's a matter of personal satisfaction for a real sailor, not just backup in case someone sits on the GPS transmitters. I could have written this in a sort of shorthand that would allow readers to work up a position while understanding little of what they were doing. I have not been tempted by that approach. Nor have I become dewy-eyed about clever computer programs that do the job for you. There's no patronising here! If you read the chapter carefully and make sure you understand the examples, you will have sufficient knowledge to move forward into the wonderful world of star navigation. You will then join a select band of brothers and sisters in a world where science meets art, philosophy is king, and only someone with the emotional capacity of a lump of granite could fail to be moved by what is going on.

There is little in the book directly linked to ocean rallies, such as the famous ARC (Atlantic Rally for Cruisers). I am not qualified to write about them since I have never been involved in one, but they have a legitimate place in today's world. I didn't always think this way, but I changed my mind when an old friend (and I mean 'old') answered this question:

'Graham, you've always paddled your own canoe. You built your own boat and you've sailed her thousands of miles. Why do you need to sign on with this crowd to get around the world?'

'Simple,' he replied. 'I'm well into my seventies. If I start a circumnavigation now at my own speed, actuarial evidence suggests that I'll be called to the big anchorage in the sky long before I make it round. This way, the team will keep me pressing on and with luck I'll be back before I'm eighty.'

He did arrive back, he did circumnavigate with the original RAFYC Blue Water Rally and he had a great time. He should know. He was a dangerous man at a party.

The book has not been written primarily as a textbook for the British RYA/MCA Ocean Yachtmaster certificate, although I am an examiner in that system. As it happens, everything currently in the syllabus is covered, together with a good deal more, so it will serve that purpose. My intention, however, was to share a lifetime of experience in all sorts of boats on seas cold and warm with my fellow sailors. Read on, my friends. May your storms be short-lived and may the trades blow for you as nature intended when the planet first went spinning on its way.

PART 1 · THE OFFSHORE YACHT

The author's Mason 44 **Constance**.

1 HULLS FOR OCEAN SAILING

Choosing a boat for ocean sailing is different from deciding what to buy for weekends and holidays in continental waters, for two reasons. The first is that the vessel is going to be home, not an occasional bolt-hole from daily life. The second is even more serious. Weather forecasting for temperate zones such as Northern Europe and North America is now so reliable that it should be possible to cruise these waters for a lifetime and never be at sea in storm conditions. Sure, the Mediterranean can still produce local gales from nowhere, but the great winds such as the Mistral and the Bora are generally well foretold. Far out on the ocean, there is sometimes no escape.

Britain's governing body of sailing, the RYA, defines an ocean passage for the purposes of its Ocean Yachtmaster certificate as being at least 600 nautical miles between ports, mostly more than 50 miles from land. The reasoning behind this is to place a yacht beyond the limits of reliable forecasting so that, as far as can be achieved without literally crossing an ocean, she is on her own and must make the best of anything that comes. Old hands will shake their heads and remark that this distance is nothing like long enough. I have much sympathy with them, but the point to take home is the essential concept that, on the ocean, forecasting – even if you can get it – isn't necessarily going to be a ticket to a safe haven. If a storm has your name on it, then your boat must be able to ride it out safely.

Yacht club bars resound with tales of '50 knots across the deck' in places like the West Solent. I've worked there much of my life and I've rarely seen anything approaching this in terms of sustained wind force. Maybe I've been lucky, but I doubt it. Fifty knots in open water with a long ocean fetch is a different story altogether for a short-handed cruising yacht. By the time it's been howling for 24 hours out in the North Atlantic, kicking up 40ft seas that march northeastwards all the way from America, you'll be wishing you were somewhere else. When the wind veers and sends the church-high waves crazy, a small crew – even a young one – may well have run out of the stamina needed to look after the boat. Sooner or later, the time comes for her to look after them. Whether a boat points two degrees higher than the average, or has a bigger bed in the aft cabin than the next boat in the show, becomes a laughable irrelevance. One message of this book is that seaworthiness is not defined simply by a set of numbers produced by authorities obliged by their calling to define the undefinable. Knowing a boat's angle of vanishing stability is helpful, but it is a long way from the end of the story.

Boat manufacturers' propaganda promises craft after craft whose spectacular performance is only equalled by their world-beating comfort and security at sea. The truth is that nothing on the ocean is given for free. A boat that really can look after herself, perhaps by heaving to with total reliability, pointing up at around 40° and never falling into the dangerous beam-on state, is unlikely to go to windward in flat water as well as one designed for the summer Baltic, with performance and space below as the main priorities. Advertisements for the high-performance yacht will show her powering along in 15 knots of breeze with a smiling crew having a grand day out. And so they are. They may stop smiling when the boat is being knocked around in a big broken sea with the autopilot disabled, the deep-reefed mainsail overpowered and the whole business having been going on for two days. Such a yacht may put in an excellent passage time on a downwind slide to the Caribbean from Europe and give grand sport on the day-sails between the islands. She may also cruise back to Europe without drama on the low-powered steamer route via Bermuda and the Azores, but should she opt to return by the exciting route up the Eastern Seaboard of North America, taking off for Ireland from Nova Scotia or Newfoundland, it could be a different story.

The bottom line to all this is to define your objectives carefully and, above all, honestly. Armed with this brief, you can then consider the choices from a position of understanding. No boat is all things to every sailor. The successful ones are those that have been chosen wisely to suit the character of their owners and to do the job they will undertake.

Hull considerations

Generalising is always dangerous, because boats do not necessarily fit into neatly defined categories. Rigs can be different too, with certain variants often being found on particular hull types, but, so long as the main hull forms are understood, an appropriate boat may be chosen. The rig can then be accepted or modified to suit the owner. It is the hull that defines all.

A modern family cruiser with in-mast mainsail reefing.

To state that the characteristics of cruising boats are varied would fall an old-fashioned sea league short of the mark. Some boats handle predictably in harbour, even steering sweetly astern in strong winds. Others, which may be fine at sea, are blown around marinas like empty crisp packets in a pub parking lot. Many that are wonderfully steady at slow speed going ahead cannot steer astern at all, leaving otherwise competent owners embarrassed on a regular basis in tight harbours, unless they mitigate the inevitable by fitting a bow thruster. Deep-sea storm survival tactics trashed as suicidal by modern writers working with fin-keeled yachts may still be reasonably safe options for traditional yachts modelled on workboats. A modern bulb-keel flyer can scud across an ocean in half the time taken by a heavy-displacement alternative. Do you care, or do you really quite like it out there and see no need to hurry? If you opt for speed, what are the trade-offs?

Among the main factors deciding a boat's behaviour is the position of her rudder, or rudders, in relation to the keel, how long the keel is and whether the rudder is hung on the trailing edge of it, or is salient, with or without a supporting skeg. Further general issues are how beamy she is in relation to length; whether she's a heavyweight or a lightweight; how heavy her displacement; whether her forefoot is deep or cut away; how well balanced her sections are when the hull is heeled over, and the windage of her topsides in relation to her underwater lateral area.

Set out here are some of the main categories.

Long or short keel

Taking shoal draught out of the equation for the moment, the most important split among monohulls is the long and the shorter keel. There are almost infinite varieties of both, but the definition is that the long-keeler hangs her rudder from the aft end of the keel itself, while the rudder on the short-keeled boat is a separate unit mounted as far aft as practicable.

As a general principle, long-keeled yachts are heavier, with deeper body sections allowing lower freeboard. They are also often steadier at sea, resisting tendencies to eccentric behaviour and broaching in gusty weather. Not all long-keeled boats steer well. Some, influenced by rating rules in the 1950s and 60s, shortened their keels in the hunt for less wetted area, with the result that their rudders are too

An Ovni aluminium world cruiser. These boats have made many fine passages and have the advantage of a centreboard.

close to the pivot point of the boat for ideal steering, especially downwind. Long-keelers are not generally close-winded and are often outperformed by more sprightly fin-keeled boats, but they are, above all things, comfortable at sea and their modest beam means their crews are not rattling around inside when the boat falls off waves in mid-ocean. Heavy, long-keeled yachts also typically enjoy more options in heavy weather survival situations where sea room is not an issue.

Long-keeled variants

Long-keeled sailing yachts fall into three basic forms, with the usual endless variety of overlaps. These are the archetypal fishing smack/pilot cutter, followed by yachts that evolved steadily out of this from around 1850 or so until the fin broke away from the skeg in the 1960s. Last comes the modern 'long keel', often with a heavily cut-away forefoot, which has departed so far from its origins that some authorities suggest it is no longer really a long keel at all.

■ The long-keeled workboat

These boats generally feature a sensible draught, moderate beam and, by yachting standards, they are of heavy displacement. British and northern French examples often have a straight or 'plumb' stem and a deep forefoot curving only a little as it joins a straight keel whose draught increases as it runs aft to the rudder. Other nationalities had different fashions, with the lovely boats of Scandinavia featuring curved stems that continue below the water to join the straight

The author's original 1911 pilot cutter, **Hirta***, dried out for a bottom scrub.*

The author's Colin Archer pilot cutter hauled out on 'Frenchy's' slip in Grenada, 1976.

keel all the way aft to the vicinity of a mast stepped well into the boat. American working craft favoured no specific shape of bow, with everything from clipper and plumb to spoon and the handsome 'Indian Head' seen on some of the famous pilot schooners of New York and Boston. No matter what their origin, however, all these boats were built with a forefoot far deeper than most modern long-keeled yachts. At the 'blunt end', sterns were either transom (planked across, with an outboard rudder), an elegant counter where the inboard rudder post ran up through the deck well forward of the taffrail or, in the case of the Scandinavians, a true double-ended stern with the planks all landing on a gracefully swept stern post from which was hung the equally curvaceous rudder.

Boats with this sort of hull often carry gaff rig to generate the power needed to drive the weight via a relatively short mast. This would in turn demand a bowsprit from which to set one or more jibs to balance the rig.

The best examples are so well balanced that they steer themselves, particularly to windward, with the helm lashed. The deep forefoot confers the sort of grip on the water needed to heave to successfully in a big sea, while heavy displacement and ballast that may well be inside gives an easy motion that would be a revelation to anyone brought up on modern yachts.

Sadly, as in all things, these important benefits don't come without a price. Bowsprits are a nuisance in marinas, and such craft were never designed with engines in mind. Most are unwilling to handle astern under power. While many of the classier survivors or replicas are capable of good passage times, they must be driven relatively hard to achieve this and the rig, unless it has been sorted by someone who really knows their business, can be unwieldy. On the other hand, they date from an era when serious men who lived their lives on deep water strove to develop forms with time-served builders who had learned from their fathers. They are therefore supremely seaworthy and it would have been axiomatic in their original design brief (had they ever had one) that they can look after themselves when the going gets tough.

Another benefit of the workboat type is that these vessels anchor very well indeed. They have no issues about carrying a great weight of chain cable and can also ship a hefty anchor or three without feeling the extra mass. The deeper forefoot delivers a sort of in-water inertia to being blown about while lying to the ground tackle, which makes the boat far less likely to pluck her anchor out in gusty conditions.

Even if such craft are not to your taste, we all should rejoice that people are now building them again, providing a viable option for those who choose them, and an improvement in the view for all the rest.

■ The classic long-keeled yacht

Yachts had shown some departure from working craft in quality of construction right from the beginnings of purpose-built leisure craft. As time passed and racing became formalised, hull forms began to come under the influence of the rating rules. These then affected yacht design, either directly or indirectly, sometimes for better, often for worse. While beam was tampered with by, among other things, the Thames Measurement Rule, which squared it in its formula, mainstream yacht profiles were not so different from their working forebears until the latter part of the 19th century. Soon, however, the underwater bow profile was hollowed to create the reverse curve now familiar on such classics as the Scandinavian Folkboat, the British Nicholson 32 and the American Mason 44, which many consider to be the epitome of wholesome form.

Like workboats, these hulls may have a counter or a transom stern. They have sensible beam and, because the hull is deep in form as well as in draught, they are not obliged to have

The author's long-keeled Mason 44 developed form a traditional race boat.

A Rustler 36 – a classic modern long-keeled cruiser.

high freeboard to achieve reasonable headroom below decks. This makes them comfortable at sea and painless for the not-so-young to climb on and off out of a dinghy and when berthing. Such long-keeled classics are generally easily driven for their displacement. They are certain on the helm when manoeuvring ahead under power or sail and are steady at sea. Their swept forefoot, however, lacks the grip of the workboat when not moving ahead, so they do not generally heave to as well as the workboat type.

Another, perhaps unexpected, benefit is that although the relatively narrow beam does not confer the extremes of buoyancy that help beamy hulls to sail more upright, it scores well in the great stability competition. It also encourages the classical accommodation layouts that work so well. Anchoring, while not quite so spectacularly reliable as a pilot cutter type, is still pretty stable. The displacement of these boats means carrying chain is no problem, and the forefoot holds the bow reasonably steady.

■ The modern long-keeler

Towards the end of the 20th century, the forefoot was cut away even more. This creates boats with sensible beam, such as the Rustler 36, that steer well when running downwind, at the cost of lost grip on the water up forward. Such craft make first-class downwind passage-makers and many are successful world cruisers, but often their handling under sail in close quarters is not as positive as either of the other types of long-keeler because of their lack of grip forward when speed falls off. Like the classic yacht, their capacity to hold their heads up to the wind when hove-to in a big sea is not nearly as good as that of the workboat. Indeed, some end up undesirably beam-on to the weather.

Such craft can also be difficult to manoeuvre in harbour in strong winds. Unlike a workboat, which has massive lateral resistance even when stationary, the lack of forefoot makes these boats the plaything of a cross wind as soon as their speed drops below that at which the keel stalls – say 1½ knots or so. I have had a number of embarrassing moments with these deep-water boats in windy marinas so, while accepting the downwind benefits, for those who intend to spend their harbour time at anchor and are prepared to live with the lack of damping effect as they blow about, I see no real advantage over a more traditional hull shape.

That said, there are notable exceptions that somehow seem to fly in the face of logic. The Nicolson 35 is a case in point. It has no significant forefoot, yet it behaves as if it has. Don't ask me why, but if you are contemplating a boat with this hull form, I strongly advise test sailing it rigorously in heavy conditions, going fast and slow. Then try your luck in a marina with a stonking cross wind.

Short-keel variants

Taken by and large, you see a lot more short-keeled boats out in deep water these days than their long-keeled sisters. Since the mid-1960s, race-boat design has eclipsed the long keel altogether, for the simple reason that a well-designed short keel will outperform an equivalent boat with lots of underwater area. If comparative sailing performance is your primary objective, then you'll be tempted by one of these boats. It does not do to forget, however, that many long-keeled yachts sail very well and that, as boats become lighter, there is a price to be paid in comfort of motion, weight-carrying and the ability to take care of herself in bad weather.

I once asked the famous designer Nigel Irens how fast he reckoned a boat he was drawing for me would go to windward in a seaway. He replied that nobody of sound mind wanted to do that anyway. The boat's first trip was from Cape Cod, USA, to the British Isles and, of course, most of the way she was downwind. Coming north from the Caribbean bound for the Azores in another boat not noted for close-winded performance and unable to lay the course, we cracked off to 60 degrees. The boat made light of the seas, didn't heel too much and still got there in good time. On the ocean, unless racing, the sort of empirical performance figures you read in magazine boat tests don't always give us the answers we need.

■ Fin and skeg

These boats began to appear when the continual shortening of the classic yacht keel had moved the rudder too close to the centre of lateral resistance for it to work properly. The logical answer was to separate the rudder from the keel and hang it right aft for maximum leverage and this is literally what took place in the mid-1960s with the yacht *Clarion of Wight*, a successful S&S-designed racer whose rudder was moved from the keel to a new skeg built as far aft as it would go. It worked, and race-boat design never looked back.

General stability ratings are promising, although fin-and-skeg yachts are often relatively lively at anchor. Most don't steer well astern under power either and, like a large proportion of the more recent hull forms, they tend to lie beam-on to the wind if left to their own devices.

A fin-and-skeg yacht with a deep body and comparatively long fin keel.

The early 'short' keels are long by modern standards; they also remain moulded into the hull rather than being bolted on, conferring handling characteristics more like a classic yacht than later short-keeled variants. The rudder is securely hung from a skeg which, like the keel, is moulded into the hull with encapsulated ballast, while the forefoot shows signs of the classics from whence it came. Such a keel is very strong and, lacking the potential weakness of keel bolts, performs well should you be unfortunate enough to have an argument with a hard sea bottom. On older variants GRP laminations are often heavy too, with lots of fibreglass between you and ultimate destruction.

One fine example of this type of yacht is the Contessa 32. Another is the old Swan 36. Unless these boats are distorted by racing rules, which tended for part of their development period to favour pinched ends, they deliver a wholesome compromise between precise steering at sea, comfort, upwind performance when required, athletic turning in harbour, sound construction and all-round safety.

■ Fin and spade

Following race-boat fashion, the obvious route for the fin-and-skeg form to take was to whittle away displacement into a 'canoe body' with a flat or flattish floor and a bolt-on keel. The keel became shorter 'from front to back' and in some cases so short that it could no longer incorporate all the ballast required. A heavy bulb then appeared at the bottom. The arrangement is more efficient to windward, especially when complemented by a deep, hydrodynamic 'spade' rudder.

Spade rudders are usually big. They have a near-vertical trailing edge, which makes for astonishingly good steering astern in marinas and good tracking in a seaway too, as long as the boat does not heel too much. They are often 'balanced', carrying some of their area forward of the stock. This makes for light steering underway, but can create some eccentric anomalies when the helm is left for more than a second or two under power in tight quarters. The other downside is that such rudders are unsupported except for the stock with its through-hull cantilever bearings or tube. Although they have overcome their well-publicised early structural problems, spade rudders remain more vulnerable than those carried by bearings nearer to, or at, their lower ends.

A moderate aspect-ratio bolt-on keel should present no special concerns in a quality-built craft, although even in these a heavy grounding can result in the fastenings being compromised. They should therefore be checked immediately by hauling out. This is not always convenient and may be impossible on a remote coral island. It has to be said that there are boats on the market that are not so well built. Well-documented instances of such craft losing their keels altogether with catastrophic consequences mean that such a vessel must be brutally surveyed before purchase and that any contact with a rock or a solid bottom must be followed by a haul-out. All keel bolts and nuts must be accessible for monitoring in such an event. You might imagine: 'Oh well, a grounding is not going to happen to me. I'm a careful pilot.' My response to this is to quote an old Yankee schooner captain of my acquaintance, who observed that 'the floor of the ocean is paved with the bones of optimists'.

Fin-and-spade craft are usually beamier than other monohull forms. Their high internal volume confers potential for roomy accommodation, although they need extra hand holds for bad weather and often do not have them. The better ones perform well in terms of speed and pointing but, while they are pleasant enough downwind, they are usually less comfortable in a seaway upwind when the virtually non-existent forefoot pounds on every other wave. Many – but not all – such cruisers can become unbalanced when they take a heavy gust of wind. This

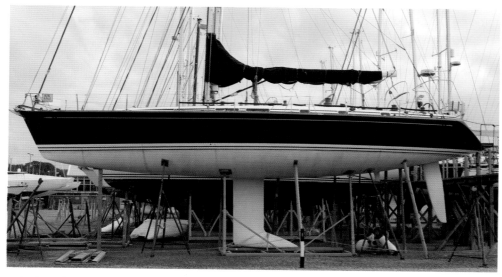

A high-performance fin-and-spade profile cruiser-racer.

A production fin-and-spade cruiser with a sail-drive engine arrangement.

leads to helming difficulties that translate into poor autopilot performance and, ultimately, into broaching when a more wholesome boat would just keep tracking along.

The salient keel and rudder, as well as the propeller, which must inevitably be outboard and supported by a bracket, are all vulnerable to picking up ropes and other obstructions that would slide off a long-keeled hull with a stern-hung rudder and propeller aperture. A bulb keel is especially vulnerable to this, unless the bulb only protrudes at the aft end of the fin. I have come on watch at dawn in a boat with a 'balanced bulb' to see two large fishing dan buoys dragging astern, their mooring lines wrapped securely around the keel, unable to slide off because the protuberance held them fast.

The pay-off for all these very real issues should be a fast, roomy downwind passage-maker, which can be a delight to steer astern.

Centreboard boats

You might imagine that, in a long-distance cruiser, draught is surely not an issue. After all, who cares if a 40ft boat draws six feet or seven when off soundings? The trouble, of course, starts when you arrive. American sailors are often tempted by the Bahamas, where an extra couple of feet of draught can disqualify a yacht from many an idyllic anchorage. Probably for this reason, the US has produced some lovely centreboard designs. One example of a classic centreboarder is the 45ft Rhodes-designed *Undina*, whose draught varies between 5ft 6in and 8ft 6in. The advantages cannot be over-stressed. Many ocean anchorages are open roadsteads. The closer a boat can lie to the beach, the quieter will be the swell that always seems to hook around the point and set the deeper yachts rolling. The benefits in shallow areas are obvious.

A shoal-draught centreboarder. Note that because of her wide, flat stern, this boat has twin rudders so that the leeward one is well immersed when heeled.

Centreboard boats are often a little beamier than their fixed-keel equivalents to take up the slack in sail-carrying capacity left by the shallower draught. This is an advantage too, as it eases space in traditional saloons and gives a bit more room along the side decks.

Dutch builders are masters of more modern centreboard construction, while such yards as Southerly in England have been producing interesting boats of extremely shallow draught that can dry out more or less vertically if required.

The handling characteristics of centreboarders are predictably similar to the fixed-keel boats they most resemble in type. Thus, the Rhodes sloop will be beautifully mannered at sea but may be a handful in a marina, while the beamy, flat-floored Southerly can play you a dirty trick or two in gusty weather and will be happier with a bow thruster for slow-speed, close-in work where her extremely shallow draught and twin rudders militate against her.

Stability is rarely a practical issue with well-designed centreboard craft. The only real downside is the question of construction. Obviously, a centreboard has the potential to cause trouble. The answer is a rigorous examination by a surveyor with experience in this area, followed by meticulous maintenance.

One final caveat. The traditional centreboarders such as *Finisterre*, designed by S&S, and *Undina* mentioned earlier have the board pivoted on a hinge so that, in the event of a grounding, it will simply swing up. The 'straight-up-and-down' daggerboards found in many designs are potentially dangerous. If they hit a rock they are immovable, so you either run hard aground and stay there, or suffer major damage as the board wrenches itself inside the hull. That said, many daggerboard boats have circumnavigated without issue, which either proves me wrong or underlines the everlasting mercy of God.

Catamarans

Catamarans are a specialised subject and deserve a whole book to themselves. A growing number are appearing on the ocean circuits, often, but by no means always, at the high end of the market. The benefits are obvious to any monuhull owner who has hung on to his glass of rum as his anchored yacht rolls her stick out, watching the neighbours in their catamaran laying out the table for a three-course dinner in the cockpit while their washing is being done for them in the machine tucked away out of sight somewhere in the forward end of the starboard hull. If the seductions of shoal draught, accommodation space and upright sailing of a mainstream 'cat' appeal, or you fancy the low-cost, seaworthiness and undisputable logic of a Wharram Polynesian

A far-ranging ocean catamaran designed by James Wharram. Numerous examples of his simple boats have made famous passages.

version, you would be well advised to study the subject in depth. Suffice it to say that, as with everything else, all that glitters may not be solid gold.

For those so inclined, multihulls have much to recommend them for deep-water sailing and far-flung anchorages. In crowded waters such as Europe, they can be an incubus for the simple reason that many marinas have no facilities to deal with their relatively extreme beam. At best, owners are charged heavily. At worst, like the rich in the New Testament, they are sent away, empty.

Some catamarans have remarkable speed potential, particularly off the wind. The fast ones are generally relatively light, with weight carrying an important factor, so you will have to watch what you are putting on board. If weight doesn't matter, the boat will, almost by definition, have relatively small performance benefits over an equivalent monohull.

One big benefit of a fast catamaran is that, given modern on-board weather forecasting, she can generally outrun serious storms. If she doesn't have the performance to make ten or twelve knots, this may not happen, so questions must be asked about how she will perform in a big sea and a howling gale.

Multihull design has produced as many variables as can be found in monohulls. For example, daggerboard catamarans generally beat upwind better than ones with some sort of keel. But to make sense of all this, if you haven't sailed multihulls in a big sea and a strong wind, do not buy one until you have. Charter options can make proper test sails a reality, so don't even be tempted by a day-sail in the Solent or the Chesapeake Bay with ten knots of breeze and a flat sea.

STABILITY

By far the greatest hazard for any sailing craft in heavy weather offshore is that of being knocked down, or even capsized, by a high, steep sea. Occasionally, boats are pitch-poled (thrown end-over-end), but here the question of stability hardly arises, since the boat is literally picked up and tossed onto her deck. This is not to say that steps cannot be taken to avoid it, but it is a rare event that comes about in only the most extreme circumstances. The majority of knockdowns are the result of being caught beam-on to the sea, and it is this condition that is conventionally considered when assessing capsize potential. An understanding of the essential theory is a great help to a skipper when deciding how best to handle a given situation and a specific boat.

Static stability

When a yacht is floating upright, her centre of buoyancy ('B') is on the fore-and-aft mid-line, as is her centre of gravity ('G'). When she heels, her immersed shape alters and B moves outboard relative to the centreline, away from G which, because it is made up of all the immovable weight in the boat, does not shift at all. We will call the shifted centre of buoyancy 'Z'. While Z is pushing up under the forces of floatation (see 'A' in Fig 1.1), G is being pulled downwards by gravity. The effect is that the boat tries to come upright. If she is rolling freely she will do so. If she is under the influence of some outside force, such as her sails, she will reach a point of equilibrium whereby she remains at that angle because the force of the wind equals her capacity to self-right.

The distance between G and Z (known as 'GZ') is a major contributing factor to capsize resistance. As the boat heels progressively, its length increases up to a maximum, decreasing once more as heel angle rises well beyond normal sailing angles ('B'). At some point, the shifting centre of buoyancy will actually pass 'under' the centre of gravity and out the other side ('C').

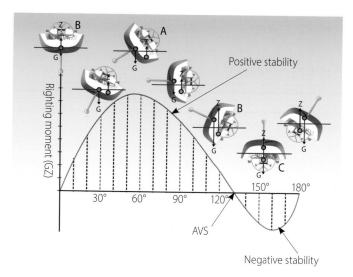

Fig 1.1 *A healthy 'GZ' Curve.*

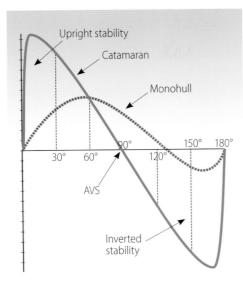

Upright stability

Catamaran

Monohull

30° 60° 90° 120° 150° 180°

AVS

Inverted stability

Fig 1.2 *Typical monohull and catamaran: comparison of static stability.*

The boat is now in dire peril because the buoyancy is still pushing up while the centre of gravity continues to pull down. These values relate to the global gravitational system rather than to any ideas the boat may have about 'this side up', and the result is 'negative GZ'. The boat is trying to invert and stay there.

Angle of vanishing stability

A GZ curve can be projected for any craft, and all builders of yachts with offshore potential should make them available to owners who ask. Inspection of her graph shows how far a boat must heel to cross the point of zero GZ. Below the zero line, GZ has a minus value, and the boat is negatively stable. The degree of heel at which this takes place is called 'the angle of vanishing stability' ('AVS').

The greater the area of graph below the line, the more stable the yacht will be upside down. Fortunately, when a boat is knocked over, the water is invariably extremely rough and it is more than likely that the next wave will flick her upright again. Nonetheless, a high value of inverted stability renders this less likely. The obvious and extreme example would be a typical catamaran, which cannot recover from capsize unassisted, but catamarans come under rather different criteria.

By comparing AVS angles from various boats, you can build some idea of how your own vessel is likely to stand up to capsizing forces, but it is important to realise that the GZ curve is only a starting point.

Further essential factors in capsize resistance

Displacement

In any mathematical formula of capsize resistance, displacement is a multiple factor. A heavier boat will, if all other factors are equal, perform better than a lighter one.

Roll inertia

This is a second element ignored by the GZ curve, but it has major significance in the dynamics of capsize. The further a parcel of weight is displaced from the centre of roll of the boat, the greater will be the arm of the roll resistance generated by its inertia. More weight means more inertia. More distance means a longer arm, or 'moment', hence greater effect. A heavy mast supplies a surprising amount of opposition to the capsizing punch of a passing wave. This is counterintuitive, but since it is already built into the centre of gravity with ballast to counterbalance it, its effect on the GZ curve is pre-ordained and may not be destructive. A heavy mast as part of the equation can thus be a powerful safety feature in the dynamic world outside the laboratory.

The authority for this proposition is the Technical Committee of the Cruising Club of America, and these first two factors explain why traditional, inside-ballasted sailing vessels such as smacks and pilot cutters were so spectacularly safe despite unimpressive GZ curves. They would have fared poorly if they ever capsized, but they almost never did.

■ Beam

High beam ratios in light, flat-floored craft confer substantial initial stability by virtue of the long righting arm as the centre of buoyancy moves outboard. The downside is that the same feature delivers a high value of inverted stability once the AVS is passed.

■ Freeboard and coachroof

High freeboard in itself does not appear to increase capsize risk, although it raises the deck so its associated weight must therefore affect the position of the centre of gravity. However, a watertight coachroof supplies an unexpected reserve of buoyancy. A 'bump' in the GZ curve for the supremely stable Contessa 32 at the angle of heel when the 'roof' becomes immersed shows this effect clearly. In terms of ultimate stability therefore, there is something to be said for the old-fashioned coachroof.

■ Long/short keel

Where all factors of beam, height of centre of gravity, depth of ballast etc. are equal, a longer keel shows no specific advantage over a short one in terms of theoretical stability. In practice, however, long keels are often associated with wholesome hull forms, moderate beam, heavy displacement, and many of the other ancillary factors adding up to better stability characteristics.

Multihull stability

Without going into too much detail, it can be said that while many monohulls of between 30ft and 50ft have an AVS of between 115 and 150 degrees, a typical multihulled cruiser becomes negatively stable at around 90° of heel. This might not sound attractive, but it must be borne in mind that such craft enjoy huge form stability by virtue of their beam and the buoyancy of the leeward hull. Their initial resistance to heeling (and hence knockdown by a passing wave) is therefore much higher. A graph of the righting energy required to capsize a monohull and a multihull of equivalent length reveals that, up to around 65 degrees, a catamaran requires a bigger slam to knock her over than an equivalent monohull, even though she is little over half the displacement. If a multihull does suffer capsize, of course, her negative stability is total and she is unlikely to right again without outside assistance.

2 SAILING RIGS FOR DEEP WATER

Take a dinghy tour around any anchorage and you'll see that although the Bermudan sloop is now the default rig, there are still many boats that break the mould. A junk-rigged schooner, perhaps, or a gaff cutter. Maybe even an unstayed carbon mast towering in aerodynamic splendour above the shining anodised forest. Who are these guys? Are they eccentrics playing out some fantasy? Are they hopeless romantics who refuse to let the past slip away, or are they innovative brains at work? They could be any of these things, but having been to sea under most sail arrangements, from square rig through gaff cutters to an unstayed carbon Aerorig, I can state with confidence that there is no such thing as an ideal formula for long-range cruising.

Racing with a full crew can be different, and proponents of various rig variants would preach otherwise, but for the short-handed yacht interested in safety and comfort as well as fast passage times, the complete answer has yet to be found. Modern Bermudan rigs are efficient upwind, as are the hulls generally sold to go with them, but, as we have seen in the previous chapter, upwind ability is by no means the final arbiter in ocean sailing. Given a well-worked passage plan and some sort of a break from Lady Luck, the rig's capacity to broad reach or run for days on end without chafing itself to pieces or wearing a crew's morale to a nervous wasteland is, if anything, more important. As in so many areas, the happiest answer lies in a compromise weighted in favour of a skipper's individual character.

This brings us back to one of the conclusions of Chapter 1. It's tempting to imagine ourselves barrelling across a strong trade wind at ten knots, or knocking up improbable daily runs, of which we can subsequently boast, while surfing the Southern Ocean rollers. While this sort of thing can be a lot of fun in the short term, it brings its own stresses. After being out there for a few weeks, a different perspective may prevail. The romance of a classic gaff rig on short trips along the continental shelf is appealing, but whether you are prepared to live with its downsides when sailing to America from Europe is another matter. You may be the sort of person who relishes a hi-tech Aerorig or a dead simple Freedom boat. Perhaps junk makes sense to you, but not everyone appreciates the aesthetics. A long hard look at the realities of the available rigs in light of an honest examination of your own character and requirements is the key.

Back in the days when sails were manhandled and there were none of the sail-taming systems most of us take for granted, Sir Francis Chichester remarked that the biggest sail a healthy solo sailor could be expected to deal with was 500 square feet. He wasn't wrong. Sail-handling systems have come on exponentially since 1965, but if they are to be trusted to give the lie to that great seaman, their reliability must be absolutely above suspicion. When a sail had only a halyard, a sheet, a vang and an outhaul and was hoisted manually when needed, there wasn't a lot to go wrong. If the worst-case scenario should come to pass – a problem with the masthead sheave – it could be dealt with as long as the sailor could get himself aloft. Given a crew of two or more, such a rig was unlikely to bring insoluble problems at sea.

Having made this point, I, for one, embrace the new technology. After a lifetime of sailing traditional gaff cutters for my private cruising, I find that a good mainsail-handling system has freed my wife and me from work on deck. As we grow older, this is very welcome and, should the system fail, it has been chosen to avoid catastrophic issues and we do have contingency plans in place for continuing a passage. I must say, though, that for a 30-year-old, such considerations should not be at the forefront of the mind. A bit of muscle work does the young no harm. Being prepared to front up to it opens the door to some exciting rigs and boat possibilities that go with them.

If you're fit, ask yourself this: 'Since going to sea in a small yacht makes no sense – it's cheaper and easier by airliner, after all – why be brutally rational about rig selection? Why not give romance a chance while you still have the strength? It will delight the eye, you'll make a lot of unexpected friends and you'll end up a better seaman. You might even find strangers buying you drinks.'

Traditionally, it was accepted that, as boats grew larger, there came a time when a small crew needed to split up the size of the individual sails. This gave rise to most of the multi-masted rig variants we see today, including the ketch, the yawl and the schooner. Sail-handling systems have had the effect of thinning out the number of these interesting craft. The sloop and the cutter are more efficient, need less gear and fewer sail covers, but they do crank up the loadings. Bigger sails may be entirely dependent on handling systems, which is fine as long as nothing vital breaks. There's no roadside breakdown service out there. When the worst happens and something lets go on an in-mast roller mainsail or a hydraulic headsail drum, you must either be able to manage without it or fix it. If you can't, you need smaller, simpler sails. It's one or the other.

Bermudan rig

Since the middle of the 20th century, this has been the default rig for ocean sailing. For most people, it will remain the rig of choice. It came about in the 1920s and 30s in order to improve windward performance in race boats and was quickly adopted by the cruising world. Nobody tried to pretend that it was any better at reaching or running than the gaff rig it superseded, but advantages in handling soon became clear. Time and technology have finished the job and today's Bermudan rigs can be a dream to operate upwind and reaching. No panacea has been forthcoming, however, for the rig's great shortfall, which is the failing of all fore-and-aft rigs – running downwind. Creative, practical minds have done much to find solutions, some of which are examined in Chapter 13.

A number of variations in the standard Bermudan rig that pass unnoticed on short trips can have considerable effects as the days stretch out into weeks.

Sail configuration
■ Masthead rig

In its purest form on a boat up to around 40ft, masthead rig offers the best rig security available. A single forestay triangulates with an equivalent backstay. Cap shrouds support the masthead via single, in-line spreaders sited about halfway up the mast at the hounds. Lower shrouds running from the hounds to a point well forward of the mast at deck level hold the rig in column from forward, while 'aft lowers' do the same from aft. It is simple and has a great track record for reliability, especially if the mast is keel-stepped rather than balanced on deck, secured only by its standing rigging. Taller masthead rigs on bigger yachts may have two or more sets of spreaders. At some point aloft, the split lower shrouds of the simple, single-spreader rig lose their effectiveness and running backstays may become desirable or even necessary.

Masthead rig came about in the 1960s, reflecting the racing rules of the day, which did not penalise big headsails. Genoas became enormous, while mainsails shrank. The rig works well upwind and reaching, but as the boat bears further off the wind, the smaller mainsail is an increasing drawback. The big fore triangle means big headsails, big winches and bigger issues when poling headsails out on a run. The relatively modest mainsail is, or should be, easy to handle.

A wholesome cruising masthead rig will be proportioned to minimise these questions and is unlikely to have a degenerate mainsail, but the size of the headsails will always be larger than on an equivalent fractional rig.

A production masthead cruiser.

■ Fractional rig

Bermudan rig is the direct descendant of gaff. When it first appeared, it brought with it the big mainsail and small headsails of its parent. In time, the default two headsails of the gaff cutter gave way to the single headsail of the Bermudan sloop. The hounds of the mast had moved up somewhat, but the forestay remained well below the masthead, creating a handy rig with the drawback of needing some sort of support for the forestay. This was generally supplied by small 'jumper struts' and jumper wires aloft, which pushed the mast back in way of the forestay, augmented by running backstays to supply the real grunt. There the matter rested until the masthead rig came along. Masthead was the standard arrangement for several decades until people became tired of the big headsails and reverted once more to the fractional option.

Fractional rig has the advantage that its headsails are far handier. Being smaller, they can be reefed later, and so will set better in a blow. They also require smaller winches; sheet loads are less, so they are safer. Booming-out poles are shorter and less of a handful. It follows that fractional mainsails are usually bigger than their masthead sisters. Mainsails are often easier to deal with than genoas because the foot is controlled by the boom. They reef more efficiently too, so shedding area from the mainsail has less detrimental effects than ditching the same amount of power from the headsail.

Staying fractional rig

The modern fractional rig does not generally employ jumpers, although these may still be seen on cutters to support the inner forestay. Instead, running backstays often appear and, in particular, aft-swept spreaders. If the rig can stand with just the aft-swept spreaders and

A classic fractional rig cutter making the most of a stiff breeze on Boxing Day. Note the Christmas tree rigged in a seamanlike manner from the masthead.

Aft-swept spreaders confer good spar stiffness but upset the mainsail when running.

In-line spreaders allow the mainsail to be squared off completely but may require occasional stiffening from running backstays on larger boats.

no runners, it is a major boon for inshore sailing. Downwind, these spreaders are a menace. They stop the boom being squared away properly, which increases weather helm and causes the sort of chafe that you can effectively ignore sailing from Cape Cod to Boston or Cowes to Southampton but that becomes an incubus on a Pacific crossing. For a race boat logging improbable speeds and constantly pulling the apparent wind forward, this may not be so serious. For an ordinary cruising boat it is really horrible.

■ Ketches, yawls and schooners

There is not enough space in this book to devote the column inches that these rigs warrant. Let it be said, though, that all exist to make life easier. The schooner and the yawl would claim to sacrifice little in the way of performance, although the schooner rig is found at its best on larger craft. Ketches can work on yachts as small as 38ft length overall.

For the record, a ketch carries her mizzen mast forward of the rudder post. The yawl's is abaft it. This means the ketch has a bigger mizzen with considerably more drive than most yawls. Both of these can carry mizzen staysails when broad reaching, which is useful sail area for free – and very easy these are to set and work, too. Big sails on a Bermudan schooner may include masthead gollywobblers, which are enough to strike fear into the heart of all but the most hardbitten speed freak.

Schooners reach wonderfully well. Their ability to point to windward depends greatly on the rig, the boat and how much the owner has spent on sails, but a good example, like the Olin Stephens-designed *Brilliant* of 1932, will still eat the wind out of many a non-racing

A schooner. Handier to sail than a big sloop and far more romantic.

sloop. On a run, they are not at their best. One sail tends to blanket the next, leading to frustration and only moderate performance.

Yawls perform more or less like a sloop and many have raced with great success. Ketches lose out upwind because their mainmast is shorter and does not generate the same power to windward. Reaching is grand, but running suffers the same negatives as the schooner, albeit to a lesser extent. Both have the option to run under headsail and mizzen in heavy weather.

■ Sail-handling systems for Bermudan mainsails

Lazy jacks and stack pack

From the viewpoint purely of setting the sail, reefed or full, together with modern conveniences to control it, the best system is lazy jacks and, ideally, a permanently rigged sail bag into which the sail is dropped, guided by the lazy jacks. For this system to work at its best, the sail will have at least some battens running right across from luff to leech. It may be 'fully battened'. This stiffens the sail, holding the leech aft as it stows, and helping the lazy jacks do their job. Such a sail will sometimes hang in the lazy jacks sufficiently neatly to require no gaskets in the short term. If a sail bag is integrated, all you need to do is zip it up and the sail is sun-protected and storm-proof.

The upside is that the sail is unencumbered by any compromise in shape. The benefits go on and on. It is also far less likely to fail and, if it does, everything is readily accessible for any proper sailor to fix in short order. That is, as long as it does not have single-line reefing. This abomination has no place in a deep-water yacht. It is prone to failure, it is inefficient, shaking out reefs can involve a trip to the boom end and it fills the cockpit with unwanted rope.

Given no single-line nonsense, the downside of the arrangement is that the battens can easily become snagged by the lazy jacks if the boat is not head to wind for sail hoisting. Vigilance and teamwork between helm and halyard are important, but the inconvenience is worth the trouble. Unmodified, production examples will probably have the reef tacks secured on ram's horn fittings at the gooseneck. Dealing with these demands a trip to the mast, which may not be palatable.

The answer is to rig tack lines to each reef, lead them through some sort of bull's-eye at the gooseneck, thence to the cockpit via the foot of the mast. The system is then as good as it gets. Far less rope than single-line reefing, much more efficient and the sail can have the full three reefs rather than the niggardly and unseamanlike two dished up by the single-line brigade. Reefs can also be winched in on any point of sail, with care and good seamanship.

All lazy-jack systems should be rigged so that the lines can be slacked away clear of the set sail when required, especially on long passages. Otherwise, chafe and inconvenience may result.

A stack pack is a permanently rigged sail bag that sits neatly (or not so neatly) on top of the boom and zips up over the stowed sail. It is integral with the lazy jacks and makes covering and stowing the sail easy. The only real drawback is appearance.

In-mast systems

For better or, some might say, worse, in-mast mainsail systems have become common even on relatively small yachts. Although thoroughly effective in removing all traces of the sail and making reefing simple and easy, with most systems the boat must be brought somewhere near head-to-wind for the sail to be rolled. This may not be convenient if manoeuvring adventurously. Another major failing is that the sail cannot use conventional

In-mast reefing is favoured by many but has considerable disadvantages.

fore-and-aft battens to maintain a leech roach. Lack of roach depowers the sail and looks pathetically underpowered, although vertical battens go some way to redressing the situation. It is not uncommon for an in-mast mainsail to crumple its leech while it is cranked in during a blow. The extra thickness catches in the groove and jams the sail half-rolled. I have had this happen at sea and it is no joke. A further disadvantage is that the full weight of the sail and all its gear is permanently aloft, even when stowed. The designers may not have allowed for this when carrying out their stability calculations and, remember, a kilo at the masthead is worth many multiples in the ballast keel. This may seem unimportant cruising along the coast in controlled weather, but when you take a knock from a sideways 40ft sea, your perspective can change rapidly, so ask the person who drew the boat if she's OK like this.

It goes without saying that if anything fouls up at the masthead, sorting out a swivel inside the spar is likely to be a lot harder than dealing with a halyard that has jumped a fixed sheave.

Despite all the negative factors, the sheer saving of manpower has found these systems an appropriate place among very large yachts. Smaller yachts whose crews do not wish to go on deck to handle sails might be well advised to consider a good in-boom system instead.

In-boom reefing has all the advantages of in-mast and with a good system none of the disadvantages, but it must be quality gear.

In-boom systems

An in-boom system rolls the mainsail into the boom itself. It presents a number of technical difficulties, often surrounding the kicker, or vang. If these are overcome, it opens up a number of advantages over in-mast systems. While the moving parts are essentially the same as in an in-mast system, they are in the boom, so they can be reached more readily if anything should fail and serviced easily if it doesn't. The better systems use a full-scale aluminium or carbon mandril that rolls the sail more effectively, rather than employing a form of headfoil inside the boom, as usually found on in-mast arrangements. If the system melts down completely, you can always ease away on the halyard and dump the sail on deck. The sail must be battened fore and aft, and there is no reason not to cut it with a full roach for power and appearance. Weight is kept low, so there are no stability issues.

Various brands of in-boom system are available. Some are poor, others first-class. It is usually a case of 'you get what you pay for'. One drawback of the cheaper units is ugly retro-fit mast tracks and riggers who insist on installing a fixed vang. The reason they do this is that an in-boom roller only works well with the boom at a precise angle to the mast. A fixed kicker, of course, ensures this, but nobody can sail properly with a fixed vang because leech tension requires frequent adjustment, particularly after reefing. The answer is to bin the fixed vang, buy a decent spring or gas kicker, lead the fall back to the cockpit winch and mark it at the correct angle. Do the same with the topping lift so they coincide and that's the boom issue sorted for hoisting, stowing or reefing. The rest of the time, set the vang for the correct leech tension on the day.

A further downside, which is generic for all systems so far as I am aware, is that reefing on a dead run is not realistically feasible. This is an inherent issue for all fore-and-aft rigged sailing craft, but it can be achieved in small and medium-sized yachts using slab reefing creatively. Unfortunately, the strain on the universal joint at the in-boom gooseneck is just too much.

That said, the author favours in-boom for his own Bermudan cutter. Well into 'retirement age', he finds the benefits of not having to go on deck and a perfectly shaped sail at all times well worth the trade-off.

Alternative rigs

Sailors are traditionally conservative with a small 'c'. The ocean takes no prisoners and most people don't care to experiment when the cost of failure may be the ultimate sanction. That's why futuristic rigs struggle so hard for acceptance and historic ideas are smiled upon, though often in a patronising way. As a tribe, seafarers are unwilling to take chances, but deep down we remain individuals, so let's take a look at some of the alternatives to triangular sails and aluminium masts. They work, they're fun, and they encourage us to think a touch left of centre.

Gaff rig

For a century or more, gaff was the rig of choice for the vernacular craft that preceded the yacht. Fishing smacks, pilot boats and revenue cutters all opted for its power, ease of handling and close-windedness. When yachting really took off in the wake of the schooner *America*, gaff was the natural option, and there is a massive library of precedent to tell us how well it functioned. It still does, in a rather 19th-century sense. Modern developments have included carbon-fibre gaffs, which keep the weight of the rig much lower, but purists argue that lightness aloft spoils a boat's motion and discourages the sail from coming down. Gaff is alive, well and full of healthy controversy.

GAFF RIG

BENEFITS

At its best, gaff is downright handsome. It is also highly entertaining to sail, delivering its pearls only to those prepared to work for them. The satisfaction that rewards anyone who gets a gaffer going really well is hard to calculate. Gaff is also the saltiest of rigs. From the smartest classic yacht to the hunkiest world-girdler, it's a celebration of the ancient arts of the sailor, with more whippings and splices to the ton than any other setup.

Gaff delivers a large, low-aspect-ratio sail area ideal for driving heavy displacement yachts whose hulls are not specially close-winded. Because the rig is short, point loadings are less than on taller alternatives, which makes it kind to a boat. Sheet loads are also reduced, doing away with the need for massive winches and ropes the size of pythons. The sails have a high stall tolerance, allowing them to set a bit oversheeted without killing the boat – a relief when you don't feel like tweaking at 0200 in the rain. The fact that low-tech spars and fittings can be repaired or replaced almost anywhere is a massive plus, as I have personally discovered. With no training and no special practical talents, I have made several major spars for my gaff cutter, including a new mast that took me from Europe to South America and home again via Canada and the stormy North Atlantic.

A hidden benefit of the gaff mainsail is that, as you reef it, the centre of effort doesn't move forward as it does on its three-cornered equivalent. This helps a hove-to boat 'keep her head up' to the wind. Factor in the deep forefoot typical on gaffers, and heaving to becomes a sure-fire formula for gale survival with no effort from the crew other than to brew the coffee.

DRAWBACKS

Despite occasional claims to the contrary, gaff is typically heavier to handle than Bermudan. Except in its most refined forms, it doesn't like pointing much above 45 or 50 degrees to the true wind. Bowsprits are vulnerable in docking situations and having to pay for them in some marinas sticks in the throat of any honest man. Also, gaff rig is a chafe monster. Great care has to be taken on long downwind passages, especially in light airs and a seaway, although a vang to the peak of the gaff can help. Like many rigs, it helps when reefing to come on to a close reach or heave to. The crew certainly have to be out on deck and, by the time everything is coiled away, the job can take several minutes on a boat of any size. It sometimes took ten on my pilot cutter if we'd left it a bit late. Extracting the best from a proper gaffer demands reasonable fitness, some degree of physical strength and high levels of seamanship, which not everyone is prepared to take the trouble to acquire.

Rotating mast rigs

■ Aerorig

This works around an unstayed carbon mast with a single boom constructed across it at gooseneck level in a sort of asymmetric cruciform. The main boom extends aft as usual, but it is partly balanced by the foreboom section, which runs towards the stemhead when the rig is set fore and aft. The clew of the loose-footed mainsail is tuned with an outhaul and a car at the boom end. The 'outhaul' for the roller jib clew leads down to a short track mounted athwart the foreboom immediately forward of the mast. By shortening or easing this, the camber of the jib and the slot between jib and main can be adjusted. The sails are trimmed at the optimum angle to the wind by a single mainsheet, which allows the whole unit, mast and all, to swivel in the massive bearings supporting it at the deck and the mast heel. Sails for these rigs are often hi-tech. The main is perhaps best hoisted conventionally via a stack pack, but versions exist with other formats. It is particularly suited to high-quality in-boom systems such as 'Leisure Furl'.

The aesthetics of the Aerorig are not mentioned here as either a benefit or a drawback, because there are two voluble schools of thought. The writer, however, confesses to being seduced by the semi-wing spar on the 60ft Van de Stadt-designed *La Novia* with which he crossed the Atlantic successfully and which went on to circumnavigate very short-handed. Some hate the look of the cruciform boom; others find it a stark, beauty-in-function artefact. Check the picture below and judge for yourself.

An Aerorig after shortening down at night. In many ways, this rig is a successful answer to trade-wind cruising, but nothing comes without a trade-off.

AERORIG

BENEFITS

A fine short-handed rig. The sheet loads are amazingly light as a result of the balancing effect of the jib boom. Reefing is a breeze on or off the wind because, to feather the rig on any point of sail, all you do is let off the single sheet and the whole unit swivels into 'spilling' mode. With the boat effectively hove-to you can then stroll forward and winch in your reefs conventionally.

Windward performance is better than adequate, but unspectacular. Tacking is simply a matter of steering through the wind. The rig does the rest, while gybing is a very soft, safe option indeed. Off the wind, these boats fly. As the jib boom moves out to weather with the easing sheet, the rig more or less balances itself. There's no call for big, challenging downwind sails and

no chafe at all. The whole shooting match spreads out like a giant sculpture in the sky, catching everything the trade wind has to offer. And if you're hit by a squall in the middle of the night, you've only to ease the sheet to spill as much wind as you like, even on a dead run. In all normal conditions it is the nearest thing imaginable to a perfect ocean rig.

DRAWBACKS

If you want to motor into a head wind, the big spar doesn't enjoy the procedure at all, although it is reported as motorsailing successfully. This is a sailor's rig, however.

It's vital to be certain of the integrity of any unstayed mast, and the bearings on these swivelling spars do take some stick. Plenty of successful long passages are on record, and although the original builder of the Aerorig went bust, the rigs continue sailing. Designer Ian Howlett now advises that new methods of construction are in place to make them even better.

Junk rig

Nobody can argue with the fact that the Chinese used the junk rig with notable satisfaction, not for centuries but, literally, for millennia. Back in the 1960s, the English war hero Colonel 'Blondie' Hasler created a modern version for his 25ft folkboat *Jester*, using it in the first Observer Singlehanded Trans-Atlantic Race. Numerous cruising yachts followed suit, including such notables as Commander Bill King's singlehanded circumnavigator, *Galway Blazer*. The rig now takes its rightful place among the options.

Junk rig uses full-length battens to shape and control sails that are semi-balanced with some percentage area forward of the unstayed masts. It generally appears in sloop or schooner form, with the schooner having the advantage of being able to sail wing-and-wing downhill.

JUNK RIG

BENEFITS

There is a certain weird beauty about junk sails that grows on you, and those elliptical leeches aren't just for show. It is perhaps the lowest-tech outfit of all; cheap to build and easy to repair wherever you are. Many junk rigs have been entirely home-constructed, including the sails. Loads are light because the sails are multi-sheeted from each batten. Chafe is minimal, as it is in all free-standing rigs. Reefing is very easy indeed, with the sail dropping into its lazy jacks like a window blind. Annie Hill, who has cruised countless ocean miles in these vessels, points out that junk rig is not notably light because most versions have comparatively heavy wooden masts, but she emphasises that this actually makes for an easier motion than super-light spars. All in all, junk adds up to low-stress yachting, if that's what you seek.

DRAWBACKS

Some versions lack power close-hauled compared with a Bermudan sloop, although care in design, a hull that can point and attention to battens can offset this. You can't do a lot to fly lightweight kites in calms, but on deep water where there is always a swell, such sails are arguably less effective anyway.

Freedom rigs

The Freedom rig was developed in the mid-1970s by former Olympic Finn sailor Garry Hoyt and designer Halsey Herreshoff. The early boats featured a cat ketch rig with free-standing spars to maintain a low centre of effort. The sails were set on windsurfer-style booms requiring no vang and were satisfyingly efficient. Downwind they winged out, one each side. Hoyt's original boat was the Freedom 40, a distinctive hull well suited to the rig. More than 100 were launched and further versions soon appeared, such as the UK-built Freedom 35. In 1987 the concept was taken on by Gary Mull with the Freedom 30 and her larger sisters. By now, the radical cat ketch with wishbones was disappearing, but the unstayed carbon-fibre mast remained, often headed up by an unconventional self-tacking jib.

Other forms now flourish, such as the Nonsuch yachts. These are generously canvassed cat-rigged yachts that stick to the wishbone boom. They are said to be well balanced in heavy and light going and are very striking indeed.

FREEDOM RIG

BENEFITS

The early boats had adequate upwind performance, but went like rockets downwind with remarkably little effort from the crew. Later boats with boomed mainsails and something of a foretriangle perform better close-hauled, while retaining the ability to tack by simply winding the wheel to windward. No need to winch the headsail. It flops across all on its own, a treat that encourages folks to sail into smaller places and get more out of their investment.

Like all unstayed rigs, chafe shouldn't be an issue, making the older Freedom rigs attractive for long downwind passages. Reefing is usually by conventional slab, and the Hoyt boats, as well as some later variants, can be shortened down easily from the cockpit. Anybody with an eye for aerodynamics can't help but be impressed by the powerful wishbone sails of the Nonsuch.

DRAWBACKS

So long as there are unstayed rigs, people will shout about them being unsafe. When asked if a lack of rigging isn't dangerous, Gary Mull had this to say: 'We note that Orville and Wilbur used wires, but Boeing doesn't.' As with all carbon-fibre masts, one drawback is getting it repaired if you have mast damage underway.

3 ENGINES

There was a time in living memory when engines were unreliable and somewhat 'second division' in the sailor's mind. Hence the term auxiliary. Fuel capacities were small and while the machinery might have enough power to manoeuvre in and out of a tricky harbour or help a yacht through a calm, they certainly weren't on the list of heavy weather survival or passage-making tools.

All that has changed. I only know of one serious cruising yacht built in recent years without an engine and even she retro-fitted one after returning to Britain from an Atlantic circuit. My own power units in early boats were so untrustworthy that I was obliged on occasions to sail on without them, more than once undertaking full ocean passages with only the wind to deliver me in one piece. Things weren't so bad for me because in those days I had oil lighting, astro navigation and no refrigeration. For my current boat to run out of auxiliary propulsion would be far more serious. It can be possible, of course, for a medium-tech yacht with wind available to generate enough electricity by renewable means to keep things ticking over, but the power demands of most of us are such that without diesel we sooner or later end up dead in the water.

Aside from maintaining charge in the batteries, a calm at sea without an engine is grim. As the yacht rolls her stick out and the sails bang and slat for days on end, even the best of shipmates can find themselves contemplating murder. To know with confidence that this will no longer happen is a huge relief. Instead of having to tolerate these horrors, I pin in the main, roll away the genny, flash up the diesel and toddle away on track at an economical five knots with a range of well over 1,000 miles. Fantastic!

The bottom line, then, is that the engine – and the generator, if fitted – are the beating hearts of a modern yacht. A diesel simply must start at the touch of the button and it must keep on running. Since diesel fuelling stations are not common out of sight of land, or on many a remote coastline, the importance of big fuel tanks to a mainstream modern cruising yacht cannot be over-stressed. Today's engines are incredibly dependable. To keep them so, they must be serviced according to the book and, in case of the occasional malfunction, skippers simply have to be genuinely familiar with the basics for getting them going again. There is no ducking this one. If you aren't mechanically minded and you don't have a crew member who is, the time to get educated is now.

Ocean sailing demands a 'can-do' attitude. The 21st century has brought reliable, computerised road vehicles and with it a generation that proceeds from the assumption that little can be done by the amateur when they stop running. The days are gone when every other young man spent his weekends coaxing life into a reluctant motor car or fixing up a motorcycle bought for pennies. Back then, a boat engine that wouldn't start was just grist to the age-old mill. To go to sea, we all must return to that way of thinking.

Accessibility

The attitude among some builders that an engine is a necessary evil has led to the odd nightmare installations. If the auxiliary gets in the way of a fine aft cabin, it is stuffed away somewhere to make room for that giant bed that sells boats to the unwary in shows. Choosing a boat for voyaging beyond outside help, the engine space must have good access. I've had some terrible times with units tucked away out of sight and mind. Once I had to cut holes in a bulkhead to access starter-motor mounting bolts. Worse frustration came when I found myself without engine or electrics after battery failure required me to hand-start a modest engine while delivering a brand-new production boat. I had already noted with satisfaction the neatly mounted cranking handle, but as I decompressed the valve gear, then inserted the handle, it became clear that the engine installation made a full swing totally impossible. I completed the delivery under sail beneath the panoply of the Prince of Darkness, reduced to shining a failing flashlight when ships came too close.

Don't let this nonsense happen to you. Look carefully at the access before you leave on a passage. Make sure you can reach the bits of the engine and other gear that really matter. This includes batteries, starter, any switching gear, alternator, fuse box, relays, dipsticks and fillers, couplings and stern tube, fuel lift pump, fuel pre-filters, fuel filter mounted on the engine, injector pump, injectors, cooling water strainer, cooling water pump impeller inspection plate, throttle and gearbox linkages. Plus, any service points such as anodes in the heat exchanger, which, if they are too difficult to reach, are often forgotten until their collapse leads to engine failure from overheating on a lee shore.

Servicing

I have found nothing in the service schedule for a modern marine diesel fitted to the sort of boat operated by an average owner-skipper that cannot be attended to by a half-competent person, given the right tools, proper replacement parts and fluids, and the right attitude.

Engine oil

Changing the oil and filter at the correct intervals is the core action of servicing. It is vital if the engine is to run and go on running for years. Given access, it is also the simplest of tasks. Make sure you have done this at least once before you leave, so as to see whether your tools work, or to discover that you need an empty can for the waste oil, and so on.

The latest engine variants often have very long service intervals, as do some modern cars. Like the cars, however, if you want your engine to keep on going until you draw your pension, change the oil at least every 200 hours. Every 100 is better. 'Once a season' might work for a marina-based weekend yacht and stretching the interval for operational reasons is OK on the odd occasion, but it's no good as a policy for a full-time cruising boat.

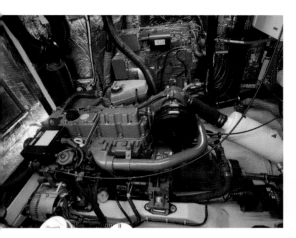

Good access.

Tricky access.

Other regulars
■ Belts and impellers

These are readily changed and, if left alone assuming they will go on for ever, are prone to failure sooner or later. Changing the oil gives you the opportunity to take a look at the belt tensions and ensure they are in perfect condition, tensioned as per the manual. If in any doubt, replace a belt with one of your spares (you should carry at least two on a long passage) and keep the old one just in case.

The almighty impeller. Change them every year and keep the old ones.

The same goes for cooling water pump impellers. The schedule may not mention these, but they do slowly harden in use and it's not unknown for one that looks OK to lack that last bit of oomph needed to overcome some other minor glitch in the system. An airlock results, with an overheated engine howling out with its warning buzzers just when you least need it. Check the front plate of the pump, too. These wear with use and when they reach a critical point, the pump loses grunt just as if its impeller were tired out. Persuading these plates to seal is a notorious problem. The gasket that is supplied with the impeller may not be enough, so be ready with the right grade of gasket goo to take up the slack.

■ Fuel filters

Part of the service should also be a change of fuel pre-filters. If the diesel is clean, these won't need doing – once a year should be enough – but you can't be sure. For what they cost, changing them every 200 hours is no bad idea. If you look after the pre-filters, the engine fuel filter should remain clean. Change it once a year, but carry spares just in case. You can't have too many spares for the pre-filters. If you're unlucky enough to suffer a filthy fill in some far-flung port, you may end up replacing them every few hours. It's well worth fitting a shut-off valve on the tank side of the pre-filter. Without one of these, you'll have to close the tap at the tank and will inevitably lose some fuel when you strip the filter to replace the element. This in turn allows air to enter the system and makes restarting problematic. The tap at the filter does away with the possibility of shunting this air further down the line into the injector pump by not letting it in at all.

■ Air filters

The engine manual may also schedule attention to the air filter. If it does, be certain to carry spares, if this is what it takes. If it's a matter of cleaning an element, do it before you leave so that you know you can.

■ Gear box

Beyond checking levels – often an awkward job – these are usually pretty maintenance free in the short and medium term, but some older units have adjustments that can be made. These should be familiarised, pending the day, and any tools needed must be on board. All boxes, whether hydraulic or mechanical, have regular oil-change intervals that must be observed, on pain of, at best, deteriorating performance and, at worst, expensive failure.

GENERAL INSPECTION

A clean engine can tell its owner a lot about its general condition.

- Oil leaks are rare these days, but they will show up straightaway and, if ignored, will usually only get worse.

- Sea water leaks are easy to spot because they often leave behind a crust of salt rather like a leaky radiator in the home central-heating system. This is corrosive and will certainly end up causing problems, so find out why it's leaking and stop it.

- Inspect all cooling-water hoses for leaks. Replace any that are showing signs of cracking and hardening when the opportunity presents itself – usually in a harbour well stocked with engineering shops. Put a screwdriver on each hose clip and make sure none have started to unwind. Pay particular attention to the elbow where cooling water is injected into the exhaust system. These units do not always last for ever and if it is showing signs of being tired, consider replacing it when you can. If it fails, it may prove beyond your powers to fix at sea without access to engineering facilities.

- It only takes a minute to ascertain the engine mounts are holding up OK. These usually involve some sort of rubber shock-absorbing and, while this lasts well, it isn't guaranteed still to be there when all hands are dead and buried, so keep an eye on it.

The drive chain

Starting at the propeller, the drive chain consists of a shaft joining the prop to the back end of the engine, usually via the gearbox. Unless the yacht has a saildrive, the hole in the boat where this shaft passes through the hull can easily be 1¼in or more. If anything should happen to the shaft or its couplings, this leaves a catastrophic way in for the sea, with a metre or so of head to encourage it to pour in. Against this ultimate emergency, any boat in which the shaft has a free route of exit (that means most fin-keeled yachts) should have a tapered wooden bung of the right size in a known location ready to drive into the hole. And the skipper must be able to swing the hammer properly to do the job.

Shaft couplings

The most common cause of shaft failure is for the coupling to come undone. I've been shocked to find people crossing oceans who don't know how their drive chain works, or even what the coupling is. I once had to float some tools down to a boat in mid-Atlantic whose coupling had let go. The crew didn't even have the spanners to reconnect it, which, it turned out, was all it needed.

The coupling is attached to a short shaft emanating from the back of the gearbox, joining this to the main propeller shaft. Couplings come in different types. Many incorporate a shock absorber or some softer material than the steel of the main unit. These may deteriorate and require periodic inspection. So do the bolts or Allen set screws holding the whole device together. Couplings often become very rusty, with their bolts beyond the power of normal tools. Maintenance and the occasional spray from a paint can will help keep this menace at bay.

Stern glands

The stern gland that keeps the water out when the propeller shaft spins round comes in two essential forms, with many variants. The traditional arrangement is a 'stuffing box', but in modern craft, the so-called 'face seal' may be preferred. Regardless of what goes on at the gland, the aft end of most shafts also features a water-lubricated rubber 'cutless bearing'. In a long-keeled yacht, this will be set into the stern tube. Shorter-keeled boats with the shaft appearing outside the hull for more than a few inches carry this externally in a bracket. The cutless bearing's job is to support the aft end of the shaft immediately forward of the propeller.

■ Face seal

This type of seal has a carbon collar secured on the shaft. It butts up 'face-to-face' against a stainless steel partner solidly clamped to the forward end of a flexible rubber bellows with a pair of hose or 'jubilee' clips. The aft end of the bellows is clipped around the inner end of the stern tube before it disappears into the hull fabric. The carbon/stainless interface is virtually friction free. The bellows are compressed somewhat when the stainless ring is being attached so that water pressure acting on the fixed stainless ring keeps the seal perfectly watertight as the carbon ring spins against it.

The arrangement is maintenance free, but it is not unknown for the bellows to perish and break up at a bad moment, allowing major water ingress. Fortunately, imminent failure can be spotted, and as long as the bellows are changed at least every eight years or so and the condition of the rings inspected from time to time, it is unlikely to occur at sea, where dealing with it can be rather difficult.

If the worst should happen, the usual first stage is that the bellows split. A temporary amelioration of the resulting leak can sometimes be managed using duct tape. Where the bellows are beyond repair, the only solution is to tear them off and try to stuff the gap between shaft and tube with rags, shoving them in with a screwdriver. It's going to leak, whatever you do, but as long as the pumps can throw the water out faster than it is coming in, you won't be a Mayday case, just another yacht without a functioning engine, sailing as hard as she can for the nearest slipway.

■ Stuffing box

The seal in a stuffing box is by courtesy of specially made waxed rope packing. This is generally square in cross section and is compressed into the bearing by either a large nut through which the shaft is passed or a flange that does the same job. The flange has a pair of bolts with lock nuts to nip it up to an equivalent flange on the stern tube. The nut on the simpler arrangement will be as large as its partner, which is very big indeed, so be sure you have spanners to fit.

If a stuffing box is going to leak, it generally gives plenty of warning by starting slowly, then building up over many hours or days. There's generally no need to haul out. The first action, after giving it a good shot of grease (if it has a greaser), is carefully to tighten up the compression nut or flange, as appropriate. This is often enough to quieten things down. If it doesn't work – and it must not be over-tightened, for fear of damaging the shaft itself – it must be repacked.

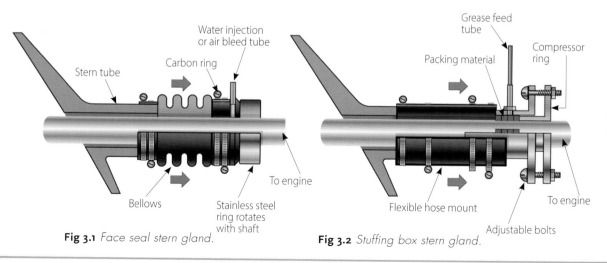

Fig 3.1 *Face seal stern gland.*

Fig 3.2 *Stuffing box stern gland.*

To repack a stuffing box, back off the compression nut or flange to expose the indent where the packing lives. Next, cut new packing into lengths equal to the shaft's circumference, wrap them around it in the form of rings and push them carefully into the aperture made for them. One may be enough, but it may take two or three. Now re-engage the compression device and tighten it down gently, ideally feeling to see if the shaft can still be turned by hand with the gears in neutral.

Unless the original packing has totally disintegrated, this can be achieved without fear of a flood. I have done it a number of times afloat with success, but cutting the rings first is a sensible precaution. If the stuffing box fails completely, you are in the same boat, so to speak, as the chap with the disintegrated lip seal. Cram rags into the gap, start pumping and sail as quickly as you can to a travel lift or a tidal beach.

The bottom line on stern tubes and glands is that you simply must be familiar with yours and have a means of reaching it if things prove awkward. Spare packing must be carried if appropriate, and if you are off around the world, a spare bellows and carbon ring for a lip seal.

The tools may be specialised if the seal carries a large shaft nut and its locking partner. A hefty adjustable spanner, which is useful to have in any case, may well be the answer. A 'Stillson' pipe wrench may even do the trick, but both nuts must be accessible and their respective spanners/wrenches must be able to turn independently. Put the spanners into position on a fine day in harbour before you find out the hard way that the ones you bought can never work.

Tools and manuals

It's been said already in this book, but I repeat it without fear of ridicule: There is no assistance out there. A boat has to be self-sufficient and if a vital tool has been left in the hardware store in Portsmouth or Alameda, that is just too bad. The same goes for manuals. I try to keep mine in a big ring binder, but as long as they are together in the same place and have been read and understood before travelling beyond the reach of assistance, all should be well.

Troubleshooting

Engine refuses to start

▪ **Engine turns but does not fire**

If an engine whips over and fails to fire, it almost certainly has fuel issues. Before investigating the fuel lines, however, it pays to ensure that the 'stop' system is not activated. Some engines are stopped by pulling a toggle that shuts down the injector pump. This is the simplest and best way of shutting down a diesel. If you have one of these, make sure it has been returned to its rest position and not left halfway out. That'll stop the beast from firing every time.

Sadly, many modern engines, my own included, shut down the pump by means of an electrical solenoid activated by turning the ignition key. I've known these to fail and when they do, they generally fail in the 'fail dangerous' position with the pump inoperative. Take a look at the

BASIC TOOLKIT

As for tools, every boat has her own special needs, but a minimum kit would look something like this:

ENGINE TOOLS

- comprehensive spanner or wrench kit (including large and small adjustables)
- Allen key set as required
- screwdrivers – large (square shafted to accept wrench), medium, stubby, small, jeweller's and electrical. Flat-head, cross-head, Robinson and/ or power-drive as required
- pliers – general purpose and sharp-nosed
- circlip pliers
- ½ in (13mm, as required) drive socket set, plastic boxed, medium quality
- ¼ in (6mm, as required) drive socket set
- sump oil pump

ENGINE SPARES

- fuel filters
- oil filter
- one complete engine oil change
- water pump impellers and gaskets
- spare drive belts
- cylinder head gasket – any upper engine job will require its replacement (even if you aren't competent to lift the head yourself, you may have to employ an engineer who does not have a gasket in stock)
- spare injector
- gasket goo

ELECTRICAL TOOLS

- various screwdrivers, including one with a 12V test lamp
- simple test meter
- 12V soldering iron, flux and solder
- crimping, cutting and stripping tool
- needle-nosed pliers
- insulating tape

ELECTRICAL SPARES

- selection of spade and ring terminals
- ditto useful wire
- fuses as required
- light bulbs as required
- spare wire in various gauges
- connectors

GENERAL TOOLS

- hacksaw, junior hacksaw and blades
- tiny spanners
- mole/vise grips, medium and very small (baby versions are exceedingly useful)
- rechargeable electric drill, high-speed metal drill bits, and centre punch bits to be kept in a screw-top jar, well oiled
- hammers – medium claw, heavy 'lump', a soft 'combination hammer' for hitting threaded ends
- set of softwood tapered bungs to block off damaged seacocks, stern tube, etc.
- a few hardwood blocks to use as drifts, anvils, etc.
- soft brass or bronze drift
- saw with at least an 18in blade, smaller for GRP craft
- two chisels, 1in and ½in blades
- portable vice or 'Workmate' and a site designated for mounting (some vices fit into a winch barrel)
- two files, a large flat/half-round combi, plus one small round
- selection of lubricants and greases
- Stillson/pipe wrench
- G cramps
- Emery paper or wet-and-dry sandpaper for cleaning terminals, etc.
- old driving mirror or 'dentist's mirror'
- seizing wire
- wire coat hangers as purveyed by dry cleaners for improvising hooks, probing, clearing tubes, etc. (you cannot go to sea without these so do not accept plastic)
- sharp knife and sharpening stone
- Araldite, superglue, epoxy repair kit, underwater epoxy putty and Vaseline for battery terminals

pump while somebody turns the key to stop the engine. You may well be able to see how it works. Then, when the horrid day dawns, you'll be able to find a way of bypassing the solenoid mechanically and delight your crew by fixing the unfixable.

■ Silence

If silence meets the start button, go straight to the voltage of the starter battery. If you don't have a gauge for this, get out the multimeter. A workable one need cost no more than a round of drinks. It measures various things, but right now we want voltage, so click it round to 'Volts DC' (direct current), choose 20V for a 12V system, place the red probe on the positive terminal and the black one on the negative and read the numbers.

A multimeter. Probably the best-value tool in the modern yacht's box.

A charged, healthy 12V battery at rest will usually read about 12.5V; 12.0V should start a healthy engine. 24V systems are 'pro rata'. When nothing is happening at all and the battery has the volts to do the job, there's either a bad connection or the switching has packed up.

After checking the obvious giant connections between battery and starter motor, the more likely culprit is going to be a small wire leading from the switch to a relay or solenoid.

Boats have all sorts of methods of connecting the battery to the starter motor. A trained eye can read the wiring diagram in the manual, but nobody can blame an average skipper for being bamboozled by these. A wire hanging off, however, is a wire hanging off, and more than likely it's the villain.

A seamanlike, systematic search has a good chance of throwing up an answer like this, so be sure to carry a plentiful supply of electrical terminals. You need spades and rings of assorted sizes, plus insulating tape, spare wire of varying gauges and cutters. If you haven't any official means of crimping a terminal, a small pair of mole grips (vise grips in US English) serves adequately.

A final possibility is that the mysterious relay that sends power to the starter motor or solenoid while protecting the wiring from the big hit has died in its bed. These aren't repairable and I find them tricky to diagnose, so carrying a spare as a last chance is a good investment. They are simple to fit.

■ Flat battery

We all know the two sorry sounds of a flat battery. One is the miserable groan of an engine turning too slowly to fire. The other is a sorry click as the solenoid in the starter motor fails to find enough grunt to engage. Power is getting to where it's needed. There just isn't enough of it.

Batteries are imperfect and they have minds of their own when they get older. A battery that seemed good in the morning can die over lunch for no apparent reason, so accept that it may have dealt you a bad card and move on. There may be sinister reasons for its flatness or it may just have decided it has had enough. In either case, the priority is to get the engine running.

- Turn off all electrics. Check that the engine battery casing is not cracked. If it is, get rid of it and substitute one of your other batteries. If you try starting with it, it may burst. The consequences are too awful to contemplate.
- Check that the voltage on the 'donor' is well over the critical 12.0V.
- Connect the two positive terminals using the red jump lead.
- Connect one end of the black jump lead to the negative terminal on the donor battery.

Ideally, the other end should go to a pain-free metal fitting on the engine. A big nut is good. Hooking up the two negative battery terminals works well, but it can spark with nasty results, so only do it if there's no other way to achieve a decent earth.

- Fire up the engine, remove the black lead from the engine or its battery, then the other end from the donor battery. Take the red cable off the donor battery first, then run the engine for at least half an hour to charge up the engine battery.

If you can hand-start the engine, go for it. If not, which is usually the case today, you must either throw the switch that connects the engine starting battery to the domestic supply or, if you don't have one, get out your jump leads. These must be of the highest quality. Rubbish may not do the job when it counts.

■ Engine overheats

As soon as you recognise that the engine is overheating, usually either by the sound of a dry exhaust or the buzzer of the alarm, shut down the engine. The problem is almost certainly that the water strainer has become blocked or the pump has ceased to function. See box on the right for what to do.

■ Engine stops in service or fails to restart after clearing a fuel filter

The most common reason for a diesel to stop is fuel blockage or contamination with air or water. A diesel cannot operate with air anywhere in its system and, if it has been struggling to pull fuel past a clogged filter, this is the inevitable result. The advent of 'bio'

DEALING WITH A BLOCKED WATER STRAINER

- Shut off the seacock and open the strainer body. A small amount of water will escape into the bilge and you will see some sort of removable gauze bucket. Lift it out. With luck, it will be clogged with junk. Clean it up and replace it, and that should be 'job done'.
- If the filter is clear, leave it with its lid off and carefully open the seacock. If water flows in, the supply is clear. If it doesn't, make sure the cock is open, then poke a long screwdriver down it to spike the plastic rubbish or the luckless jellyfish. You may have to remove the inlet pipe at the seacock before poking around.

Old-fashioned strainer.

diesel additives has aggravated the dreaded diesel bug which clogs pipes and filters. Be careful where you fill up and always add a fuel treatment. It's worth every penny.

SORTING OUT A NON-FUNCTIONAL PUMP

- If water still fails to circulate after the above procedure, the pump is generally the bandit. Follow the pipe from the seacock to find it. It is usually the first fitting in the line on the body of the engine itself.
- Shut the seacock and carefully unscrew the face of the pump. If the impeller inside is damaged, withdraw it, install one of your spares, grease the ends of the lobes to ease the passage until the water arrives, and start her up. If the impeller looks OK, take it out for inspection anyway. Often, one or more lobes will have deteriorated sufficiently to reduce performance below a critical level.
- Check also that the face plate of the pump is not too worn. A worn plate can have a surprisingly dramatic effect, so replace this with your spare if in doubt and try again.

BLEEDING THE SYSTEM

- First, shut off the fuel and change the pre-filter in the fuel line. A badly clogged filter will be visibly filthy, but do not despair if it isn't. Make sure the bowl of the filter is spotless and note any water or dirt that you find in there to chase up later. Turn on the fuel and make sure that the filter body is full of diesel before you try to restart the engine. Sometimes this can be achieved by manually cranking the lift pump on the engine, but if the filter is high up, you may have to top it up from a remote source of diesel. I keep a gallon can full, together with a handy funnel for this.
- Many modern engines self-bleed. If yours is one of these, keep cranking on the starter motor after you've sorted out the filter and it should eventually start. Give the batteries a chance, however, and only crank it for six or seven seconds. Let the starter and batteries rest for half a minute before repeating the procedure.
- You can help a great deal by bleeding the filter, however; if the engine is not self-bleeding you'll have to anyway. Slack off the bleed screw on the top of the filter (if there is more than one filter, tackle the one nearest the tank first), then operate the manual pump handle on the side of the lift pump. Keep working this up and down until the bubbles stop and clean fuel runs out. Some filters have an inbuilt pump to deal with this contingency. Now nip up the screw and hit the starter.
- Make sure you have plenty of kitchen roll handy when you are bleeding a fuel system. A flexible plastic container is also vital.
- If all else fails, carry out the same procedure with the engine fuel filter. If this doesn't get it going, crack a bleed nut or screw on the injector pump itself. The manual will indicate where they are, but, if in doubt, try any hexagon on the face of the pump to see if fuel begins to flow. If bubbles appear, keep cranking the lift pump until they stop, then try a restart. This time, it really should run.

4 STEERING

Rudders

In Chapter 1 we established that three types of rudder predominate in modern cruising yachts. Each brings its own benefits and drawbacks to the table. Understanding what these may be helps a lot when persuading a boat to steer herself.

Keel-hung rudders
■ Transom and Norwegian sterns

From the viewpoint of reliability and ease of maintenance, these are the best rudders you can have. They generally steer the boat well because they are right at the stern, as far away from the pivot point around which the boat turns as possible. They can be solidly attached, with a meaty bottom pintle set into a massive female fitting at the heel of the keel taking the brunt of the strain. This is backed up by further pintles and gudgeons up the stern post. A transom stern can even have an extra set above the waterline, which is a luxury denied the Scandinavians by their sexy curved stern posts.

A stern-hung rudder is usually protected against ropes or other foreign matter creeping into the gap between it and the stern post by a heel fitting that effectively stops off the aperture. Given this, such a setup is as near bulletproof as mankind has yet contrived.

A transom-hung rudder is easy to maintain and typically strongly mounted.

The Norwegian stern also allows the strong pintles and gudgeons, although the curved sternpost negates any mountings at the top.

The rudder can be dropped readily to check or renew the pintles. Every bit of its mechanism can be visually inspected. The trailing edge can also be pressed into service to run the simplest of servo windvane self-steering systems by the addition of a basic trim tab. What more could one ask?

■ Counter sterns

A long-keeled yacht with stern overhang in the form of a counter enjoys many of the benefits of the transom-hung rudder, but she does suffer the complication of a tube, or 'trunk', through the counter to carry the rudder stock up to deck level. This apart, the mechanics are the same. At its best, the trunk holds the upper part of the rudder stock in place effectively. As it grows older, however, any glands supporting the stock and keeping the water out grow tired,

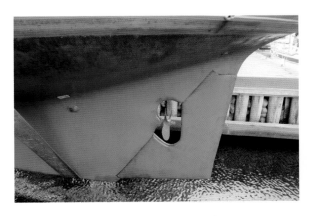

The counter-stern rudder can be strongly mounted on a stout bottom pintle, although dropping it for maintenance can pose problems.

things start to slop around and it becomes another headache for the poor owner's creaking bank balance. Such a rudder is far more of a challenge to drop for inspection and service than its transom-hung cousin, and it cannot run a trim-tab servo self-steering system. The counter-stern rudder isn't bad, but the simpler system is better.

Skeg rudders

In the absence of the after end of the keel from which to hang a rudder, the fin-and-skeg profile yacht grew a 'skeg' well aft to serve instead. A skeg-hung rudder has the same benefits and drawbacks as the traditional counter-stern alternative, but the skeg brings scope for some degree of sophistication.

The strongest skeg rudders sit vertically for maximum effect behind a full-length skeg and enjoy the pay-off of a bottom pintle. Ideally, a second pintle will be found halfway up the skeg to the hull, whereafter the stock is supported by the trunking. A skeg, if shorter than full length, offers the additional option of a balanced rudder.

A balanced rudder carries some of its area forward of the stock so that when the main body of the rudder turns to port, the balanced section swings to starboard. Any balance cancels its own area in terms of helm weight, yet the efficiency of the blade is not much compromised. The result is a lighter helm. You might argue that a well-balanced yacht should not need this sort of assistance

This skeg rudder is well supported by the rudder trunk and the lower brackets.

and I would not disagree, but such rudders have proliferated and in the right conditions they make helming a delight. A heavily balanced rudder, such as one finds on many general-purpose cruising yachts, can take charge if the boat is left unattended under power for more than a second or two. The results are always alarming and can become expensive in crowded waters.

Spade rudders

Spade rudders are the most efficient of all when it comes to performance sailing. To prove it, just about every race boat has one. They may be balanced, with the usual joys and griefs, or they may not. All, however, are supported only by bearings holding the stock in the trunk. The forces on a rudder are substantial. If it is held at the bottom as well as the top, they present no special problems. When the rudder is maintained only by a cantilever system in the hull, you don't need to be an engineer to realise that it is a source of potential weakness. Most yachts that lose their rudders have this type of arrangement and, while big strides have been made in construction since the spade rudder first made its appearance, they can still catch a big fishing net while sailing at 7 knots. Strong they may be, but they are by definition vulnerable. Such an accident is virtually impossible for the long-keeled yacht under sail and not half so easy for one steered by a well-designed skeg rudder.

The spade rudder is more efficient than the others, but is far more vulnerable to damage.

Tillers and wheels

Tillers

I love tillers. They have the massive advantage of being perfectly simple; no mechanism to fail, no wires and pulleys to lubricate and replace periodically, nothing to adjust in impossible places. In fact, nothing to worry about at all. The worst scenario is that they actually break. I had this happen in a North Atlantic storm many years ago. I was young and didn't have a spare. The result was a night I'd rather forget, spent hanging over the stern of a Norwegian pilot cutter endeavouring to cobble up something to retain the rudder, with my wife grabbing on to my wellies as wave after huge wave broke over us both. Any yacht with a tiller must have a spare, unless the original is iron, as mine was on my second tiller-steered pilot cutter. The boat would have taken off and flown to America before she broke that one, but, just in case, I carried a standby that I used for steadying the rudder in harbour while I removed the lovely curved metal bar for painting.

Tillers have the dual benefits of being cheap and virtually foolproof, so if you are thinking of building a boat and she's the right sort of shape, forget the wheel, leave months earlier with the money you've saved and enjoy nights free from a bad conscience about those steering wires you know you really ought to have changed.

Wheels

The best wheel steering I ever went to sea with was on my 1911 pilot cutter. It had been fitted to the 35-ton gaffer in 1952 to replace the original tiller. When I sold her in 1995, it was working perfectly and had never needed to come ashore for service. It was a simple rack-and-pinion arrangement, which a previous owner had pulled off a big 1930s racing yacht. The 'rack' was a quadrant through-bolted to

The author's daughter at the wheel of his 35-ton 1911 pilot cutter in 1982. The mechanism was removed from a scrap racing boat in the 1950s. It needed no maintenance beyond occasional greasing and worked perfectly for decades.

the top of the rudder stock, the wheel ran on basic bearings we lubricated daily at sea with an old-fashioned oilcan, and the direction of its travel was turned by a couple of bevel-cut gears. The whole issue was kept liberally greased with lanolin supplied by a lifeboatman who had shepherded swimmers across the Bristol Channel. It had stopped their skin going crinkly and it kept those gears in perfect condition for thousands of miles and five decades. With the boat at rest in the water you could spin the old-fashioned wheel from one lock to the other, three turns in all. The huge rudder was in more or less neutral buoyancy, so it didn't wear out its bearings and was always easy to move. Quite why all wheel steering can't be like this, I don't understand, but it isn't.

A good wheel-steering system will, on all but the best-balanced yachts, be lighter and less tiring to operate than a tiller. The sort of heavy-duty below-decks autopilot it favours is easier to use and usually has more long-term reliability than a tiller pilot. Nothing is perfect, unfortunately, and wheel steering can lead to potential – but usually soluble – issues with a windvane.

The bottom line with any wheel-steering system is that it must be carefully maintained. Unless rod-driven, it has sheaves running on spindles, which wear, as well as wires that strand and stretch. All this is typically tucked away out of sight and out of mind below the cockpit sole. On my current boat, as on many others, getting to it is no fun at all for anyone bigger than a two-year-old and with less strength at arm's length than a gorilla, so it's 'groan you may but go you must' for the annual inspection. We have to become familiar with the whole arrangement and monitor its condition closely and regularly. That way, the worst should never happen. If it does, we are at least in with a fighting chance. If you've never seen the steering gear until the night it lets go, you'll be joining that queue of optimists waiting outside the pearly gates for their inevitable comeuppance.

Self-steering

My wife once observed that she'd rather go to sea without a cooker than with no means of self-steering. In any short-handed boat, and most real cruising yachts are just that, nobody wants to steer for any distance. In fact, solo watch-keeping on passages of ocean scale is impractical in real terms if the poor soul looking out for his or her sleeping shipmates is under the cosh from what has been aptly described as 'the tyranny of the tiller'. Windvane or autopilot, whichever is selected, must work and go on working. Each has its strengths and weaknesses. The best answer is to opt for both.

A properly set-up windvane or a suitable autopilot with a bulging spares box will steer across an ocean under sail, as long as the boat is well balanced and remains so in gusty conditions, even if hard pressed. Sadly, flat-floored cruisers abound that do not behave like this. I have sailed many a wretched yacht that gripes to windward when hit by a few extra knots of wind, leaving an autopilot labouring to maintain any semblance of control. Even competent humans have a hard time, but because they can be proactive and apply extra weather helm in good time when the boat starts to heel, they can usually keep her on her feet. Not so the autopilot, which can only react to what has happened in the way of yawing off course. A sophisticated unit can take steps to deal with this characteristic, but, in the end, it will always be beaten. Even a windvane struggles. Such yachts have no place in the long-distance sailor's world.

Autopilots

Electronic autopilots are easy to operate and require no special skill once they have been set up. They fall into two essential categories: the cockpit-mounted tiller pilot or its wheel-driving equivalent and the full-on, heavier-duty autopilot mounted below decks.

■ Tiller pilots

The tiller pilot comes under various brand names, but they all have common features. They are self-contained units carrying the four main elements of an autopilot within a surprisingly small casing.

The electronic 'brain' of a typical modern autopilot safely out of the weather.

All that is needed to mount a tiller pilot is to secure a bracket or female socket to the boat – often the cockpit coaming – and bolt a small 'pip' to the tiller. A modest 12V connection is also required. The device is literally slotted into the bracket while a hole in the end of the ram is lowered on to the pip on the tiller. Plug in the power and away you go.

A cockpit-mounted wheel equivalent pilot is somewhat more involved, using a clutch and a belt drive. It may also have a remote control head, but it is not generally as powerful as an autopilot mounted below decks.

FEATURES OF A TILLER PILOT

- The drive is delivered by an electric ram.
- The control head is a simple device that may or may not offer some degree of sophistication on how the boat is steered by...
  - a basic course computer
  - and a fluxgate compass tucked away somewhere in the casing.

PLUS FACTORS

Above all, a basic tiller pilot is cheap – so cheap that any issue of carrying spares becomes redundant. If the thing only costs £350, you may as well ship a whole unit to produce like a genie from a lamp when yours dies the death, as it surely will sooner or later on planet-scale passages. This may sound like prodigal advice, but back in the days when I felt mugged at paying £1.50 for a pint can of varnish, my father observed: 'It may seem a lot now, but when placed at the foot of the ledger of human misery, you won't even notice it.' For 'human misery', we sailors can, of course, read, 'the shocking costs of running a boat'. As to the issue of expense, when confronted with a nasty-looking bill from some far-flung boatyard, I am mindful of the Royal Navy's dictum: 'If you can't take a joke, you shouldn't have signed on!'

Apart from ease of installation and cost, the other major benefit of a tiller pilot is that, in fair weather at least, it consumes remarkably little power. In easy conditions on the right boat it may ask for as little as 1 amp, with 3 amps being the most a big one is likely to guzzle when working hard. Clearly, under engine, these figures make power consumption irrelevant. For the sort of small boat that might be tempted to use one under sail, it may become an issue.

A rather off-centre benefit of a tiller pilot is that it can serve to drive a windvane system in conditions where direct wind power is proving problematic. It can also be hooked up to the windvane gear's servo unit as an under-power autopilot, doing away with the need for an expensive in-boat installation (see page 65).

DOWNSIDE

Tiller pilots have all their components out in the air and the spray. As long as the seals hold up this is no problem, but it is not an ideal situation, so care should be taken to keep them protected wherever possible, especially when not in use.

In my experience, there is a limit to what can be expected from a tiller pilot under sail. A perfectly balanced Harrison Butler classic might sail across an ocean with one, but this would be the exception. Put simply, they end up burning out, so if yours is important to your overall comfort, carry a spare.

Some manufacturers offer a fancier, more powerful tiller pilot with its compass, computer and control head remote from the ram. This has obvious advantages, but it winds up the cost and the installation effort.

■ Below-decks autopilots

A wholesome yacht with a decent below-decks autopilot can steer herself across an ocean with no other assistance. While windvanes offer big advantages for committed, long-term, short-handed crews, people with boats much over 50ft or merely on a one-off Atlantic circuit may not feel them worth the bother. Such craft are often already fitted with a serviceable autopilot.

FEATURES OF A BELOW-DECKS AUTOPILOT

PLUS POINTS

- Intelligent features

I've been impressed in recent years by how much more reliable and intelligent the best autopilots have become. My own B&G unit with its smart course computer does far more than simply react to a heading alteration as the boat yaws. Among other smart tricks, it 'learns' the yacht's characteristics, reacts to rudder loads and can steer a compass course or a course relative to the apparent wind. My boat is easy to steer and copes with wind shifts and gusts in a seamanlike and docile manner, so the combination with the pilot is remarkable. If I could rely on it totally, I'd be content to set out with no further assistance, except for the matter of the drain on the batteries.

- Out of the weather

All the delicate parts are down below out of the weather. The compass is remotely mounted in a sensible place away from deviating ferrous metal, and the control head is so user-friendly a novice can operate it. The latest units do not even have a remote compass.

- Wheel backup

An unexpected bonus from the electronic autopilot is that it can and should be linked directly to the quadrant on the rudder stock of a wheel-steered yacht. Not only will this take the strain completely off the wheel mechanism all the time the pilot is engaged, it also means that, should the wheel and its connecting system fail in some way, the boat can be steered to a safe haven using only the autopilot which is, of course, unaffected by the damage.

DOWNSIDE

- Ultimate reliability

I started delivering yachts way back in 1970. In those days you were grateful if you arrived with the autopilot still working after a few thousand miles. Huge improvements in reliability have made them a serious proposition today, yet they are not immune to failure. On a previous yacht of mine, a top-of-the-line Raymarine unit died after logging a mere 4,000 miles. The message on the control head advised that the drive unit had malfunctioned. This proved not to be the case. The processor, or 'brain' had failed, but it took some serious diagnostics to ascertain the problem. Replacement solved it.

Reliability is now much better, and failure a lot less common, with electronic autopilots. Generally pretty solid, when they do break, there isn't much most of us can do, although cross-examining the manufacturer about what might go wrong and carrying any recommended spares makes a lot of sense. Drive units relying on electric motors are a case in point. Although extremely consistent in their performance, many battle-hardened ocean wallopers still carry at least one extra. Some carry several. The hydraulic rams that are an option with larger units seem more reliable.

A further issue is that, as autopilots become more sophisticated, setting them up becomes an interesting mix of art and science. My current B&G unit is a miracle at keeping a course, but setting it up in a remote area without access to expert assistance proved a challenge requiring patience, a cool head to analyse the manual, and an understanding of the mechanics of sailing.

- Power consumption

Unlike the tiller pilot, where power consumption finds itself in the plus points, the serious autopilot lands on the other side of the equation. On a modern 45ft yacht, the pilot may well burn between 3 and 6 amps – more on full load – as it munches its way through a fully charged 105AH battery in 24 hours. A yacht with a nominal 420AH capacity is, in reality, kitted up with more like 250 safely usable amp hours. Add to the autopilot's requirements the demands of all the rest of the stuff without which few of us are now prepared to go to sea and you will realise that this is a major issue. Crossing the English Channel or the Gulf of Maine it's no problem, because the yacht will hook up to a marina on the other side after a day or two. On a long ocean voyage it means that serious charging arrangements must be in place.

- Cost

Also on the negative side of the scales is the cost. Smaller yachts and any tiller-steered boat will be well advised to consider the benefit of a tiller pilot or its clutched-in wheel-steering equivalent instead.

CONCLUSION
Having laid out the indictment, I have to say that I love my autopilot and would be reluctant to go to sea without it.

The author's cockpit instruments, with the autopilot control head on the right.

Windvane self-steering

For far-voyaging sailboats, this is really the Holy Grail. Windvanes are not cheap, unless you build them yourself, but they steer effortlessly and silently, they make no demands at all on the ship's batteries, the harder the wind blows the more powerful they become and they can be almost frighteningly reliable. The only downside of a windvane is that it steers by the apparent wind rather than the compass, but on an ocean passage this is of no significant consequence. Indeed, it can even be a benefit when close-hauled or running near the gybe point.

I fitted a Gunning pendulum-servo gear to my 32ft Colin Archer gaff cutter in 1975 and almost never steered her again until I sold her three years and several major crossings later. It couldn't cope under power, but it steered my boat beautifully on or off the wind. The Gunning followed the shifts close-hauled and gave reliable gybe protection on a broad reach. When the occasional part failed, it was so agricultural that I was able to fix it from on-board resources. It was the perfect solution.

Sadly, Gunning gears have not been available for decades, but a number of honourable alternatives are on the market, most of which perform equally well.

■ Pendulum-servo gear
Discounting miracle workers like pioneering solo circumnavigator Joshua Slocum in *Spray*, it was the first singlehanded races in the 1960s that finally cracked the self-steering nut. Sir Francis Chichester's 'Miranda', which employed a small sail pulling the helm, missed the bull's-eye by a long sea mile, but Blondie Hasler in the Folkboat *Jester* carried the day with a touch of genius. His pendulum-servo system still forms the basis of many of today's most successful gears.

The pendulum-servo gear uses water flow to beef up raw wind power. The vane is adjusted so as to feather when the boat is on course. When she wanders, the vane receives wind on

The Windpilot Pacific pendulum-servo gear gives the author a cushy ride in some heavy weather.

one side or the other. Whether vertically or horizontally mounted, it reacts by pivoting. This activates the servo paddle, which is a deep blade cutting through the water beneath the windvane. The paddle is hinged fore and aft, so that as it is twisted off the 'feathering' position by the vane, it is kicked up sideways like a pendulum by the water flowing past it. If you doubt the power, try it with an oar when buzzing along in the dinghy.

This swinging movement to one side at a time is transferred to the helm by lines joining the paddle to the tiller, or to a drum on the wheel. As the paddle is displaced, it drags the helm with it. This steers the boat until she is once again sailing at the original angle to the apparent wind. Vane, and hence paddle, now return to the 'feather' position and the process ceases until repeated again. The net result is a surprisingly straight course in most conditions. Users are strongly advised not to get trapped between the tiller and a cockpit bench with the gear in full cry. I have suffered nasty bruising and on one wild night I almost ended up with a squeaky voice.

The only downsides I can think of for a gear like this are that it doesn't enhance the appearance of the stern, and mean-minded harbourmasters may bang you for an extra pound or two for the added overall length. If it uses turning blocks, it will pay to carry a few spares as the constant working can wear them out, but not for a long time if they are any good. The same goes for tiller or wheel lines. Vanes are removable, so a spare, or at least a suitable sheet of plywood and a likely counterweight, can be a lifesaver.

There's an Aries Servo-Pendulum windvane in there somewhere!

Some of the gears are produced by real enthusiasts who look after their customers like members of a family. Windpilot (www.windpilot.com) is a case in point, with after-sales service that is second to none. This is Rolls-Royce equipment. If your budget is straitened and you relish a moderate-skills DIY task, the Hebridean unit (www.windvaneselfsteering.co.uk), which you build yourself from a kit for extremely modest money, is well worth investigating.

■ Trim-tab servo gears

These are usually home-made by sailors with a bent for engineering. The price is therefore what the 'manufacturer' chooses to make it, but it is invariably popular compared with the commercially produced alternatives.

All that is required is a stern-hung rudder with an accessible, straight trailing edge. A full-length trim tab is hinged to this. The trim tab is operated by a windvane and some suitable linkage. That's the clever bit, but it has not been beyond the ingenuity of a number of my friends. The tiller is left free and the windvane set up to feather when the yacht is on course. When she wanders the vane senses it and passes the message to the tab, which turns. The rudder, by basic fluid dynamics, swings the opposite way and stays there until the vane feathers again. The system is beautiful in its simplicity. It works for aircraft trim tabs and it works on yachts too. My chum Nick Skeates has circumnavigated a number of times in his home-built steel gaff cutter *Wylo II*, using no other form of self-steering.

■ Auxiliary rudders

The auxiliary rudder windvane is less powerful than a pendulum servo, but shows good results in well-balanced yachts. A substantial rudder is hooked up directly to a windvane. Together, they form a removable unit. The boat is placed on course and her main rudder is locked when she is stable. The vane is then activated and, while the main rudder handles steady weather-helm issues, deviations from course are taken up by the auxiliary rudder. For a yacht that suits it, the system has one huge advantage: the gear is, effectively, a built-in emergency rudder. Hydrovane make a well-proven example.

Hermaphrodite systems
■ Pacific Plus windvane

Because of the inherent difficulties attending the connection of a straight pendulum servo to some yachts' wheels, Windpilot produce a stand-alone unit that uses a pendulum servo to operate an integral auxiliary rudder. The main rudder is set on course, the vane is weathercocked and the gear does the rest. It sounds complicated, but it is engineered in Germany, has a good reputation and many trouble-free passages lie behind it. Like the Hydrovane with its auxiliary rudder, Windpilot's Pacific Plus can be used as a rudder of sorts in the event of the main steering failing.

The Windpilot servo gear on the author's 22-ton gaff cutter being driven by a tiller pilot.

◾ Tiller pilot/windvane

I found out about this hybrid system for myself before realising that others were also using it to great effect. All it needs is a servo windvane system, the smallest, cheapest pilot available and a little lateral thinking.

Initially, I set up a tiller pilot I had bought on an optimistic whim directly on to the tiller of *Westernman* (a 20-ton gaff cutter I owned for 13 years from the mid-1990s). The pilot stood no chance, until one day I rigged it between the taffrail and the windvane unit, discovering as I did so that Peter Forthman of Windpilot had already thought of this. The windvane casting had a mounting already in place for the tiller pilot. Instead of trying to shove the mighty iron tiller across, all it now had to do was tweak the servo paddle. No longer driven by the wind, the paddle of the steering gear was adjusted continually by the tiller pilot, which was steering a compass course. Because the arrangement proved equally effective when sailing, I often used the pilot in preference to the vane if the wind was shifty, when I needed a steady compass course or running in light winds when the vane didn't work so well.

Battery drain with such a system is negligible, since the tiny motor in the autohelm hands all the tough stuff straight over to the pendulum-servo paddle. This revels in its labour. The faster the boat goes, the harder it pulls, and the boat steers herself without fuss for thousands of miles.

It's a sweet mix of old and new technology. There's more than one way to skin a cat, as the bosun's mate said to the man lashed to the grating.

Experimenting with a hybrid system.

5 SYSTEMS

When I first went out on the ocean as a lad, the question of what systems to install centred around what sort of stereo tape deck to buy and whether or not to equip the boat with a ship-to-shore radio. As to the latter, we didn't bother. We carried 45 gallons of fresh water, 15 gallons of diesel and around 10kg of propane for cooking. We gathered rainwater in tropical downpours and on one occasion we were 42 days between ports without any discomfort.

Today, some would still consider my yacht to be rather light in the radio department, but she has a powerful generator, a four-burner propane cooker with solenoid shut-offs for safety, a 110V fridge-freezer, pressurised water with hot on tap, electric winches, windlass and black- and grey-water holding tanks, as well as on-board PCs that navigate, communicate and entertain. Because these days I favour higher latitudes over the more crowded tropical routes, I threw out the mains-powered air-conditioning units I inherited and installed a solid fuel stove. Most people would have plumped for warm-air heating with more electrical reliance and diesel consumption. I have LED lighting and, if my tanks weren't so enormous, I'd also fit a water maker.

The list seems endless and it pays to remind ourselves that nearly all this kit has arrived on the scene since the days of classical yacht cruising when Eric Hiscock, Erling Tambs, Bill Robinson and their ilk made safe, successful voyages with none of it.

The conclusion must be that all systems fall into two categories: gear we need and gear we'd like to have. Gear we need is vital to our safety, happiness and the successful conclusion of our voyaging. Gear we'd like contributes to our creature comforts, our social life, our interests and, perhaps, our fun. If a particular item in the 'like to have' bracket fails on passage and can't be fixed on board without making our lives a misery, we should be able to carry on merrily without it.

Which division an item ends up in will depend on how you view life, but I had some of my best times cruising in a boat whose engine fell into the 'like to have' category. When it failed semi-terminally from an obscure complaint in South America, I sailed all the way to the United States before it could be fixed. The trip took six months with no battery power. We had oil lamps, a well-found boat and sextant navigation. We hardly noticed its loss until we arrived at civilisation and needed it to motor up the Intracoastal Waterway. It was then upgraded to 'must have' and, sure enough, the time produced the man. A retired chief artificer, US Navy, happened by and solved my problem without fuss, free of charge, in his basement workshop. That was 1976. I still have the tiny vise grip he gave me to complete my tool kit.

This chapter concerns itself with some general education about boat electrics, then concentrates on the sort of upgraded kit that is important on ocean passages but might not be found on all coastal cruising yachts. I have, for example, left out any mention of LPG safety because this is dealt with in my book *The Complete Day Skipper* and is assumed knowledge at this level.

Electricity

The basics

Whatever systems we choose to install, unless we are taking an aggressively Luddite route, we are all going to require some level of electric power. Almost all yachts operate primarily on a system of low-voltage direct current using power stored in accumulators generally known as batteries. The batteries are charged by various means, but the core source is usually some form of alternator driven by the main engine or a dedicated generating engine. Once charged, the batteries hold on to the power rather like a fuel tank until something starts using it. How long the tanks hold out depends on what the user is, and the time they take to refill is governed by the capacity of the charging device. There is a multitude of modifying factors, but these are the rock-bottom lines.

Direct current: nuts and bolts

■ Volts

In our situation, voltage can be taken as a measurement of the energy contained within an electric circuit, at a given point. The absolute definition of voltage involves the tricky concept of 'potential difference', but fortunately we don't need to go into this. As long as we know that voltage is a vital factor in determining how much power we have left, how much we are using and how much we are putting back into the system, that will suffice.

Yacht systems use either 12V, 24V or some combination of the two. In a 12V setup, healthy, fully charged batteries at rest should sit at around 12.7V. Some may be less than this, but if the reading is below 12.3V after an idle period of some hours, the battery is not happy.

On charge, voltage may rise to well in excess of 14V in the early stages, falling to a little over 13V when fully charged. If charging continues in this condition, the battery is said to 'float' and as long as the voltage has fallen to around 13V, no damage will ensue. When the charging is discontinued, either by shutting down the engine or disconnecting a shore lead, voltage will fall away to its at-rest state.

If voltage drops to less than 12V, the battery is in a parlous condition and must be charged soonest. A lead-acid battery left like this for more than a few hours will begin to 'sulphate'. Its interior chemistry is receiving a hammering and its plates are starting to coat over with lead sulphate. Once this happens the battery may well be on the skids, so it pays big dividends not to flatten your batteries. As one electrical engineer eloquently put it: 'Few batteries die a natural death, most are murdered.'

Although voltage varies as a battery is put under load, the table on page 68 may prove useful for owners whose boats have digital volt meters but no inbuilt 'percentage of charge remaining' meter.

Percentage of charge	12V battery voltage	24V battery voltage
100	12.70	25.40
95	12.64	25.25
90	12.58	25.16
85	12.52	25.04
80	12.46	24.92
75	12.40	24.80
70	12.36	24.72
65	12.32	24.64
60	12.28	24.56
55	12.24	24.48
50	12.20	24.40
45	12.16	24.32
40	12.12	24.24
35	12.08	24.16
30	12.04	24.08
25	12.00	24.00
20	11.98	23.96
15	11.96	23.92
10	11.94	23.88
5	11.92	23.84
Discharged	11.90	23.80

WATTS = VOLTS × AMPS

watts = volts × amps

Because watts = volts × amps, it follows that

watts ÷ volts = amps

This means a 12W light bulb in a 12V system will draw 1 amp (12 ÷ 12)

If it is illuminated for 1 hour, it will draw '1 amp hour'.

■ Amps

An ampère, more commonly known as a humble 'amp', is a unit measuring electrical current as it flows through a conductor from positive points to relatively negative points. For 'conductor', read 'light bulb', 'fridge', 'radio', 'autopilot', etc.

More current, more amps; more amps, more drain if it's coming out of the battery; higher charging if it's going in.

■ Watts

A watt can be defined as the rate at which work is done when 1 amp of current flows through an electrical potential difference of 1V. In practical day-to-day life on a voyaging yacht, it is the measurement of how much power a conductor or utility (see above) will demand of the battery.

■ Power consumption

All power consumption is governed by a simple but fundamental formula that determines how much battery a utility will drink up (see panel below left).

■ Amp hours

The amp hour forms the core of all battery management. By using easy mental arithmetic, we can assess accurately how much it will 'cost' us in power terms to run anything on board. See the example on page 69.

■ Battery types

Batteries vary hugely in price and, to some extent, in performance. The high-end units are so expensive that there is much to be said for choosing a moderate-spec, economical make, with sealed caps so that they can't spill if the yacht is knocked down. Whatever you go for, they will probably need replacing every five years or so. In order fully to understand the options available for yacht batteries, it's best to consult a specialist book or website such as www.integrelsolutions.com/blog/2019/06/19/choosing-right-battery-for-yacht/.

Batteries on board have to deal with two different types of task. It's important not to mix them up.

■ House batteries

The domestic supply or 'house batteries' should be of the 'deep cycle' variety. These hold their voltage levels high under moderate load. They continue to do so as they run down until finally the levels drop dramatically and it's all over until they are recharged. They are designed to stand this sort of treatment by using heavy, relatively low surface-area plates. While too many deep discharges are not good for them, they can handle a moderate amount of abuse. The benefits are obvious. On a long night with no engine running, what is required is voltage that holds up right through and can be recharged at convenience, not a battery whose output is steadily diminishing under load.

Capacity in amp hours

The capacity of a deep-cycle battery is rated in AH (amp hours). This is exactly what it says. A typical 12V, 105AH unit can, in theory, push out enough power to run a 12W light bulb for 105 hours. Reality is different. While a new battery can deliver a large percentage of its theoretical output, it is far better for its long-term health if it is only rarely asked for more than half. Thus, in practical terms, the 105AH battery can be expected to dish up 50 or so amp hours from full charge. Given proper, managed charging and sensible use patterns, it should continue to do its work for many years, with five being a realistic target.

A typical 45ft ocean cruiser will have 400–500 nominal amp hours' house capacity. Smaller yachts less, bigger ones more.

AMP HOURS

An incandescent 25W bulb, as is found in a masthead tricolour light, will draw approximately 2 amps (25 ÷ 12), and hit the battery for 20 amp hours if left on for a ten-hour night.

By contrast, old-fashioned bulbs in lower running lights typically rate at 15W, so a port light, a starboard light and a stern light add up to 45W, drawing 3¾ amps (45 ÷ 12), or 37½ amp hours over the same period. Quite a hike over the tricolour.

Three modern LED running lights typically add up to a mere 6W, giving an amperage of 0.5 (6 ÷ 12), and 5 amp hours overnight. Makes changing any remaining incandescent units a no-brainer, doesn't it!

Read the spec of any battery carefully before choosing.

Charging

It makes no sense to have a huge battery bank if your charging unit consists only of the unmodified alternator supplied as standard with a 55HP diesel. Not only is this too small for a sailing yacht, it is also restricted in output by voltage regulators designed for continuous use in power-driven vessels. The bottom line is that you'll be running the engine for far too long. Whether you opt for a powerful wind generator, a towed generator, the ever-improving solar panels or a 'genset' with a serious charger at its heart, you'll need something to back up the main engine. The absolute minimum on a really basic boat would be to install a 'smart charging' regulator that at least allows the alternator to achieve its full potential without blowing up the batteries.

As we shall see, it's easy to run away with 100AH in a 24-hour day. Even with a smart charge regulator, a 50 amp alternator is absolutely not going to make that good in two hours because, although theoretically capable, the general reluctance of batteries

A 12V system charging hard.

A North American 110V mains power system cranking out about 2½kW.

to accept charge as they fill up will strike it out. You need to consider which of the various alternatives will deliver the goods reliably and cheaply, then decide on the one that suits your boat and your character.

Some people love the simplicity of a wind generator. I hate the noise most of them make. It winds me up, so it's off my list. Right now, I'm using a very quiet 5kW diesel generator, which also runs my hot water and my refrigeration, but I'm sitting here writing a book and not sailing round the world with a limited supply of fuel. If I were, I'd certainly look into using the water flowing past my hull. I'd also think hard about modern solar power, which has made colossal strides in efficiency, especially if I had a catamaran with a big, permanent Bimini that incorporated the panels and I planned to sail the tropic seas.

■ Engine start batteries

Engine start batteries are different. Rather than a steady, moderate delivery, they must be capable of shoving out a massive punch in short bursts. This surge of current is needed to start a cold engine. Once the engine fires, the alternator begins putting the charge back into the battery, so there's every chance it will go through life without ever being drained below 20 per cent of total capacity. Even if a number of 'starts' are demanded, such as may occur while bleeding a fuel system, a well-chosen start battery will be able to cope. In order to achieve this heavy current, an engine battery uses thin plates to increase the active surface area.

Cranking amps

Engine start batteries may have an amp hour rating, but the important figure is the 'CCA' (cold cranking amps). You may also see an 'RC' (reserve capacity) rating, which represents the number of minutes that the battery can deliver 25 amps while keeping its voltage above the sudden-death level of 10.5V.

A dedicated engine-start battery for a 55HP diesel. Note the high CCA-value on the spec.

A typical deep-cycle battery has up to three times the RC of a start battery, but will only push out half to three-quarters of the CCAs. A dedicated deep-cycle battery will hold up after several hundred total discharge/recharge cycles. A start battery won't enjoy going totally flat at all.

■ Battery maintenance

Various grades and varieties of lead-acid batteries are in the marketplace, as are gel units and some ultra-light, extremely expensive power sources that don't use lead. Any lead-acid units must be sited in a well-ventilated space and monitored for physical condition. It pays to smear Vaseline on the terminals to discourage corrosion. If the cells are not sealed, open them up and check the level of the electrolyte periodically. Never let a plate become dry at the top. They should all be covered by a centimetre or so. Use only distilled water to top up the cells, except in an emergency. The small amounts of impurity in tap water will ionise in the acid and do some degree of permanent damage.

■ Battery failure and backup

Most of today's engines cannot be hand-started, but usually they fire up readily enough. If a motor is growing sulky at start time, it's vital to seek the reason before it becomes a serious problem just when you don't want one. Occasionally, even a healthy engine needs more 'starts' than usual. For this reason, a plentiful supply of CCAs is an axiomatic 'must'.

As long as the domestic bank remains in good fettle, this can easily be hooked up to the engine start battery if it goes flat, either via a permanently mounted emergency link, or simply by a serious set of jump leads. The house units won't boast the CCAs of the engine battery, but they'll have plenty of grunt to get it going if they are charged. It is by no means unknown, however, for some oversight or malfunction to flatten all the batteries together. In a well-found modern yacht, this may theoretically be impossible, but it has happened to me more than once. What then? There's no roadside assistance out there to come and bail you out.

A classic long-term cruiser charging set-up. Wind and solar.

Wind chargers really come into their own at anchor.

Some people carry a petrol-driven, hand-start generator. The trouble with this apparently useful solution is twofold. You might not want petrol on board, and even if you are comfortable with this, it will still take at least 15 minutes – probably more like half an hour – to liven up a dead battery to engine-starting status. Even then, it won't have much life in it for a while longer.

The alternative is either a spare cranking battery kept fully charged in the battery box, ready to hook up via the jump leads, or an emergency start pack such as may be bought in any decent motor factor outlet. These latter are the sort of thing carried by roadside breakdown mechanics. They work well and are less money than a generator, but beware cheap and nasty ones that look like a good deal. I have personally had one of these refuse to start a healthy two-litre petrol engine when the thing had been on charge as specified and was less than a year old.

A power pack or a battery can be charged either by hooking up to the main bank from time to time, or by rigging an inexpensive dedicated trickle charger. My own preference is for a high-quality spare battery. I use this to power the tiny pump that inflates my dinghy, and each time I blow up the flubber I recharge the battery. This stops it being left in a dusty corner to deteriorate. A quality power pack is just as good an answer, but do be sure to source a high-spec example. The poor ones are notorious for failing to crank when jumping a totally flat battery.

Armed with this information, we are now in a position to assess which systems we can 'afford' electrically and which we may prefer to leave ashore, or at least to shut down at sea.

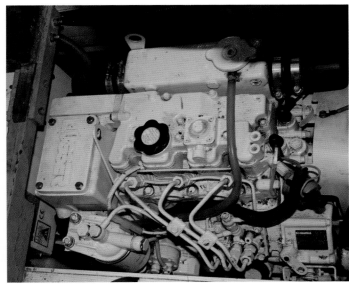

A 5kW diesel generator.

'Need-to-have' systems

Cooking stove

These are dealt with in Chapter 6, but since this chapter deals with questions of battery drain and power supply in general, it should be noted that if you are tempted by the very safe option of electric cookery, you are going to need a mains-power genset to run the stove. Also, you and your crew have to accept that every time you turn it on, the generator will either start automatically or you'll have to flash it up. In very large yachts, with generators running most of the time in harbour, this is not a problem. In any boat that is likely to be rubbing shoulders with her peers in a crowded anchorage, you may find yourself unpopular with yachts downwind of your exhaust.

Refrigeration

Refrigeration on modern cruising yachts is now virtually a 'given'. However, if your budget and battery capacity are both severely limited, don't forget that you can still opt to have none. Fridges have only arrived in general use since the 1970s. Before then, virtually everyone managed without. My wife and I have owned three ocean cruisers with no refrigeration and have lived on board in the tropics without it. One or two of my friends still do, and so if times are tight, it's better to go sailing and put up with warm beer and no milk than it is to wait months to save up for a fridge, only to have it break down when you think you need it most. Always remember, harbours are well stocked with sailors searching for a 'fridge man'.

A heavy-duty holding plate.

■ Types of refrigeration

Holding-plate fridges use a remote compressor to freeze a 'cold sink' in the fridge filled with some high calorific value product, often a liquid or gel. Once frozen down in a well-insulated box, they hold their 'cool' remarkably. The cooling process is a one-stop job for a compressor. This may be an AC unit deriving power from a generator or shore hook-up. It may also be a direct-drive system via a belt from the engine. Even better, and today's default choice, are the increasingly popular 12/24V compressor units now available, the best of which are downright frugal in their power grab. AC units are power hungry, but given a good holding plate and efficient insulation, 1–2 hours a day will often suffice, during which time the generator also charges batteries, heats water, etc. This arrangement is becoming increasingly outdated, however, with solar and wind generators delivering sufficient power to keep a 12V compressor well fed at anchor, backed up by an in-water 'green' generator at sea.

■ Power consumption

A modern Technautics CoolBlue 12V compressor-driven fridge-freezer of 7 cubic feet (200 litre) capacity, is going to draw under 30AH daily, given good insulation, less than overpowering ambient heat and that it is cold to start with. Solar and wind can easily supply this. A unit using an engine or generator compressor will demand up to two hours' running per day, but during this time other electrical demands on the batteries can also be taken care of. At sea, you may well be wanting to replace the 100AH or so grabbed by the lights, navigation system, radar, autopilot and the rest, plus heating shower water into the bargain. If your 'green' systems fall short of this, perhaps giving the diesel a two-hour stint doesn't sound so bad after all.

These are murky and highly specialised waters. To make recommendations is beyond my competence, so I'll resist the temptation. I've seen many different arrangements work well, but I've also experienced endless frustrations when cheap, poorly installed refrigeration fails in remote parts of the planet not yet discovered by the fridge engineers.

It's best not to be totally reliant on the fridge. Then, if it does go down, you can carry on enjoying life. You may be obliged to give away a few joints of defrosting meat to neighbouring yachts, but you make good pals doing that. And in the absence of cold beer, you can always drink rum and water with a squeeze of lime as the sun goes down. From whole-life experience, I recommend this without hesitation.

Water makers

Water makers are far from cheap and they are fairly heavy. They represent yet another demand on the batteries and are relatively complex, requiring a surprising amount of plumbing and more than one through-hull fitting. They need spare parts and proper maintenance. They also only work well in clear water so they aren't going to help you in the English Channel, but all these drawbacks come to nought in seas where filling water tanks is impossible or, at best, a recurring misery.

■ Types

If you have an AC generator and an AC-driven fridge, you'll be running the genset for upwards of two hours per day. You may well be doing so for batteries in any case. To operate the pump necessary for an AC water maker won't inconvenience you at all. It will draw 25 AC amps or so, but it will deliver 20 imperial gallons in an hour, which will do nicely. If your crew are using more than 40 gallons in a day, it's time you paid them off.

If you don't have a genset, you can fit a similar output pump to the engine via a simple belt drive. Otherwise, it's back to the dear old DC mains again. For a unit that makes up to 10 gallons an hour, you can expect to draw anything up to 25 amps at 12V, although efficiencies are being gained each year and performance as good as 20 amps for 12 gallons is claimed. A lower-powered unit may only grab 8 amps, and if 7 gallons or so per hour sounds useful, this conversion rate is achievable using modern hydraulically boosted low-pressure pumps off the ship's 12V mains. Such systems are in successful use on ocean rowing boats charging batteries by solar panels only.

One downside of DC units is that unless the batteries are in top condition, the actual quality of the product may suffer. Some salt then appears in the drinking water, so, assuming you have more than one tank, it pays handsomely only to top off a single source from such a water maker. If you lose one tankful of fresh water it's a nuisance. To lose the lot might prove catastrophic.

Holding tanks

More and more cruising venues are, quite reasonably, insisting on yachts using holding tanks for 'black water' until well offshore or at a pump-out station. As green awareness grows, this is not specifically an ocean sailing issue, but it is worth making sure before leaving on a cruise that your tank is sound and, in particular, that its hoses are of the expensive, no-odour variety. When it gets hot down below, anything given half a chance to smell will do so, and waste pipes are the champions of pong. Unless your boat is very upmarket, the builder will have put in cheap plumbing. Change the hoses for the best that money can buy and you won't be sorry.

'Want-to-have' systems

What items fall into this category will depend on whether you consider your yacht as a boat, with all the necessary drawbacks and the enormous benefits of life afloat, or whether you prefer to see her as a shore home away from home. It's a grand thing to be on a yacht with a washing machine, but in order to service this luxury she must also have a lot of mains (AC) power and large amounts of water, plus, in all probability, various pumps and through-hull fittings. Plenty to go wrong, in other words.

Microwave ovens are considered essentials on some boats. I've even seen craft with no oven but the microwave. Lovely as long as the AC keeps on delivering and you don't mind a generator running every time you fancy a hot pie. Others may disagree. If you want a free microwave, the one that came with my boat may still be in the dumpster in Southampton where my wife threw it, before baking a couple of perfect loaves in her propane stove.

Cabin heating and cooling don't really belong in this section. Depending on where you plan to cruise, one or other is likely to be essential. Not knowing your plans, I can't say which, so I've entered them as options instead.

Air conditioning and keeping cool

Air conditioning (A/C or aircon) can really only be powered by alternating current at mains voltages. Units are readily sourced at quite reasonable prices, but installation is not simple and additional through-hull fittings are required. Because of the need for mains power, aircon is only available to yachts with generators, or those content to enjoy the cooling flow of air when lying alongside, hooked up to the town services. That said, anyone crazy enough to be in Florida in summer is either going to have to fit aircon or spend most of his days in a cool-air bar. Anywhere in the tropics where a refreshing breeze is not guaranteed is much the same. With the sun overhead, the afternoon heat is pretty hard to take.

Fortunately, if you can't afford full-on aircon, you don't want all those holes in the hull or would rather use the locker space more usefully for wine and other essentials of life, help is at hand. It is possible to buy carry-on aircon units, which do the job reasonably well as long as you can offer the beast a mains power socket. Dometic in the US can supply one that is designed to fit in a forehatch. Just plug and play.

Any 12V aircon I have seen has been somewhat Mickey Mouse for marine use, and the general domestic portable units, while excellent for what they do, always seem to demand large-diameter exhaust hoses that are never long enough to reach a hatch.

■ Natural cooling

Thank Heaven the Almighty has given us an alternative to aircon, free of charge, as long as we anchor and keep in the tradewind belts. Most American yachts and many from the Mediterranean countries have their skylights and forehatches hinged at the aft end. When propped open, these act as wind scoops. A yacht designed with a good supply of these generally vents like a vacuum cleaner in a good breeze, so if your hatches are mounted the other way round, flip them before you leave and enjoy God's free air-conditioning service. If you can't flip them, look into rigging some canvas wind scoops. These can be made from a bit of old sailcloth that you find lying around. Better is to buy them. Some of the commercial ones are amazingly effective.

For Bimini cockpit shelters, see Chapter 6.

Cabin heating

The ins and outs of blown-air heating are so well documented elsewhere that it seems superfluous to include a commentary on them here. The upsides are obvious; instant, dry warmth at the touch of a button in every cabin where an outlet has been installed.

The downsides are more insidious and seem never to be mentioned in mainstream publications. A blown-air system involves a lot of big-bore, insulated ducting to transfer the heat to where it is wanted. It uses up valuable locker space. In my experience, reliability starts to deteriorate after five years or so. I have even shipped out with units that rusted out altogether in the humidity and heat of the tropics. The exhaust is noisy. The roaring sound can ruin that magic moment on a still, frosty evening when you take your crystal tumbler of malt whisky on deck to enjoy the moonlit anchorage, only to be assailed by a sound akin to what the Pentecostal disciples described as 'a mighty rushing wind'. Then there is the drain on what may well be precious diesel (around half a gallon in eight hours) and the load on the poor old batteries to the tune of up to 2 amps once it is running.

The alternative is a solid fuel stove. I have had these on all my deep-sea yachts. I have burned chopped wood all the way from Nova Scotia to Ireland which, although free, was very space-consuming. I have squirrelled away half a ton of smokeless coal on my 50ft pilot cutter and run the stove continuously from the UK to Norway, then on to Greenland and Newfoundland. More recently, I installed a small stove in my GRP Mason 44. I can easily 'lose' 100kg of smokeless fuel in clean, sealed bags around the ship and run my heater silently and without other loss of fuel, amps or anything else at sea and in harbour whenever I choose.

The late Ed Burnett, the designer, once said to me that he loved solid fuel heaters because they gave off what he described as a 'thick heat'. Nobody can define this, but it's true. The warmth is more satisfying. Plus, Man needs fire. It is a special thing. It sets us apart from the animals. Show me a male human and I'll introduce you to someone who secretly enjoys lighting a fire and carrying out the ashes once a day.

Nothing warms the toes and the heart like a real fire. It burns coal, peat, driftwood, even the harbourmaster's fence posts.

Installation is low-tech, but you'll have to build some sort of fireplace and tile it. You may also need to have the flue and chimney custom made. On the Mason I ran my flue up through a convenient dorade box, but suitable deck fittings are still available from real chandlers such as Arthur Beale of Portsmouth.

Luxuries

Mains-power items aside, most other things boil down to a question of power drain, cost and ease of installation/portability. The choice is entirely personal. CD players are now largely superseded by tablets, iPods and the rest, which can load all the music most of us will ever need, then play it via whatever system suits you. I am a music fan, but I don't really need monster woofers to be happy. My boat has a sophisticated stereo system with big speakers, but these days I mostly just use my tablet and a quality 'boom-box', which picks up its signals via Bluetooth. No cockpit speakers for me. I just carry out the box and fire it up.

TV is another puzzle. Most of us don't go cruising to watch *Coronation Street* or *Neighbours*, but plenty of us would like to enjoy a movie on a damp dismal night when we're alone. The answer is either to use a laptop with a big screen built in, or to kit the boat out with a larger flat screen and hook this up to the PC. Within reach of solid internet wi-fi, catch-up sites allow us to watch sport, news or whatever else takes our fancy, so bothering with a full-on TV is really too much trouble for most folks in these electronically enlightened times.

System Management

Although each system can be considered a stand-alone unit, any piece of equipment requiring fuel or electrical power in a yacht must be seen as part of a total management system. Whether it's a fridge hammering an AC generator, or a stove needing space to store coal, they all relate to one another. The subject is considered in more detail in Chapter 14.

6 ACCOMMODATION

An ocean-cruising yacht is going to spend weeks at sea and probably months in harbour. People will live on board, maybe even with no other home. Her accommodation should therefore be a homely, reassuring, comfortable, convenient, safe place to live. It must feature the following:

ACCOMMODATION

- Sea berths, one for each crew member and, for couples who want it, a serious double bunk for harbours.
- Somewhere on deck and down below to sit in comfort on either tack where the crew can read, eat, play with children, listen to music, or drink and yarn with fellow-rovers.
- A safe, comfortable cockpit that remains so at any angle of heel.
- A galley that works as well at sea as it does upright in a marina.
- A decent heads compartment that can give essential satisfaction at an angle of up to 30° – on either tack. If it has a proper shower, so much the better.
- Copious guaranteed dry stowage for food, drink, spares, tools, books, charts and all the necessities of voyaging life.
- Good headroom for the more mature. Young adults don't need it.

OK. That's about it. Next time you visit a boat show, take a critical look at what's on offer. You will discount many of the offerings on sight. We'll go through the boat now, paying attention to what counts.

The saloon

This is the heart of a cruising boat. How you create atmosphere will be up to you. Some folks like a minimalist approach. Personally, I enjoy a few cushions around the place and a more homely feel. Knick-knacks can always be stowed for sea and they make a home in harbour. The vital component is that whoever you are and whatever your personality, the saloon absolutely must feel secure and reassuring at sea. When all hell is breaking loose on deck, you really need a good place of retreat.

The saloon aboard my Mason 44 cutter **Constance**.

A long-range cruiser often develops a real character below decks. Souvenirs from distant ports find homes in odd corners, and so on. I love to have pictures on my bulkheads, but you won't find a photograph of the yacht sailing. There's more than enough of that going on outside. Our favourite image is one my wife and I have had ever since our first boat. It's a small, oak-framed reproduction of a 19th-century Sutcliffe glass-plate image of a ploughman with his horses, taking a break under a low hill with the team steaming gently in the morning air. You can almost smell the turned earth. It's like a steady hand on the shoulder when the seas are running houses high, the boat has been hove-to for 24 hours and you are starting to wonder why you bothered.

General arrangement

The best arrangement of all is the oldest, but it does have limitations as boats have grown bigger. The simple bench settee down either side with a table between is ideal, and if you don't try to cram in too much else there's plenty of space to angle the seat backs sweetly for comfort, rather than leaving the wretched incumbent perched against a vertical support that never, ever works.

Lockers can proliferate outboard of the seat backs, while at shoulder level, book shelves can accommodate all the reading matter for a prolonged cruise. If you prefer to read electronically you can use the shelves for something else or box them in tastefully and have even more lockers. The settees have the advantage that one is always downhill and both are usually in the part of the boat with the least motion. That means a short-handed crew can use them as sea berths – very useful in a boat with a double in the fore cabin, for example. On my boat, we have an offset aft cabin forward of the aft cockpit that does have a usable sea berth, but when the going is tough and we're two-up, we prefer to sleep one at a time in the saloon.

As beam increases, the classical format may be less successful. At their best, dinettes can work brilliantly and on some of the Scandinavian boats they are a wonder of clear thinking. If they aren't properly considered, however, a poor dinette is a disaster. They are often too short to sleep on or, worse, are curved tastefully to render them useless except to impress the unwary in a boat show. They have vertical seat backs that guarantee discomfort instead of a nicely canted setup, and many are all too often difficult to manoeuvre the human frame into. Treat dinettes with suspicion and don't confuse them with well-designed settees with athwartships legs fore and aft, where the outboard side is at least 6ft 6 inches long.

As for 'island' seating in the middle with a linear galley outboard, this is an abomination. It just doesn't work. It's OK for a charter boat where, all things being equal, life will go on mainly out in the cockpit and few, if any, meals eaten at table at sea but if a yacht is ever to feel like home, forget it. The cook will tumble over the midships seat, and when he has regained his feet, he will very likely be brained by cans, bottles and even, in one memorable case, a large Polish sausage plummeting out of the galley lockers. What's more, all hands will have to spend their evening looking at the washing-up until some poor masher finally volunteers to deal with it.

I once made a passage on such a boat with my wife. It was an upmarket 45-footer and had cost the owner a packet. It sailed very well, I must admit, although it slammed horribly when going uphill, but the galley was a joke. We had to handle a long leg with the cooking on the uphill side. My wife, who, in a proper boat, has turned out full meals for a crew of seven bang on the dot three times a day while working to windward across the Greenland Sea in gale force conditions, was barely able to rustle up a cup of tea. Don't be tempted by such yachts, and if the salesman advises that many are even now circumnavigating, smile kindly and spare a thought for the poor, suffering incumbents.

Sea berths

The first thing to say about sea berths is that they must be in the right part of the ship; low down and either well aft or at least amidships. Absolutely not forward of the mast. Nobody deserves that fate.

Years ago, people in the know used to reckon that a proper sea berth was narrow. I have found this not to be true. Many of us like to sleep in a foetal position, and it is perfectly possible to jam either back or knees against one side or the other. Given this, and the obvious proviso that a berth needs to be long enough to stretch out, the main demands are support from both sides, somewhere to lean back against to drink one's pre-watch tea, and a good reading light. In other words, if you can't sit up in bed, you aren't going to have a good time. It may not be necessary on a race boat where the watch turns in totally bushed, but in a cruiser whose people want to read, bunks without bed ends or, more usually, well-sited bulkheads, are a misery.

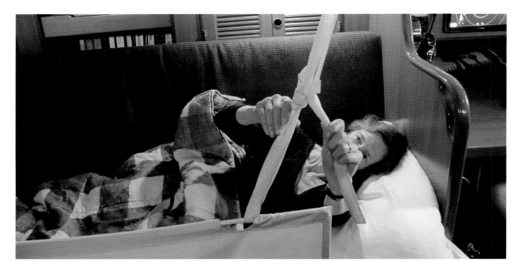

If there's no solid leeboard, a well-designed lee cloth with a stiffener at the top and easily adjustable tapes is a good working substitute.

The reading light must be specific to the bunk and it must really work. I have sailed in many a yacht whose designers or builders were clearly illiterate and expected their victims to be the same.

As to support when sleeping, the ideal is some sort of leeboard a foot or more high. We have managed this by having the lower part of the saloon seat back lift out and drop into slots on the inboard side. It's easy, it transforms a seat that may legitimately be rather too narrow for sleeping into a decent-sized berth, and as a bonus, it creates a cave behind the leeboard when it's back in place as a settee in which the ex-sleeper can stow the bedding. If you can't manage this, the only answer is a leecloth. This must be deep enough to hold you comfortably and have enough spare material to secure well under the bunk cushion. To be successful, it also needs a stiffish batten along the top. The webbing or lines that secure it to robust rings in the deckhead or high on a bulkhead should tie off within easy reach of the sleeper and be tensioned downwards so he can pull himself in.

The galley

Like cooks, galleys come in many shapes and sizes. Some are wonderful. Some, as noted, are disastrous. How effective the galley is depends in the end on just a few demands. It must work at a steady angle of heel. It must be tight enough to stop the cook being rattled around if the yacht is rolling and backed up with a bum strap as required. It must have plenty of work surfaces with high fiddles (see page 78). Sinks must be deep enough not to throw the water out and if space exists for two, the opportunity must be grabbed. Washing up at sea is easy with a spare sink. With only one, draining plates must be balanced somehow and if, like me, you won't have anything to do with plastic tableware, they may be smashed. Any fore and aft lockers must have high fiddle rails inside the doors, and bulletproof stowage for crockery and glasses is vital.

Cookers

Unless sited athwartships, cookers must be mounted on gimbals. They all also need solid fiddle rails and pan clamps. You may have to manufacture the rail yourself as the ones that come with most marine cookers are flimsy and would struggle to do their job in a

A gimballed cooker with a custom-made fiddle rail is usually safer than the standard item.

caravan. It is hard to find a cooker with a separate grill. Most have these inside the oven, which is a shame. Manufacturers come up with all sorts of arguments as to why it is a good idea. None have convinced my wife, a sea cook of huge experience. If you can find one with the grill between the oven and the hobs, clutch it to your heart and never let it go.

■ Gas/LPG

The issue of gas safety is so well understood that no extra is required here, except to stress that the most likely failure in a modern galley is the solenoid switch in the gas locker. If this packs up, as it did on me on a sail-training schooner, you can't even get a coffee until you have either contrived to bypass it or replaced it. The answer is always to ship a spare. It's an important piece of kit and you don't want it letting you down a week out from the Canaries.

It is impossible to carry too much cooking gas. Systems for replenishment vary in different countries and filling up isn't always straightforward. Also, the bottles can be a bear to hump around when you have no car. Therefore, the rarer an event this is, the better for all hands.

On my previous boats with which I sailed the oceans, I carried three 13kg propane bottles in self-draining lockers. This delivered cooking for a crew of up to six for three months, including baking bread. On the Mason 44, the locker only allows for two of these bottles, but we sail her mainly two-up, so they last three months with ease. I'd be unhappy with less. I once ran out of gas a day short of Ireland after a ridiculously long passage from Nova Scotia where, in a 32ft gaff cutter of substantial vintage, I encountered three weeks of strong easterlies. You never know how long it's going to take, even if you do arrive with your mast intact. We were eating cold baked beans out of the can by the time we got there.

A solenoid shut-off in the gas locker has much to recommend it.

■ LPG safety

There are still some hard-core safety buffs out there who absolutely refuse to sail with LPG gas, but for most of us it has provided the best cooking option for well over a generation. Safety is, of course, paramount with gas. Easy-to-use shut-offs at the bottle, backed up by gas sniffers strategically placed in the bilge, are a good start for preventing an explosive build-up in the bilge. I always feel the best system is one that measures pressure in the delivery line between bottle and cooker. With both switched off the pressure ought to hold up. Should it start to drop, you know what to do!

If technological avoidance of the big bang isn't your bag, the old standby of soapy water will not let you down. Mix up a strong solution of washing-up liquid, whisk it up with a 1-inch paint brush and apply liberally to all unions in the gas system. Run the cooker, then turn it off. Leave the bottle valve open. Any gas leak will literally blow bubbles. These may be tiny, but you can't miss them and there are no gauges to go wrong. I do it regularly anyway as a save-all.

■ Alternative cooker fuels

Diesel cookers

Diesel cookers sound fine and there are people out there who love them. They do away with LPG, of course, and are generally very safe indeed, but they are rarely fitted on cruising yachts because of the following general drawbacks:

They use your main fuel supply; most, if not all, require a deck exhaust fitting; and they tend to be slow to heat up and cool down. They also require an electrical connection and are voltage sensitive in use, so if the batteries are low, they have been known to conk out, just as the cook was perfecting his fluffy rice for the crew's curry while approaching the ice edge.

Paraffin/Kerosene

Despite the obvious advantages of LPG cooking, there is still a reluctance in some quarters to abandon the pressurised paraffin cookers that preceded it. These work by way of a hot pre-heated burner that vaporises the liquid fuel under pressure. They do the job, but nobody but the most dyed-in-the-wool enthusiast would try to suggest they are anything like as easy to operate as a modern LPG unit. The fancied advantage, apart from the fact that a Taylor's cooker looks extremely salty, is that of safety. Paraffin doesn't explode, it burns. I witnessed one gas explosion and I never want to see another. I have been involved personally in two major galley fires, both involving liquid fuel cookers. One makes one's own peace with the situation, but whichever fuel is chosen, it must be treated with the greatest respect.

Electric cookers

Once again, the great advantage of these cookers is that they are the nearest thing to complete galley safety that can be achieved. However, they have a huge downside for any but the largest yachts. To learn about this, flick back a few pages to Chapter 5 and take a look at the section on galleys. Electric cookers are dealt with there because they relate directly to power consumption, which forms a major section of the chapter.

Sinks

These always end up by blocking. Clearing them isn't always easy, so take a really good quality 'plumber's mate' plunger along. The best ones come from the US, so buy one while you're there. While you're in Uncle Sam's hardware store, load up on small rubber builder's buckets too. Nobody makes 'em better.

The universally useful plumber's mate.

Fiddles

You can always recognise a serious cruiser by her fiddles. Any fiddle that's going to be called upon to hold a mug must be at least an inch high. 1¼ is better. Smaller than this can lead to a false sense of security. The inside edge must be vertical. If it's bevelled, it merely serves to accelerate the sliding plate on its way to the cabin sole. The outside can be any shape, but a bevel looks good and takes some of the feeling of weight out of it.

Fiddles can be a nuisance on a saloon table in harbour. They can get in the way on chart tables also. The answer is removable units with pegs on their underside, which drop into holes in the table top. On

If a galley doesn't have decent fiddles, don't buy the boat!

Westernman we used two at sea on the dining table; one at the edge on the downhill side and one at the inboard edge of the lifting flap, 15 inches or so from the lip on the uphill side, so that those eating there could let their plates slide off until they rested against the fiddle. It was ideal. In harbour we just lifted them off and enjoyed a fiddle-free dinner.

Hand holds

The wider and more spacious a yacht becomes, the greater is the need for hand holds down below. Injuries are not uncommon where crew members have been flung across a wide open space with nothing to hang on to. Narrower yachts have fewer problems with this, but they still need plenty to grab. Think it through, for all compartments. Even in the heads, a grab handle with which the enthroned skipper can ensure security of tenure when an athwartships mounted bowl is on the uphill side can make a big difference to life.

Lighting

An ill-lit yacht is a wretched thing where joy is hard to find. My early boats all had their primary lighting from paraffin lamps, so the ambience was lovely. We rigged one or two electric spots for reading small print and sewing and we had the perfect combination. Nowadays, with soft, dimmable LED lighting available, it makes a lot of sense to specify this. It's easy on the batteries and as long as care is taken with choosing and positioning lights, a lovely feeling can be engendered. I still hang a carefully secured oil lamp over my saloon table and a second smaller one on the forward bulkhead. There is absolutely nothing to beat the light from a real lamp, well trimmed, when two or three are gathered together, the rum bottle is halfway down and the tales are getting taller than the seas in a fine October gale.

On deck
The cockpit

Before specifying a boat, it is critical to think about where you intend to cruise. It's possible to work the Atlantic trade winds to the West Indies and return along the low-powered steamer route via Bermuda and the Azores without ever experiencing more than a modest force 8 gale. If this were your passage plan and you got lucky, a broad-beamed yacht with a summer cockpit and an open transom would not seem out of sorts. If you intend making passages in higher latitudes, experience may bring a different point of view. To feel safe in a cockpit in rough seas, it must have coamings that protect, rather than sides that leave the crew vulnerable. In any yacht under 50ft, an aft cockpit is going to be safer and more comfortable than a centre equivalent for the simple reason that you sit lower down further from the action up forward and may well have more room to move around into the bargain. Basically, the deeper the cockpit, the better.

Sunshades

On a happier note, anyone intending to cruise on the equatorial side of around 45 degrees latitude will be well advised to take a serious interest in sunshades. The only real answer is a 'Bimini'. This must be strong enough to stand in a gale because, if it's big enough to be any use, stowing it is going to be a production.

If in doubt about how to do it, buy a cheap ticket to the States, have a holiday and see what the professionals do. Summers are hot there and the Bimini originates from the islands in the stream off Florida. The trouble with Biminis is that you can't see the sails. This leads to all sorts of aggravation, so try to have it made with a Perspex panel, or some sort of opening flaps so you can check what's going on aloft. Sun hats are all very well, but once you've sailed in the tropics with a Bimini, you'll know that doing without one is tough. Being at sea anywhere with a poor one is worse, so make sure you get it right.

A 'Bimini' is a life-saver in high sunshine, but it can make sail trimming an awkward business.

Aft cockpits are generally safer. This one is emphatically not so. Note the author literally hanging on by his boot straps in reasonable weather.

PART 2 • OCEAN NAVIGATION AND DEEP-SEA SEAMANSHIP

7 WEATHER

It may at first sight seem odd to include ocean weather in a section dedicated to navigation. Thirty years back that would have been so, but times have changed, and with them the navigator's priorities. Ever since Odysseus went astray on his way home from Troy, the top priority of any navigator has been to determine position. In 1973, four years after my own inaugural ocean passage, Whitbread Round the World Race boats were finding where they were by sextant and RDF. This was often an imprecise art, and exercising it took up much of the navigator's energies.

Having fixed one's position, the next job was to decide how to get from where you thought you probably were, to where you knew you were supposed to be bound. From the 1990s on, location has no longer been in doubt. GPS has supplied 24/7 fixes of staggering accuracy at the touch of a button. Today's ace navigators expend most of their labours considering polar performance diagrams and the options offered by computerised weather routeing. Even we lesser mortals in cruising boats are still more concerned with the best way to go than with where we are. The answer is often weather-dependent, and therefore I put ocean meteorology upfront in this section without apology. Everything depends on it.

The big picture

I'm assuming that before picking up a book on ocean sailing, readers will have a fair grasp of the essential anatomy of mid-latitude wind systems. The life, death and likely movements of a frontal depression are assumed knowledge. If you don't have this information securely on board, I suggest you consult my previous-level book, *The Complete Yachtmaster*, or at least read, mark, learn and inwardly digest some suitably detailed online descriptions. It's not enough to read about it and tick the box. Thorough knowledge of air masses, the significance of isobars, frontal anatomy and surface-pressure synoptic weather charts is axiomatic.

The stylised diagram of an Atlantic weather chart sums it up: In the northern half, a clockwise-circulating mid-oceanic high-pressure system creates the right conditions for anticlockwise depressions in more northern latitudes to wind up a westerly airstream between about 40 and 55 degrees. Along its southern limb, the same high-pressure circulation generates the northeast trade winds. In the slack isobars of its centre lies the Sargasso Sea, where breeze can often be hard to come by.

A similar arrangement exists in the South Atlantic with circulations reversed to keep the westerlies and the trade winds where we expect to find them, with parallels in the North and South Pacific. It was in the North Atlantic, however, that the term 'Horse Latitudes' was coined by explorers and conquistadors bound towards the New World with a full complement of beasts of war and burden. If their ships wandered from the trade routes into the airless centre of the high, they encountered Sargasso weed swirling aimlessly inside the system of currents that follow the ocean winds. As day followed airless day and the ship's water began to run out, they threw the horses overboard to conserve their own essential supplies. These ill-fated mariners would have been well served by a pilot chart (see Ocean Passage planning on page 164).

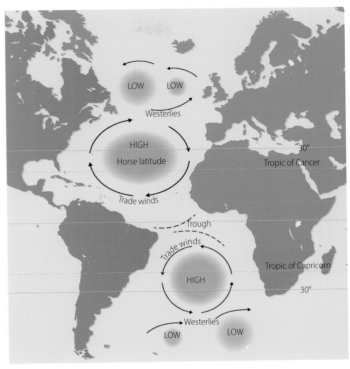

Fig 7.1 *Stylised Atlantic synopsis with typical pressure distribution. The Intertropical Convergence Zone lies in the vicinity of the Equatorial trough.*

On the polar side of the mid-latitude depression centres, one does in theory encounter some easterly winds. These form the so-called 'Northern Route' across the North Atlantic, while, far to the south, desperate square-rigger crews used to search for the easterlies, hacking ever towards the Antarctic ice, questing for a slant around Cape Horn. I can personally testify that one year when I crossed the North Atlantic westbound via Iceland and Southern Greenland, these following winds were a figment of the met books' propaganda. We beat more or less the whole way, and highly unpleasant it was too. Perhaps others have had better luck.

Knowledge of this general circulation will be of use in planning a passage and it is worth noting that, on the whole, ocean currents, forever intertwined with the prevailing airstream, follow the same pattern as the winds.

Practical forecasting for mid-latitude weather

Outside the tropics, ocean weather behaves more or less as sailors accustomed to conditions on the continental shelf might expect. There are, however, two striking differences. First, because there is no running away from it, you will generally experience more heavy weather on ocean trips than ever has blown your way in coastal waters. The major tactical effect is that there are

Ignore a halo like this on the sun or moon at your peril.

no harbours to escape to and no snug berths to hide in while a gale blows itself out. It goes without saying, therefore, that your boat must be properly found to cope with heavy weather. Waves will often be bigger than coastal sailors are used to, but there is a bright side even to this situation – there's nothing much to hit out there. No rocks and no lee shores complicate our tactical decisions. Except in extremis, we are probably safer out there than nearer home, though there are times when it doesn't feel that way.

The second feature about weather far out at sea in the 'forties and fifties' is that depressions behave far more like textbook cases than is often the case near a land mass. Without continental land to distort their purity, they tend to appear on synoptic charts as they are depicted in textbooks. The results are dramatic.

Fronts associated with ocean depressions are normally obvious. Cold fronts can be particularly lively, with winds clocking sharply toward the pole and a change in precipitation that you cannot miss. While this may rattle our cages for a short while, it's comforting to know that the depression centre has already moved past you and that before long life will improve. In fair weather, the warm front that heralds a depression can usually be seen approaching for some time. First comes a fine array of high cirrus cloud spreading over the western sky, perhaps accompanied by a halo round the sun or moon. Some, relying on downloaded material outdated by events, might ignore these portents, but it is invariably unwise. The next thing is that the barometer begins to tumble, while the wind shifts and hardens. When it's going to blow, a swell coming from the upwind direction is also usually apparent.

If the glass is falling at one millibar in three hours, you can be reasonably sure that something unpleasant is on the way. Two millibars per three hours normally heralds gale-force winds, especially if this sort of drop continues for eight hours or more. If the dial collapses by five millibars in three hours, you're in for it, with storm-force winds shortly to become your portion.

These signals are so unmistakable in deep water that they are usually all a sailor needs. The use of more modern methods to keep out of trouble will be considered later, but the truth is that in medium and high latitudes you will probably have to put up with most of what's coming unless you have a fast boat and access to regular forecasts. At least, this kind of hands-on 'single-station forecasting' prepares you for the worst. It may be reassuring to hear a voice on a long-range radio tell you it's only going to blow force seven, or peer at the wind arrows on an internet download, but out there at the coal face it's reality that counts.

Tropical weather

Contrary to what you might imagine after reading the travel brochures, many tropical areas do not enjoy a year-round idyllic climate. A typical example is the situation in the Windward and Leeward Islands of the West Indies. This sometimes-ideal cruising ground sits plumb across the tropical belt of the western North Atlantic. From early winter until early summer, the area has more or less reliable trade-wind weather of the sort many of us leave home to find. In high summer, however, the cool, steady breeze gives way to hot, airless days, winds can clock into the dreaded west, from which shelter is sparse, and for all but the southernmost islands, there develops the lurking threat of a major beating from a hurricane.

Similar scenarios exist in many tropical locations. As a result, it is as important to make sure that you are in the right place at the right time in low latitudes as it is in high. The consequences of being too casual may be less obvious, but they can be dire indeed.

Trade-wind sailing

As the airstream flows around the equatorial quadrants of the mid-ocean 'highs', it settles into the trade winds. These steady easterlies, relied on by ocean merchants in the days of sail, follow the track of the isobars. Since these tend to 'flatten out' parallel to the equator, the winds often stay consistent in direction for hundreds, even thousands, of miles. According to accepted theory, the trades bring fair weather and blow at a mean speed of around 14 knots. A pretty picture indeed, but reality can be different. Reading cruising classics from the 1930s, you might be forgiven for believing the trade winds to be as reliable as sunrise, but it does seem that they have become less predictable, with yachts reporting crossings bedevilled by light and variable conditions where there should have been a fine following breeze. Even strong head winds are reported from time to time.

Sometimes, the trades can blow great guns. In the West Indies, for example, the so-called 'Christmas Winds' are exceedingly stiff. I recall spending one festive season anchored in the lee of St Kitts in a howling wind that made it impossible to row ashore with 7ft oars in a fine stem dinghy to replenish the necessities of celebration. We sailed for eight weeks that winter with two reefs and a spitfire jib on a 35-ton cutter, and we were not under-canvassed.

Squalls

Trade-wind squalls are sometimes more common than you might expect and they can raise the wind speed substantially. If you cannot see the horizon underneath a cloud, expect rain for sure and probably a blow lasting anything from five to twenty minutes. If everything seems to be turning white underneath the cloud, with driven spray shutting down visibility, you are about to cop a White Squall. These can be very nasty, but generally don't last longer than the others. Just watch out for them, especially if conditions are unstable.

A heavy squall like this will certainly bring rain and very probably increase and shift the wind.

If you are reaching or beating, squalls can be handled by bearing away to reduce the apparent wind and the heeling effect. The blow may last a little longer than if you press on regardless, and you may be giving away a mile or two of weather gauge, but at the time it will seem cheap at the price. Soon it will pass; with luck the wind will return to normal, the sun will re-emerge and you can get back to watching the flying fish play.

Working across or against the trades

When considering a route that involves reaching across the trade wind, or one that would place you as close to the wind as you can comfortably lie, most cruisers will end up steering at least 60 degrees off the true wind. You may even plump for more. There is generally an eight-foot sea running in these latitudes and you won't enjoy pointing up any higher, unless you happen to be racing. It will all even out in the end, however. It's better to arrive with the teeth still in your head and the mast on your boat than to hammer yourself to pieces trying to fight the unconquerable.

If you are considering a trip that may involve beating a serious distance against the trade wind, there is only one answer. Don't – if you can possibly go somewhere else. There is usually a current running down the trades; tacking against it can be like trying to weather a major headland against a foul tide that will never turn. The only instance I can think of where someone successfully crossed an ocean against the trades was the 65ft Steve Dashew-designed long-range motor yacht *Grey Wolf*. They worked north from the South Pacific until they found the ITCZ (see opposite page). The trades fizzled out and they even discovered a counter-current to help them along. The option is not open to boats driven primarily by sail, but, given enough range under power, *Grey Wolf* and her bold crew have proved it can work.

The Intertropical Convergence Zone

This is a trough of low pressure extending across the oceans between the influences of the north and south high-pressure systems. It represents the convergence of air from the two hemispheres and, while not technically a weather front, it does display front-like characteristics when sailing through it. Known universally as the ITCZ, this band of recognisable weather stretches across the Atlantic and Pacific Oceans all the year round. In the Indian Ocean it is sucked north on to the continent of Asia during the Southwest Monsoon and is of no interest to the sailor.

The ITCZ is generally at its widest on the eastern sides of the oceans, where the widespread calm, or rainy and squally conditions are known as 'doldrums'. Further westwards, the northeast and southeast trades come ever closer together, sometimes merging into a general easterly as the ocean's western extremity is approached.

Sailing across the ITCZ can be almost unnoticeable or it can be pretty nasty. Sometimes the sultry calms mentioned above are a real problem, at other times they seem barely to exist, being substituted by days of grey, rainy weather punctuated by squalls of varying violence. In the Atlantic, a south-bound skipper's dilemma is typically that the further west the yacht crosses the line, the less trouble she will have from the ITCZ, but the more close-hauled she will be when she picks up the southeast trades and has to weather the corner of Brazil. Life is rarely perfect for the ocean sailor.

Monsoons

Just as temperature variations of land and sea on a coastal summer's afternoon cause pressure differences resulting in sea breezes, far mightier results occur on a global scale from similar causes. In the summer months, pressure generally falls over the continents as land masses cook up. It remains comparatively high over the oceans. The reverse effect occurs in winter. In some areas the outcome of these phenomena is a predictable, reversing wind circulation known as a 'monsoon'.

Indian Ocean, South China Sea and northern Australia

The effects of low pressure over northwest India from May to September are felt right down into the southern hemisphere. The pressure gradient stretches into the southeast trades of the Indian Ocean, which are drawn northwards to cross the equator, veering as they become part of the southwest monsoon circulation. Any northeast trades in the northern Indian Ocean, and as far away as the western part of the North Pacific, are knocked out completely and replaced by the monsoon sou'wester.

This southwest monsoon is an extremely wet wind in the Bay of Bengal and it blows hard. In the China Sea, it is less violent and considerably drier. Here, its flow is often east of south, but despite its comparatively well-mannered appearance, it can still generate typhoons right into October. Cyclones in the Indian Ocean are also prevalent towards the end of the period.

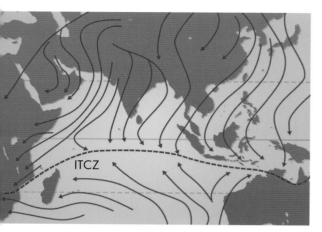 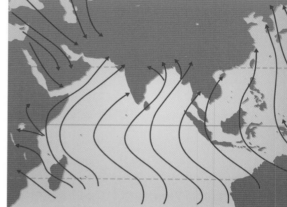

Fig 7.2 *Monsoon in January.* **Fig 7.3** *Monsoon in July.*

From October to March, the Indian Ocean comes under the influence of a huge high over Siberia. This funnels a more pleasant northerly airstream over the area, which starts northeasterly, gradually backs northwest as it crosses the equator and reaches the top of Australia under the name of the 'Northwest Monsoon'.

In the northern half of the Indian Ocean, this monsoon is dry and usually brings the fair weather that drove the sons of Sinbad south in the dhows of Arabia to Zanzibar. Further away, along the China and Indochina coasts, winds are stronger. Between January and April, particularly later in the period, overcast weather with prevalent drizzle known as 'Crachin' occurs over the South China Sea.

Other monsoons

In West Africa, a southwest monsoon blows into the Gulf of Guinea from June to September. Its effects can stretch to 20 degrees South. Low pressure over the Amazon Basin causes a northeast monsoon tendency down the eastern coast of Brazil from September to March. There are also frequently disguised monsoon cycles in other areas, including the Gulf of Mexico.

Tropical revolving storms

The tropical revolving storm (TRS) is the planet's most extreme system. Under their various guises of hurricane (North Atlantic), typhoon (China Seas) or cyclone (Indian Ocean), these cyclonic disturbances cause more mayhem every year than most commentators would care to quantify. In 1970, a cyclone rampaged ashore on the Bay of Bengal, killing half a million people and unleashing energy that has been likened to many atomic bombs.

It isn't only the Third World that suffers from these terrible storms. New Orleans was shattered by a hurricane in 2005, while Hurricane Andrew back in 1992 left upwards of a quarter million homeless in Florida and ran up an unsettled account for US$25bn. Life aboard a yacht at sea in such conditions is effectively indescribable. Knowledge is power, however. To make certain that it doesn't happen to you, the nature of the beast must be thoroughly understood. Later in this chapter, we will consider tactics to weigh up if you ever find yourself peering into the wrong end of this grizzly gun barrel. First, we'll take a look at what makes it tick.

Early life and nature of a TRS

Most TRS activity originates from shallow tropical wave depressions running down the trade winds, or major cloud disturbances associated with the ITCZ. They demand a limitless supply of moist air, for which the critical criterion is a sea temperature of around 80°F (26°C). This is only achieved in tropical seas after they have warmed to late summer and autumn levels. The proposition holds good even in the Indian Ocean and Arabian Sea where, although a TRS can occur at either change of monsoon, they are at their worst in the usual northern hemisphere danger months of July to October.

These storms cannot form any closer than 5 degrees to the equator, because the Coriolis force of the turning Earth that sets all weather systems circulating diminishes as the equator is approached. At anything less than this critical distance there simply isn't enough 'spin' to crank up the action.

As moist air rises over the warm sea, an area of low pressure is formed, which may develop a circulatory motion if it becomes enough of a feature for the Coriolis force to grab hold of it. Once this occurs it is designated a 'tropical depression', defined by winds of force 7 or less, but it now has the potential to wind up into something far worse. The rising air in the centre of such a system sheds latent heat as its moisture precipitates out at higher altitudes. The freed heat keeps it rising until it runs out of moisture at anything up to eight miles high. The newly dried air is spun out at the top of the depression as it begins to circulate with real power. The air now travels to the outer limits of the centre's influence, to be sucked down towards sea level again. Close to the water once more, it loads up on moisture, spirals inwards towards the centre and repeats its journey at ever-more frenetic velocity.

As this huge heat engine spins ever faster, winds near what is now the eye increase to anything from 35 to 55 knots and, before long, force 12 is reached. This is 60 knots, and a full hurricane, cyclone or typhoon is born.

The storm can be anything from 50 to something approaching 1,000 miles in diameter, although typical sizes range between 150 and 250 miles. Wind speeds may rise into the realms of the unimaginable.

A mature tropical revolving storm with a clearly defined eye.

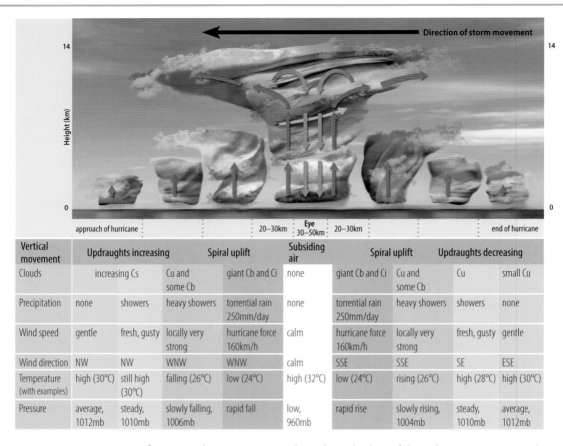

Vertical movement	Updraughts increasing		Spiral uplift		Subsiding air	Spiral uplift		Updraughts decreasing	
Clouds	increasing Cs	Cu and some Cb	giant Cb and Ci	none	giant Cb and Ci	Cu and some Cb	Cu	small Cu
Precipitation	none	showers	heavy showers	torrential rain 250mm/day	none	torrential rain 250mm/day	heavy showers	showers	none
Wind speed	gentle	fresh, gusty	locally very strong	hurricane force 160km/h	calm	hurricane force 160km/h	locally very strong	fresh, gusty	gentle
Wind direction	NW	NW	WNW	WNW	calm	SSE	SSE	SE	ESE
Temperature (with examples)	high (30°C)	still high (30°C)	falling (26°C)	low (24°C)	high (32°C)	low (24°C)	rising (26°C)	high (28°C)	high (30°C)
Pressure	average, 1012mb	steady, 1010mb	slowly falling, 1006mb	rapid fall	low, 960mb	rapid rise	slowly rising, 1004mb	steady, 1010mb	average, 1012mb

Fig 7.4 *Anatomy of a TRS. Observations are taken along the line of the advancing eye. Wind direction will be approximate. Note that Ci = cirrus, Cs = cirrostratus, Cu = cumulus and Cb = cumulonimbus.*

Hurricane Gilbert wound up to 160 knots in 1988, Luis managed 130 knots in September 1995 and rampaged through the Caribbean with terrible results for St Martin and Antigua. Speeds of 180 knots have been mentioned, but a more typical wind speed, for Atlantic hurricanes at any rate, is around a hearty 90 knots.

Life in the storm's eye, or 'vortex', is remarkable for the fact that an observer may well have clear blue sky overhead while the mighty clouds of the eye 'wall' tower up on all sides. Rainfall in the circulatory system will have been phenomenal and seas will have built to enormous proportions. Once in the eye, rain stops while the seas, temporarily bereft of the wind that was giving them some discipline, become chaotic and mountainous. As the eye passes, the wind returns from a different direction, the rain begins once more and the seas slowly sort themselves out, although this is purely relative.

Mid-life, routes and death of a TRS

A TRS normally grows as it travels. Its pressure may not sound staggeringly low to a sailor from higher latitudes used to winter depressions of 950mb. A TRS may only run to 960mb, although far lower readings, such as the exceptional central pressure of 888mb achieved by Gilbert, have been recorded. What is extraordinary is the pressure gradient, which can be as much as 10mb over 50 miles with even greater falls towards the centre.

It is impossible to be specific about the movements of a typical TRS, but it can be said, with only rare contradiction, that most Atlantic and Pacific examples begin their lives on the equatorial side of their mid-oceanic subtropical 'high', sometimes a good way east. They then travel west or northwest (southwest in the southern hemisphere), slowly at first, before accelerating to 10 or 12 knots as they approach the 20th parallel. Somewhere around here, many storms 'recurve' in a clockwise direction (anticlockwise in the south) towards the pole and move at increasing velocity away from the tropics. This may also carry them further from the continental land mass on the west side of the ocean, but it doesn't help Bermuda or any Pacific islands in the way. The centre of recurvature of a storm is called the 'vertex' of its track, which is not to be confused with the 'vortex'.

In the most general terms, a recurving TRS will follow the isobars of the mid-latitude anticyclone, or 'high', but even with modern computer models and all the other wonders of science, TRS tracks remain notoriously unpredictable. Storms have even been known to perform a full loop, which forecasters may at first assume to be the recurring process.

As a TRS travels towards temperate latitudes after recurving, its size increases and ultimately it loses its tropical identity by developing into a frontal depression or becoming absorbed into the circulation of a temperate system that has already formed.

The alternative scenario is that the recurving procedure does not take place and the storm goes barrelling ashore with catastrophic results. It is not unusual for this to happen when a North Atlantic hurricane piles into Florida or enters the Gulf of Mexico after marching down the Greater Antilles chain. It then turns right and pulverises the Deep South of the US. Another area where recurvature tends to fail is the Bay of Bengal, leaving the low-lying Ganges delta and the Sunderbunds a helpless victim.

When a tropical storm comes ashore, its days are numbered and it is doomed literally to 'run out of steam' from lack of the water that fuels its engine. Occasionally, however, it has enough inherent energy to leapfrog the land and reappear back at sea to be rewound. This can occur in Central America, while cyclones have been known to travel clear across India to re-establish themselves in the Arabian Sea.

Navigating in the vicinity of a TRS
Strategic avoidance

The primary factor in dealing with the TRS menace is to arrange your life so that the issue of how to survive one never arises. Every passage-planning guide, all the world's pilot charts and every internet site worth anything at all will give the times of year when the TRS factor must be considered. Because of the unpredictability of tropical cyclones, you can never be absolutely sure of missing them by working the seasons, but you can easily whittle down the chances of being hit from a measurable possibility to the almost negligible. Nobody is going to put his hand on his heart and say: 'Cross the Atlantic from the Canaries to the Caribbean at Christmas and I promise you won't see a hurricane.' You can, after all, be run over by a truck on London's M25 even if you use both mirrors, but those of us who have made such crossings in winter have not spent our time nervously scanning the sky and tuning our PCs to the hurricane advisory service. Find out about the local TRS season, and go sailing somewhere else.

Sometimes, it may be necessary to be out on the ocean at times when TRS activity is a measurable possibility. An example would be a decision to sail to Bermuda from the US in late October. You might do this in order to miss the beginning of the New England winter before moving south to the Caribbean a few weeks later when the hurricane season is virtually closed. Hurricanes can form in October and do sometimes recurve towards Bermuda. It happened in 2014, but, on the balance of probabilities, the chance might be felt worth the taking to avoid more certain horrors further north, especially with a clear forecast to start the trip. The bottom line is that unless you plot your whole cruising curriculum with TRS avoidance as the sole item on the agenda you must accept the possibility, however remote, that you may one day be hit.

So what are the signs that a tropical storm is coming your way?

Warnings from your own observations
■ Barometer

Just as it is in more temperate latitudes, the first telltale is usually the dear old barometer. In the tropics, the 'glass' generally stands rock steady for days on end within the limits of the phenomenon known as 'diurnal variation'. Typically, this involves a rhythmic pulsing of pressure of 1–1.6mb either side of the mean. The cycle happens twice a day, with 'highs' around 1000 and 2200 local time, and lows corresponding at 0400 and 1600. Mean pressure comes an hour or so after noon and midnight.

You soon get used to diurnal variation when sailing the tropics, and if the pressure nudges up a notch outside yesterday's high, watch out. There might be a TRS 500–1,000 miles off. If the glass now starts to drop, note readings regularly. A drop of 3mb or more means you should take matters seriously. A 5mb drop means that you could well be within 200 miles of a TRS.

■ Swell

It will come as no surprise to learn that a TRS shoves a mighty sea in front of it as it moves. A high swell with a rapid period can be a sure-fire sign. It might even be the first indication that all is not well because these seas can extend up to 1,000 miles ahead of the system. They move faster than the storm, so you may become aware of them a day or more before the barometer starts playing tricks.

Don't make the mistake of assuming that the eye of a TRS is advancing at 90 degrees across the wave pattern. It may be, but, as we shall see, the outer winds do not run directly along the super-tight isobars. In any event, unless you have other information, the storm could well have changed course since it kicked up the waves that are passing you at any particular moment.

■ Sky

Visibility sometimes becomes crystal clear during the approach of a TRS. Evening and morning skies may be vividly coloured as cirrus cloud develops, sometimes in a series of 'vees' pointing towards the distant eye. Cirrus is seen 300–600 miles from the vortex and, together with the swell, may be the first indication that all is going to be far from well. As the storm approaches, the cloud levels lower, with altostratus and fractocumulus giving way to driving, rain-soaked black scud.

■ Wind

Because there are no fronts in a TRS, the airstream runs directly around it, more or less without interruption. Winds spiral anticlockwise in the northern hemisphere and clockwise in the southern. In the outer regions, considerable in-draught can be experienced as the air tries to flow across the isobars into the low pressure at the centre. At 200 miles from the eye, where the wind will typically be blowing force 6 or 7, this can be up to 45 degrees. As the eye-wall approaches, the centrifugal force of the high-velocity airstream virtually defeats the pressure difference and the winds rattle straight round the circle.

In the absence of any radio forecasting, this information is critical for locating the storm centre as it approaches. At first, therefore, if you face the wind, the eye of the storm will be around 120 degrees over your right shoulder (left in the southern hemisphere). As things hot up, the angle will decrease until the vortex is at hand, at which point its middle should be square across your outstretched arms.

Tactics and storm management

With a TRS moving at 15 knots or so, the idea of the average cruising yacht outrunning one in a straight foot-race is rarely a possibility. It can, however, be entirely realistic to sidestep its worst effects.

First, the storm's relative position and track should be ascertained as closely as possible by applying the above principles, coupled with regular weather reports when these are available. Now comes the big decision about tactics. The best action will depend upon which 'quadrant' of the approaching TRS you seem to be in. For clarity, we will consider a northern hemisphere TRS, but note the opposite wind directions, etc. for the southern hemisphere.

■ Dangerous semicircle

This is the semicircle on what we might call the storm's 'starboard side' as it advances. Because of the anticlockwise circulation of air and the forward motion of the storm that creates its own apparent wind, the generally easterly wind across the deck of a stationary vessel on this side can be 20–30 knots greater than that on the opposite side, where the velocity of the system's progress is effectively subtractive from the true wind speed. Furthermore, because it is to this 'dangerous' side that the storm will recurve if it hasn't done so already, a boat caught here may be in for a 'double whammy'.

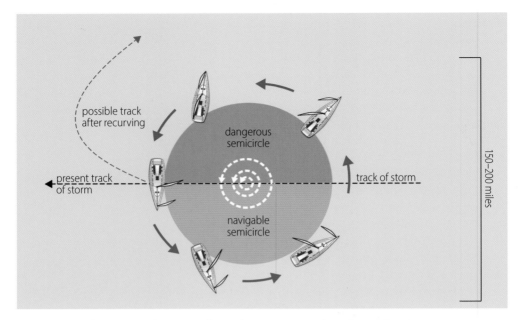

Fig 7.5 *Tactical anatomy of a Tropical Revolving Storm (northern hemisphere).*

■ Navigable semicircle

Life in this half of the TRS will still be hell, but the chances of a safe exit are better than those dealt out to the poor souls on the side away from the equator. You also have a better probability of being able to give the slip to the worst of the action as it approaches. The danger of a cruelly timed recurvature is almost (though never totally) non-existent, and in order to increase your distance from the track of the approaching centre, you can reach bravely with the wind exactly where you want it. You might even be making some sort of progress towards your destination.

■ Actions to take in the dangerous semicircle

A yacht trying to evade the eye from a position within the dangerous sector will have to attempt to sail close-hauled or pretty near to it, as fast and as far as possible to escape the worst. Anyone who has tried this in 45 knots of apparent wind in open water will understand that even to contemplate it in 60 knots or more is a non-starter for a cruising yacht. Therefore, if it seems that an approaching storm will catch you in the forward quadrant of this semicircle, you need a quick decision. Either you must beat as far beyond the track of the centre as you can while you still may, taking your chance on a recurvature hit, or you should put the wind on the starboard quarter and run or broad-reach as fast as you can, trying to reach the slightly less awesome 'navigable' semicircle.

A further problem associated with the dangerous semicircle, or at least its forward quadrant, is that a yacht caught in it and not making way will be carried into the track of the eye. So, if you find yourself in this most wretched of circumstances without the option of running out of it, you have little choice but to make what ground you can by sailing or motorsailing with serious dedication on the starboard tack. When either you or the boat can stand it no more, you must heave to on that tack, if you can still carry any rags of canvas, batten down and take a serious look round the accommodation on the assumption that you may well be knocked down or capsized. The deck needs a cynical inspection as well. In one dramatic incident, a pal of mine with a big gaff schooner opted to leave his topmasts up with extreme weather approaching. All his booming-out poles were lashed on deck. When he came out the other side, the deck had been swept clean, but the topmasts were still standing. Makes you think, eh?

That done, you can only settle in to read a good book, ideally strapped into your bunk, then trust in fate, your god or whoever rigged your boat.

Even when the north–south line of the moving storm's eye has progressed west of your position, your problems are not over in the dangerous semicircle. You are now in its less lethal quadrant, but the wind is still driving you towards the centre. Your only comfort is that as long as the brute doesn't recurve on top of you, the TRS is on its way to bother somebody else.

The nature of the dangerous semicircle is so uncompromising that if it seems likely to become your lot in an approaching storm, you simply must opt for positive action before it is too late, either to avoid it by getting well clear on its windier side and taking your chance on an unlucky recurvature, or by muscling your way across its bows to the navigable semicircle.

Given reasonable warning of the storm's approach, getting into the navigable semicircle if you aren't there already may prove a realistic possibility. If you seem poorly placed, remember that, while the TRS is advancing at 10 knots, it could still be 300–400 miles away. This means you may have manageable winds for another 15 hours, possibly longer. Most modern cruisers can readily achieve 100 miles in that time; some can do more, and every yard counts. If a 75-knot storm looked like catching you 50 miles from the centre plumb in its dangerous semicircle, a determined effort across its approach line would place you at least the same distance on the safer side, experiencing the dismal reality of 60-knot winds rather than the appalling prospect of 90 knots. What is more, since most boats can run in far heavier going than that into which they can beat, you will still be able to sail towards clearer conditions long after you'd have had to give up on the other side.

Ocean weather forecasting

Voice radio weather forecasts

It isn't such a long time since the only weather reports for ocean mariners came in Morse Code down short-wave sets, usually driven by professional radio operators. Today, not only can yachts receive comprehensive weather information by voice, there are even interactive stations where sailors can discuss their situation with experts ashore.

It's important that you do your own 'homework' on weather stations before you leave, because availability varies from ocean to ocean. It also depends entirely on what equipment you have and how much you are prepared to spend.

The essential reference work is the *Admiralty List of Radio Signals*, Vol. III, Part 2: Radio Weather Services. This gives the word on official marine weather broadcasts via HF (SSB), VHF,

Weatherfax and Navtex. In addition to this government information, many voyage routes are covered by ham nets and private individuals whose lives are dedicated to assisting sailors. In the previous edition of this book I gave details of a number of private and official weather services that I and others had found helpful. Editing this edition, I discovered that virtually all of my recommendations were no longer extant. Public services had moved on and each of my individual forecasters had retired or perhaps even gone to the great cloud system in the sky. The bottom line is that ocean weather forecasting is improving and changing constantly. Finding a station or site that will serve you best is not an onerous task using an internet search engine or the latest word from ocean cruising clubs, such as the OCC. Very often the best source is the relevant ham network.

All these stations are available on a good-quality pocket-sized short-wave receiver, available in your local radio store for around £200. You may not even need to rig an outside aerial. The Sony package comes complete with a suitable length of reeled-up wire and a connector to hook it up to the usual telescopic aerial you would find on any portable VHF receiver. I have draped mine around the deckhead of my navigation station and picked up Perfect Paul, Herb and others satisfactorily. You could even take it outside and clamp it to an insulated backstay. It doesn't stop the gales, but at least I know what to expect.

Internet and data transfer

Digital weather data are becoming more readily available as year succeeds to year. Weatherfax information has been used by yachts for some time now, giving current synoptic charts as well as prognoses. Already, however, some of those who want to remain in touch with the world ashore prefer to hook up via satellite to the internet through their on-board PC.

Weather services available on the internet are many and seem sure to proliferate. Various providers offer synoptic charts, full forecasts and much smaller GRIB files. By comparing these, together with any accompanying comments and data, sailors can form conclusions about which outfit is currently to be preferred for their needs. For those who want to spend the money, tailor-made forecasts can be issued to you personally.

Detailed internet information on TRS development is astonishing, in the North Atlantic at least, where hurricanes can be tracked by courtesy of at least five different providers. All deliver coloured maps, histories of current storms, forecasts and numerical data.

In the South Pacific, providers such as the excellent Bob McDavitt, aka www.metbob.com, offer tailor-made reports to clients and a useful synopsis with comments to anyone who cares to hook up. In this area particularly, general forecasts are unlikely to pick up some of the small, but virulent, local weather systems that people like Bob keep tabs on.

Sea-ice data proliferation is not far behind the American hurricane advice. Armed with such information, via satphone or SSB, a yacht has a better chance than ever before of staying clear of trouble. See Chapter 22 for information on the options for acquiring it.

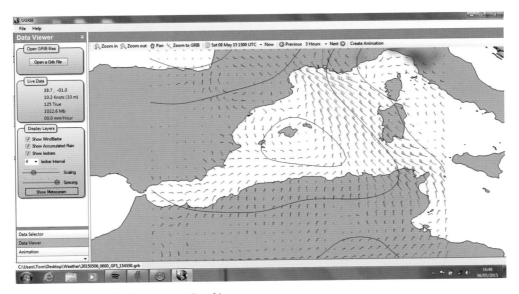

Fig 7.6 *A downloaded GRIB weather file.*

Conclusions

As recently as the early 1990s, the majority of ocean cruising yachts were 'single-station forecasters'. They left port with what general and preliminary information they could gather, then set sail with only a barometer, the sea and the sky as their guides. There will always be sailors who prefer their voyaging like that and choose to keep it so. For the mainstream, however, the long-term future lies in a 'laptop' hooked up to the world, interfaced with GPS and an electronic chart-plotting program. No longer will most of us sail free under the heavens, content to make the best of what comes and with only a general idea of our whereabouts.

Instead, we will watch our yachts crawl across a screen, our position defined to within a boat's length. Wanted and unwanted email messages will flow from our PCs, while an accurate, up-to-date weather chart will be overlaid on to the ocean we are sailing. It's progress. Some will choose to reject the changes, but growing numbers would feel uneasy without them, for we live increasingly in an age of certainties.

8 HOT AND COLD

Back in the 1960s and 70s, very few sailors ventured into higher latitudes other than those who found it necessary to round the great Southern Ocean capes. Lord Dufferin had cruised up to Bear Island in 1856, but things were so different in his day that, finding himself unable to understand a word his Icelandic hosts said on his way north, he and the locals in Reykjavík were reduced to communicating in fluent classical Latin. This may cause us to reflect on the state of education in the internet age, but that is probably not why most readers have picked up this book.

Instead, we can take note that, today, more and more people are heading north and south to find true seclusion and untamed wilderness. Changing global conditions have made ice in general a lot less impenetrable now than it was on my first visit to Greenland in 1983, but sea ice and passing bergs remain a reality that must be considered long and hard. Meanwhile, the tropics continue to draw blue-water pleasure-seekers who find themselves taking more than a passing interest in coral.

Neither subject appears in the British RYA Yachtmaster curriculum. Nor are they to be found in many other nations' courses, yet both form an integral part of the complete ocean skipper's compendium of skills, so a few words here will perhaps not go amiss.

Ice

Ice navigation is a subject worthy of a whole book. All I can offer here is a brief introduction, which may whet the appetite or put readers off completely. Those determined to pursue a cruise to the far north or south are urged to read the British Admiralty *Mariner's Handbook* for further hard information. Other textbooks exist, but none of them seem to be produced with yachts in mind. Fortunately, we are blessed with a growing canon of fine literature on the subject written by such masters as HW Tilman, Alvah Simon and, if you can get hold of his wonderful papers via the Irish Cruising Club, John Gore-Grimes. Accounts by them and many others will prove as helpful as most textbooks. Since sailors who go to the extremes of the planet are generally interesting people, they are usually a grand read too.

Ice charts

These are available via the internet. For the North Atlantic and Greenland, they are issued by the Danish and Norwegian authorities and are generally updated two or three times per week. In order to make sense of these, sailors must be aware of some basic definitions.

A grand sight under the northeast Greenland high-pressure system.

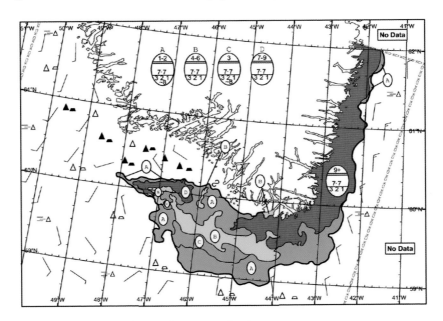

Fig 8.1 *A downloaded ice chart for southern Greenland.*

■ Ice types and other definitions

Although ice is found in many, many variants, five distinct types must be understood. These are fast ice, drift, pack, icebergs with their attendant chunks, and icing in the rigging and superstructure.

Ice accumulation on ships

From time to time, especially in winter, the UK Shipping Forecast mentions 'icing', often in Southeast Iceland. This may be light or heavy. It refers to ice precipitating on to rigging and superstructure, the weight continuing to add up until the vessel becomes less stable, or even unstable altogether. This can happen to yachts at any time, given the right conditions of temperature and atmospheric moisture. Air temperatures of −2°C or less are usually needed, and things deteriorate rapidly after the wind exceeds force 6.

You don't have to be navigating the high Arctic for this to come about. I have known it on yachts bound south for the Caribbean in early winter from the northeast United States. In that case, chunks of ice fell from the sails and rigging and the yacht became distinctly 'crank'. Other than shaking the rig to try to loosen accumulations, the only advice I can offer if icing becomes a serious issue is to lessen the causes. Do whatever is possible to lower any apparent wind speed and don't carry too much sail.

Fast ice

This is sea ice attached to the shore, or more or less permanently attendant upon some shoal, long-grounded berg or group of bergs. It may be formed in situ, or it may have arrived as wind-driven drift ice that has become attached. Fast ice can extend for a few metres or hundreds of miles. It is found in areas where a thaw is rare or non-existent, such as northeast Greenland or parts of Antarctica.

Drift ice

Drift ice is the name given to free-moving areas of frozen sea. It may consist of larger or smaller floes with greater or lesser leads or spaces between them. Unless you are proposing the risky business of entering a full-on pack through a stray lead, drift ice is the most likely heavy ice to be expected by high-latitude voyagers.

Pack ice

Pack ice is a loose definition for any tightly packed drift ice, but the term is tending to fall out of use. It sometimes appears as a synonym and will be found in many pre-1990 accounts.

Ice berg

A berg is a massive piece of ice more than 5 metres in height. It is free-floating unless aground and has usually broken free from a glacier. Bergs come in many forms, such as tabular (table-like), pinnacled, dome-shaped and so on. Southern Ocean tabular bergs can break off the ice shelves surrounding the continent and as such may be enormous, perhaps miles in length. Most North Atlantic bergs originate from Greenland glaciers and are thus

If you're lucky with the weather, it's worth braving the cold and the distance to see sights like this.

The remains of a growler.

PACK OR DRIFT ICE

- *Very open pack* of $\frac{1}{10}$ to $\frac{3}{10}$ cover is perfectly navigable by a well-found yacht, although there will be more ice than you expect and you'll be obliged to do some ducking and diving.
- *Open pack* at around $\frac{6}{10}$ cover can be penetrated as the large floes are not technically in contact with one another, but it should not be attempted voluntarily without previous ice experience.
- *Close pack* ice at $\frac{8}{10}$ cover and more will stop any small boat.

fresh water. Melted down, they make the perfect accompaniment to malt whisky. Those formed on the east coast drift south to round Cape Farewell and proceed up into Baffin Bay. Here, they join their chums from west Greenland and continue south down the Canadian side of the Davis Strait, finally to melt when they meet the Gulf Stream off Newfoundland where the detritus they have left over the millennia has formed the Grand Banks.

Bergs are generally associated with lesser ice pieces such as *growlers*, which do not exceed a metre in floating height above the sea, but can easily be the size of a motor car. These don't show up on radar in a typical sea and so are dangerous to yachts in fog.

Bergy bits are larger pieces of floating glacier ice that do not reach more than 5 metres above sea level.

In addition to these, smaller chunks of ice still large enough to hole a boat are often found close to bergs.

Ice blink and sea temperature

Approaching distant drift ice in good visibility, a whitish glare can be seen reflecting on low clouds. This is called ice blink. When coupled with a sea temperature of 2°C or so, it is a sure precursor of ice.

Cape Brewster, northeast Greenland, with grounded bergs.

Percentages of ice, and ice passage planning

Ice charts show areas of the sea, sometimes in different colours, depending on concentrations of ice. What percentage you consider navigable will depend on your experience, your boat and, of course, the likely weather. Ice conditions can change rapidly, such as occurs often in the Denmark Strait between Iceland and Greenland in July and early August. At this time, the drift ice that has beset the entrance to Scoresby Sound, for example, may well be retreating day by day.

If you can download charts as you go, you are privileged to have the latest data at all times. If not, you are best advised to wait at your jumping-off point within reach of wi-fi, keep downloading until things look tenable, then make a dash for it. Make sure you have enough time to get out again before the ice closes in once more, unless you plan on wintering iced-in. My pal Annie Hill and others have done this, but it stays dark for a long time and may not be your idea of a large night out, especially if unplanned.

It's not unusual for ice to extend out to sea beyond a destination, but a broad lead will allow you to work inshore. As long as the drift ice is retreating, this is a fair policy.

Fog and sea temperature

Ice in the open sea seems to generate fog. Keeping an eye on sea temperature can be a good guide as to the likelihood of ice if you can't see beyond the yacht's pulpit. 2°C is a sound point at which to assume you are in among it.

In my experience, one encounters a lot of fog when sailing around the outside of ice areas. On a passage to Greenland in 1983, the visibility almost never relented. We saw bergs and growlers going by in the murk, but no towering ice-cream castles glittering in blue seas as per the brochures. That came on a second trip where, by courtesy of the general warming of the Arctic, we were able to penetrate Scoresby Sound (70°N) and enter the influence of the Greenland high-pressure system. Then we saw the wonders of the North in all their glory. On our return through the Denmark Strait a couple of weeks later, it was back to the salt mines; hard head winds with prolonged heavy squalls ripping off the ice cap, steep seas, low-flying growlers and wall-to-wall fog.

For all the danger and the challenges it presents, small-craft voyagers in high latitudes become members of an exclusive club that has no black-ball rite of passage and no annual subscription. Working into icebound coastlines, one becomes fascinated by the history of polar and sub-polar exploration. The loneliness and sheer savagery combine with moments of ethereal beauty to make us feel that, in the humblest way, we might perhaps sit down in the next world at a rough-hewn cabin table lit by an oil lamp, to raise a glass with such great names as Scoresby, Franklin and Bill Tilman.

Coral

Unlike the rocks of temperate latitudes, coral is a living thing. When justifying an out-of-date chart of, say, the west coast of Norway, we might observe with some complacency: 'Ah well, at least the rocks don't move.' And we'd be right. They've been there since before Eric Bloodaxe cut up rough in the tenth century and are unlikely to shift now. Coral, while less fickle than a Thames Estuary sandbank, is not as reliable as granite. It grows, it dies and cannot be relied

A coral reef, great for diving, bad for anchoring.

Water colours can be read like a book by an experienced pilot.

upon as it's always on the move. Furthermore, charts of tropical seas aren't usually surveyed with the diligence and frequency of those serving Long Island Sound or the English Channel. One way and another, coral needs treating with respect.

Coral is nasty stuff, unless you are diving on it and enjoying the underwater view. Even before eco-awareness dissuaded us from even trying to anchor on it, you couldn't anyway, because either the hook refused to bite or, occasionally, it caught around some projection and wouldn't let go. If you run on to coral, it makes a horrible mess of a yacht. The trouble is that piloting into many a tropical anchorage demands cutting coral-bordered corners pretty fine, so we need a plan to miss it. This does not include the chart plotter and electronics in general. So close to doom in such places, these are emphatically not to be relied upon. We need to train our eyes and to read the beautiful colours of reef-strewn waters.

Don Street, the guru of West Indian sailing, said to me when he was well into his eighties that so long as he kept to the seas only between 0900 and 1500 local time, he reckoned he could probably navigate anywhere in the Lesser Antilles with only a gas-station road map and a Boy Scout compass. Earlier or later than this and the sun is too low to light up the seabed with any degree of reliability. Also, it always seems to be in your eyes just when you need it behind your shoulder. Polaroid sunglasses help a lot, but they can't beat the glare of a low sun.

WATER COLOURS

Here's how to read the colours in good light, and believe me, it is dramatically obvious.

- Dark blue — deep water
- Paler blue — bottom coming up, but still deep
- Greenish tinge to the blue — getting shallower now. Could well be down to 4 metres or a couple of fathoms
- Greener still — 4 metres, coming down to 2
- White, as clear as a gin and tonic — less than 2 metres and white sand bottom
- Brown — coral! This shows up clearly. If you have to work through a lagoon with growing coral heads that certainly won't be on the chart, you'll see them OK as long as you concentrate.

ALOFT

If you're expecting a lot of reef work, it pays to rig simple ratlines in the shrouds, leading to a more comfortable platform of some sort, so that a keen-eyed crew can go aloft when entering a lagoon or 'eyeballing' through coral. The same applies to working through leads in drift ice. I'm not suggesting a full 'crow's nest', although traditional rigs as illustrated can organise luxury aloft so much better than modern. For those stuck with bare stainless steel, a wooden batten that won't cut into bare feet 20ft up with ratlines leading to it works well.

THE TOOLS OF OCEAN NAVIGATION

Now that astro navigation has taken a back seat, piloting a yacht on an ocean passage is not as different from a coastal trip as it once was. However, travelling to places far from the beaten track brings some surprising challenges to modern instrumentation and reminds us that the philosophy of navigation has not, in fact, changed at all. The remote, but genuine contingency of total electronic failure is always with us, and many ocean sailors choose to become masters of celestial navigation just for the joy of plotting their position on planet Earth using a Victorian instrument to observe impossibly distant bodies plummeting through the unfathomable mystery of outer space. Here, then, are some thoughts on the tools of our trade in the third millennium.

Charts

In 2014, the Volvo Round the World Race boat *Team Vestas Wind*, manned by professionals and guided by a highly experienced navigator, piled up on the Cargados Carajos reef in the Indian Ocean. Listening to what that navigator had to say about it, I realised that, seven years earlier, I had been called as an expert over a parallel incident involving the loss of a cruising yacht. The mistakes made were eerily similar. Both skippers had planned their passage using vector charts of the sort loaded into the plotters on many of our bulkheads, computers or tablets. Neither had seen the reefs across their path. As their boats smashed into the shoals that wrecked them, neither knew what he had hit and assumed the hard stuff was either a floating container or some uncharted danger.

In fact, both reefs appeared on the paper charts, even at a global scale of 1:20,000,000. They had been known for two centuries or more. The one hit by the race boat is almost double the length of the Isle of Wight at 40-odd miles. The coral hit by the cruising yacht was less extensive and wasn't revealed on the vector chart until zoomed in to a piece of ocean little bigger than my village pond. No wonder the guy missed seeing it, yet it was shown on the paper chart of the world.

These are not isolated incidents. According to *Yachting World*, a dozen or so yachts are wrecked every year on reefs around Fiji, and it seems reasonable to assume that at least some of these have fallen into the same error.

So what goes wrong? Are the charts at fault? Or is it some human blunder? Either way, how can we make sure it doesn't happen to us?

Vector charts: the dangers

Electronic navigation charts (ENCs) have revolutionised navigation in a generation. Used properly, they make life so much easier for the navigator that the day's work has become unrecognisable. Abuse them and we end up on the reef. It's as simple as that.

■ Zooming and panning issues

Whether they are viewed on a PC or a hardware plotter, all ENCs suffer from the fact that the bit we're looking at just isn't physically big enough. Actually, it's not the chart that's too small. That's as extensive as we could ever want. It's the kit we have for displaying it, but it comes down to the same result in the end. Zooming and panning an ENC is the process of magnifying and shunting what you are seeing sideways to reveal what's off the screen. With a paper equivalent, this is never more of an issue than sometimes having to fold it creatively. With ENCs on a 15-inch screen, let alone the more usual 8- or 12-inch unit, zooming and panning have become a skill of their own.

There's more to zooming a vector chart than might meet the eye, and one of the main reasons for the yacht-on-reef situation is tied up with it. Vector charts are stitched together so that users can move around the globe at will until they run off the bit they've paid for. The result is that the 'chart' is carrying far more information than it can show. If you were looking at the North Atlantic and the electronics displayed everything they had, the chart would be unreadable because of all the clutter. To combat this, the software and/or the chart reduce the data to 'layers'.

Starting at full zoom in the marina, it gives us the lot. Entering the sound outside the breakwater we can't see the other shore on the chart at marina-scale level, so we zoom out a bit. As the area we need for plotting a course appears on the screen, some details disappear.

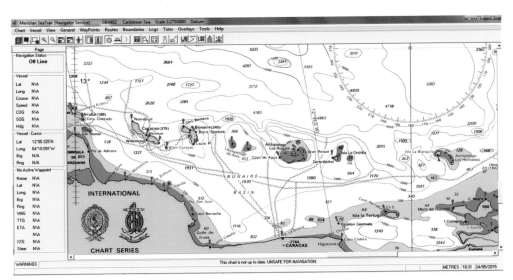

Fig 9.1 *An Admiralty raster chart of the southern Caribbean. Note that all the major offshore rocks are clearly indicated.*

By the time 50 miles of sea is in the frame, little detail remains. At oceanic scale, there may be nothing left but the outline of the continents and a few islands of major importance. As detail is 'layered out', vital dangers have a nasty tendency to vanish as well. The only way to find them is to zoom in again, which you may not wish to do if you're planning a long passage. Zooming in to make the screen a mile across while planning a 3,000-mile trip is so tedious it's unrealistic and, in any case, who knows exactly what track the boat will follow as she makes the best of wind and weather? It won't be the Great Circle or the rhumb line, you can bet on that.

So how do you discover what might, or might not, crawl up from the depths to bite you on the behind? You look at the paper chart, that's what, or its raster equivalent (see Fig 9.3). Remember, my paper charts at 1:20,000,000 showed the reefs that sank the two yachts as plain as barrels on a brewer's dray, yet both remained zoomed out and hidden from the navigators as they sailed along into deadly danger.

■ Datum shifts

An ENC will nearly always be accurate in terms of how one headland or pier relates to another, so it's natural to assume that the boat sailing merrily across the chart is placed equally precisely. While this is generally true – though not invariably – in northern European, Australian, New Zealand or continental North American waters, in far-flung places it may be anything but. GPS can only think in terms of lat/long. The graticule of lat/long lines over our charts was not placed there by God, but by a cartographer working to some sort of protocol. Not all authorities operate to the same one. GPS defaults to an American horizontal datum called WGS84. When this doesn't concur with the chart's original graticule and datum, and no compensating software is in operation, the boat won't appear in the right place relative to any physical features.

If a 'datum shift' is likely, a paper chart or its raster equivalent will carry a note to that effect. Vector charts generally do not. Yet in far-flung places like the Pacific, these shifts are often measured in miles rather than yards, so relying implicitly on a vector chart with no notes on it to qualify positional accuracy may lead to a wretched outcome.

By no means all of the UKHO or US chart portfolio works to WGS84 and much of the material from remote places relates to no known datum at all. The UKHO suggests that, without WGS84 referencing, no ENC can be official. Unofficial vector charts are available for just about anywhere for very little money or no money at all. Before using them, you have to ask yourself how the providers of these charts handle the fact that the datums are unknown. Then you must find yourself a robust stance for

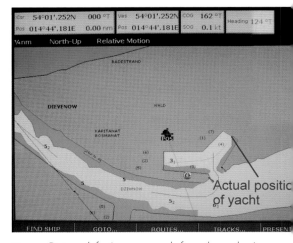

Fig 9.2 *Datum shift. A screen grab from the author's bulkhead plotter using popular vector charts.*

coping with the double-hit of uncertainty. A good start is to have an alternative type of chart handy when planning the passage and to keep it by you to check every so often. This policy lines up with classical navigating philosophy, by which nobody was ever satisfied with a position until confirmed by at least one different source of data.

Alternative charts: paper and raster

The paper chart is well known to us all. For long-range cruising voyagers, the sheer numbers required have always been a financial burden and a space-consuming commitment. If you have a huge folio they are also the devil to correct, but at least that service is free. I remember well the desperate chart-swapping that used to go on in the ports of the world as crew after crew hunted for someone on a reciprocal heading who was ready to hand over the charts they no longer needed for the ones of where they were going in return. Now that paper is largely relegated to backup and planning (see Chapter 11) for a lot of us, we don't seem to need so many of them, but to leave without any at all is asking for trouble. Happily, a viable alternative is at hand.

Vector charts are generated from vectorised data supplied from survey by the world's charting authorities. A raster chart conforms to IHO (International Hydrographic Organisation) specifications and is produced by converting paper charts to a digital image by scanner. To all intents and purposes, an Admiralty or NOAA raster chart is exactly the same as the paper chart of which it is an electronic facsimile. It looks the same, has the same boundaries, is drawn to the same projection and uses the same survey data and corrections, all of which can be readily inspected. Even the notes that come with the paper chart are there, which means you can assess the likely quality of the survey to which it is drawn. There is no chart interrogation to discover hidden details as there is with vector charts, no layering and no zooming. If you don't like the scale, you bring up the next chart. In fact, what you see is, literally, what you get.

The result of this is that a raster chart that works perfectly with a plotting program and GPS can safely be used for passage planning, just as if it were paper. However, it takes up no space at all.

A balanced chart kit

There is no denying the benefits of vector chart coverage on at least one plotter aboard a cruising boat. I, for one, wouldn't want to be without them. They are, however, rather like motorcycles, which the ill-informed often damn as 'dangerous'. Bikes are nothing of the sort and neither, in general, are vector charts. Both are as safe as the person controlling them – and this statement takes account of the old chestnut: 'I was riding along minding my own business when a car pulled out in front of me and I had no chance.' This is precisely paralleled by the man who hits a reef, which he says wasn't on the chart, only to discover it later by zooming in. Vector chart coverage is worldwide and relatively cheap, so discounting the system would be crazy. However, it absolutely must be viewed intelligently by navigators who understand the possible shortfalls.

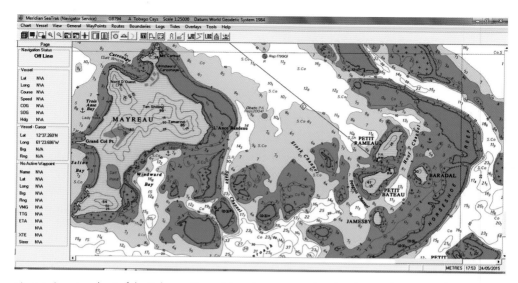

Fig 9.3 *A raster chart of the Tobago Cays. Note the superior detail to that on the vector chart below.*

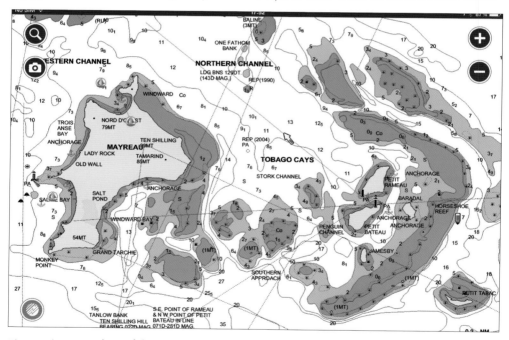

Fig 9.4 *A vector chart of the same piece of sea. Beautifully clear but short on detail.*

Given a good, up-to-date vector chart system on my hardware plotter, I run an ARCS raster chart simultaneously on a PC. I use it to check the vector and, between you and me, if the scale is good, I navigate on it too, because I prefer the way it looks. It is clearer, it is drawn by cartographers who know their business and because there are no zooming issues I find it easier to operate.

Finally, I always sail with a usable paper backup. Because of the 'rasters' I do not expect to have to bring it out too often, and I don't carry all the detailed charts I did when paper was undisputed king, but I have enough to reach a safe haven no matter what may befall. Paper charts remain the rock on which my castle is built.

Electronic hardware

This subject is so well understood and so diverse that little will be served by spelling it all out here. Today, a well-equipped yacht will have a bulkhead multi-function display for radar, AIS, chart plotting and the rest. She will also probably have a PC operating charts of some sort, and most will have a tablet too. Add a basic 'nav app' for mobile phone and you are better covered than anyone could have dreamed of even at the turn of the century.

Radar

While any serious yacht sailing in mid or high latitudes would surely understand the desirability of radar, it is sometimes argued that boats spending most of their time in the tropics do not need it as the visibility is generally pretty good. Readouts of AIS (Automatic Identification System) on a plotter screen add to this sense of security. However, it must

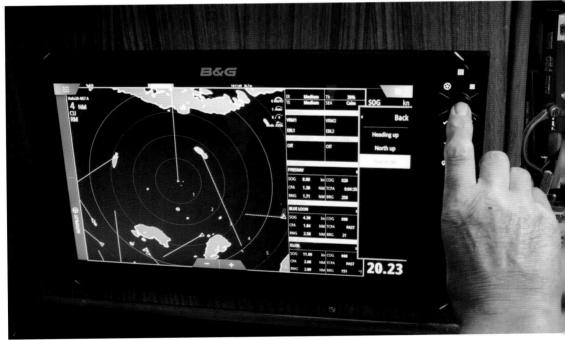

Linking AIS to radar transforms collision avoidance techniques.

Icebergs making clear radar targets in the Denmark Strait.

be understood that not all vessels have AIS, while anything under 300GRT is not legally required to deploy it even if she is in possession of the hardware. Radar, on the other hand, sees more or less all, so on a short-handed yacht where watch-keeping far from shipping lanes may fall short of official requirements, a glance at the radar screen every ten minutes as part of the routine look-around can be a major contributor to safety.

A generation ago, radar was prohibitively power-hungry for small sailing yachts. With modern equipment and power systems, this is no longer so. Having the radar on stand-by asks little in terms of power and switching to active mode for a minute or so is simply a matter of pressing a button. Even when transmitting, power demands are a fraction of what they once were, while the weight of a scanner up a mast is similarly dramatically reduced.

Off-watch single-handers can leave the radar scanning with a guard zone activated so that, in the event of a target coming closer than the distance which the skipper has set, an alarm turns him out of his bunk.

Radar is an almost magical tool for spotting approaching squalls, and using the electronic bearing line to see if they have your name on them soon becomes second nature. It is also handy when anchoring in a tight cove. Distance estimation using the human eye is subject to all sorts of errors, but radar will tell you exactly how far you really are from that threatening cliff face.

Those of us who sail in high latitudes know the value of radar for spotting bergs in thick visibility and, of course, should GPS be disabled for any reason, radar emanates from the ship herself and will continue to function, giving an electronic means of establishing an accurate position in coastal waters.

As you see, 'you pay your money and you takes your choice.'

The author's chart table – paper charts inside, bulkhead plotter for radar/AIS, PC for raster charts, log book, clock (GMT) and barometer. And Lord Nelson ensuring fair play.

Traditional tools

Pelorus

Chapter 10 deals with checking the steering compass at sea by taking bearings of the sun as it rises or sets. The simplest method is to sight it directly across the steering compass. This is only possible where the instrument is binnacle-mounted, unless you have shipped out with one of those excellent Sestrel compasses sited on the coachroof ahead of the cockpit that can be read either from side or top. Otherwise, you can only observe bearings relative to the ship's head by some mechanical means. The classic instrument is a pelorus with proper sights and a finely graduated scale, but these are expensive, space-consuming and I have yet to see one on a yacht.

HOME-MADE PELORUS

Here's a piece of DIY that absolutely anybody can manage:

- Find a redundant square transparent plastic CD case and clear out any paper contents.
- Take an old chart with a good 360° compass rose.
- Cut out the compass rose carefully with scissors.
- Stick it face up in the circular depression used for the CD.
- Make a small hole at dead centre.
- Stand a toothpick (or similar) vertically in the hole and lay the case fore-and-aft on the deck where it can 'see' the setting sun. The shadow picks out the reciprocal of the bearing.

A home-made pelorus is ideal for compass checking on a budget boat. Mine uses a long matchstick as a post, which makes for a beefy shadow. I read off the average 'middle of the shadow' as the boat yaws and that gives a perfectly respectable result. If you can contrive a finer post with a toothpick, so much the better.

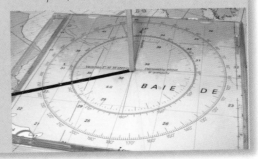

Chart protractor

Nearly all of us use a chart protractor of some description for our paper charts. If this is set up on deck with zero degrees on the ship's head, its index arm can be swivelled towards the sunrise to deliver a surprisingly reasonable relative bearing. Just take some care to note the sun's average position as the boat yaws from side to side of her course.

Sextant

The sextant is the core of traditional ocean navigation. It is so called because its calibrated arc is one-sixth of a circle, or 60 degrees, and the Latin word 'sex' had a rather different meaning to that ascribed to it in modern English. The mirrors double this to 120 degrees. The instrument is made up of a frame with a handle, a moving 'index arm' with an index mirror at one end and a micrometer at the other, and a fixed 'horizon' mirror in line with the optical axis of the telescope. On a classic unit, this mirror is half silvered, half transparent.

Look more closely at the fixed mirror and you will realise that the two halves hold the secret. Some sextants today have a magic horizon mirror that, rather than being half-silvered, somehow becomes transparent when required, but it's all the same in the end. Light from the sun is reflected through safety shades by the index mirror down on to the horizon mirror. This reflects it to your eye via the telescope. If you've set the instrument up properly and you are seeing the horizon through the plain glass with the reflected image of the sun apparently perched neatly on it, the sextant's graduated arc and micrometer read the angle between them to decimals of a minute of arc. This potential level of accuracy from a non-digital tool is nothing short of phenomenal.

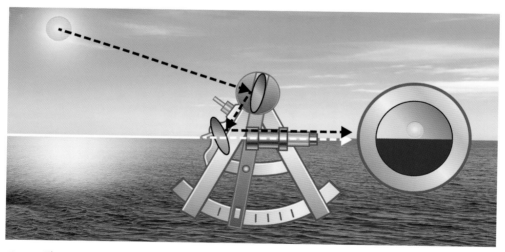

Fig 9.5 *The sextant in operation.*

In order to achieve such results, the sextant must be adjusted for the following errors in this order:

SEXTANT ERRORS

ERROR OF PERPENDICULARITY

Effect: Images side by side.

Cause: Index and horizon mirrors out of parallel.

Action: Adjust the index mirror with the tool supplied in the sextant box. Set the index bar to something like 60° and look across the face of the sextant towards the arc so that the image of the arc in the index mirror runs into the arc itself.

It may be necessary to remove the telescope to achieve this. If the line of the arc where reality joins the image is broken by a step, there is an error of perpendicularity. Adjust the mirror screw until the line becomes unbroken and the index mirror is now 'true'.

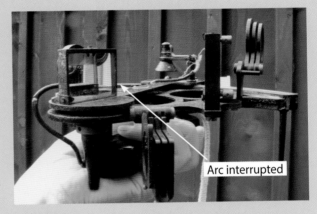

This sextant has an error of perpendicularity. The index mirror is to be adjusted to remove the 'step' in the arc, and bring the image of the arc into line with the true arc.

Arc interrupted

After adjustment, the arc appears as a flowing curve from mirror to reality with no step to disturb its sweep.

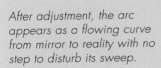

Arc in a clean line

SEXTANT ERRORS

Fig 9.6

Fig 9.7

SIDE ERROR (Fig 9.6)

Effect: When the two images (one seen through the transparent horizon glass, the other via the index mirror and silvered horizon mirror) are superimposed, as illustrated, there is no side error. If one sits beside the other, side error must be removed.

Cause: The horizon mirror is out of line.

Action: First, find a distant vertical line such as a lighthouse. Sight on it with the sextant set to zero. The horizon mirror has two adjusting screws. One of these moves the mirror laterally, the other up and down. Use the lateral one at the side of the mirror and take out the error. This may induce a large index error, but see immediately below for the answer.

INDEX ERROR (Fig 9.7)

Effect: With the instrument set at zero, the horizon or a distant rooftop appears as two images, one above the other.

Cause: Horizon mirror out of adjustment in the 'up and down' plane.

Action: Remove the error using the second screw on the horizon mirror until the two horizons, or perhaps two images of a likely star, become one. This sometimes causes a reintroduction of side error. You can live with a little of this. If it seems too much, play one adjustment against the other and try to eliminate both. If you can't, the one you'll have to settle for is index error. Once this value has been established, it remains pretty stable with a good sextant and can be built into all calculations as a matter of routine. Up to two or three minutes of arc can be tolerated and should be labelled *on* or *off* the arc.

If the sextant reads, say, +2 minutes, the index error is *on* the arc and all subsequent readings should subtract 2 minutes to render them true. If it reads 58 minutes with the horizons together, the error is *off* the arc and is added to all subsequent readings. To sum up:

When it's **OFF** the arc, add it **ON**.
When it's **ON** the arc, take it **OFF**.

■ Care of the sextant

Handled carefully, a good sextant requires minimal attention. Its moving parts are surprisingly robust, and an occasional drop of light machine oil is all they need. Deterioration in the mirror silvering is the most common source of poor performance. Silvering is surprisingly delicate and is easily damaged by sea water, so a rinse in fresh water is important if the instrument takes a soaking. Resist any temptation to polish your sextant regularly. It looks great, but the rubbing and the compound in the polish worry away at the inscribed gradations on the scale. If you have a brass telescope like mine, get out the Brasso and shine it up to your heart's content. Using the sextant is described on page 139.

10 ESSENTIAL CELESTIAL NAVIGATION

Celestial navigation, or 'astro', is where art, philosophy and science meet. With backup GPS and other satellite processors tucked away all over the boat, including our phones, and even our watches, it's possible to circumnavigate without needing even a passing glance at the heavens, but sometimes there's more to life than pure pragmatism. At the time of writing, the British authorities insist on basic astro for an Ocean Yachtmaster certificate. So do the US Navy. They are right. It may be hard to imagine but, as the poet observed: 'The day may come/When Man's fine chattering machines are dumb.' Finding oneself in mid-ocean with no means of ascertaining a position is a grim prospect, so for a little work and some investment in beautiful instruments that you will hand on to the grandchildren, you can remain in control of your destiny. If all the satellites were to fall from the sky, nobody on Earth would notice except for a few navigators and the millions of clowns in cars who have forgotten how to read a map. Should the sun decide to do the same, loss of position would be the least of one's worries.

The trick about celestial navigation is to take it on board one step at a time. Do not move on from one section of this chapter until you have thoroughly mastered its concepts. If you do, all will be lost. As long as you take the trouble, the whole thing is surprisingly accessible. For want of space, and also to keep things as simple as possible, I have confined this chapter to considering only the sun. Should you be fired with enthusiasm and wish to see the whole wonderful picture, with morning stars giving fixes of staggering accuracy, Polaris offering latitude on a quiet middle watch when the moon has lit the horizon like the loom of a mystic city, and a cross-fix on the old gods, Saturn and Jupiter, buy a copy of my modest little book *Celestial Navigation* (published by Fernhurst Books). I wrote the text when I still used my sextant on a daily basis. Although I was never a dab hand at figures, the methods described in it have served me well.

Earth and the heavens

Astro navigation requires one or two adjustments in how we view life and the universe. The first is that we must unlearn all we know about the cosmos. For the purposes of this chapter, the Earth, known as the *terrestrial sphere*, is a round ball exactly in the middle of everything. Out in the big beyond, another sphere – a hollow one with us at its centre – marks the perimeter of the universe. This is the *celestial sphere* and all the heavenly bodies can be taken to move in their courses on its inside surface. Don't worry if this bizarre view of reality offends your sensibilities. We aren't all astrophysicists and navigation has been done this way since long before Hubble opened our eyes to an expanding universe.

Terrestrial sphere

Any location on the Earth's surface is expressed in terms of latitude and longitude, which are angles measured from the centre of the Earth.

■ Definitions

• *Meridians of longitude* define east–west position. The meridians are Great Circles (see Chapter 12) converging at the poles and running directly between them on the surface of the terrestrial sphere. They are numbered by their *angular distance* (see below) east or west of the zero meridian. This is called the *Greenwich Meridian* because it passes through the Greenwich Observatory in London. Sadly, there are some who choose to live in denial of Britain's major contribution to astronomy. These sorry specimens call the zero meridian the *International Reference Meridian* or the *Prime Meridian*. Whatever your political views, longitude is measured in degrees east or west of Greenwich. Rudyard Kipling observed that 'never the twain shall meet'. Although generally a shrewd observer, in this he was wrong. East and west do meet, somewhere in the fastnesses of the Pacific Ocean.

• *Parallels of latitude* define angular distance north or south of the equator, which is the only parallel that is a Great Circle, being on a plane at right angles to the Earth's axis halfway between two poles. All the others are *Small Circles*.

• *Geographic position* (GP) is any point on the terrestrial sphere defined by latitude and longitude.

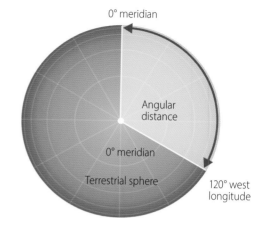

Fig 10.1 *Looking down on the Earth's axis from the Pole. An observer at 120°W longitude is at an angular distance of 120° west of the Greenwich Meridian.*

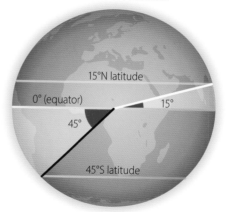

Fig 10.2 *Latitude – the Earth (the terrestrial sphere) viewed from the plane of the equator. Latitude is expressed as an angular distance north or south of the equator, measured from the centre of the Earth.*

■ Angular distance

'The man on the Clapham Omnibus', the ordinary reasonable man of the common law, expresses distances in linear terms such as miles or kilometres. This convenience enables journeys to be calculated by means of speed measured in time and distance, such as miles per hour. For the celestial navigator, the system doesn't work. Nobody could realistically handle the north/south distance between Sirius and Betelgeuse in terms of miles, but to measure it in degrees from the centre of the Earth is comprehensible and simple to work with.

At the equator, the Earth turns through around 25,000 miles in a 24-hour day. In northern Norway it's nothing like so far, but this awkwardness can be neutralised by forgetting miles and, instead, thinking of the Earth as turning through 360 degrees in a day. When dealing with spheres, therefore, the most convenient unit of distance is one degree of angular distance. This is the same in Svalbard, Australia's Great Barrier Reef or the palm-fringed beaches of Trinidad, only 5 degrees off the equator.

■ Subdivision of degrees

Degrees subdivide into 60 minutes (60'). In days gone by, a minute was broken down by 60 again into seconds. Today, this has mercifully been superseded by decimals of a minute. As it happens, one minute of latitude is equal to one sea mile at all latitudes. A so-called 'nautical mile' at 1,852 metres is an arbitrary, human dimension. The sea mile is defined by nature in degrees and minutes. It is therefore much to be preferred. A tenth of a mile is around 100 fathoms, the length of a single anchor cable in Nelson's Navy. Hence, the unit of distance of 'one cable', which comes in at something near a convenient 200 yards.

One minute of longitude equals one mile at the equator, but diminishes to zero at the poles. Working out what it represents in between in terms of miles is a potential brain-twister nobody needs. Angular distance is the answer.

Celestial sphere

All the main features of the terrestrial sphere are mirrored in its celestial counterpart. The terrestrial poles projected outwards from the Earth's axis on to the celestial sphere form the *celestial poles*. The terrestrial equator is reflected by the *celestial equator* which, like its terrestrial counterpart, is equidistant at all points from the celestial poles. A ship's position on the terrestrial sphere is defined in lat/long. In the same way, the position of the sun, or any other heavenly body on the surface of the celestial sphere, can be defined by its *celestial co-ordinates*. Achieving a firm grip on how these work is the key to understanding celestial navigation.

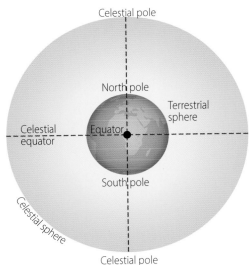

Fig 10.3 *The celestial sphere is an imaginary sphere enclosing the Earth, with its own poles and equator. For the purposes of navigation, all celestial bodies such as the sun and the stars are positioned on the surface of this sphere regardless of their actual distance from the Earth.*

2014 APRIL 19, 20, 21 (SAT., SUN., MON.) 83

UT	SUN GHA	SUN Dec	MOON GHA	v	MOON Dec	d	HP
19 00	180 11.7	N11 04.1	312 41.8	6.8	S18 46.6	1.5	58.7
01	195 11.8	05.0	327 07.6	6.7	18 48.1	1.3	58.7
02	210 11.9	05.9	341 33.3	6.6	18 49.4	1.3	58.7
03	225 12.1	.. 06.7	355 58.9	6.7	18 50.7	1.1	58.7
04	240 12.2	07.6	10 24.6	6.6	18 51.8	1.1	58.7
05	255 12.3	08.5	24 50.2	6.6	18 52.9	0.9	58.7
06	270 12.5	N11 09.3	39 15.8	6.6	S18 53.8	0.7	58.7
S 07	285 12.6	10.2	53 41.4	6.6	18 54.5	0.7	58.7
A 08	300 12.7	11.1	68 07.0	6.6	18 55.2	0.5	58.8
T 09	315 12.9	.. 11.9	82 32.6	6.5	18 55.7	0.4	58.8
U 10	330 13.0	12.8	96 58.1	6.5	18 56.1	0.3	58.8
R 11	345 13.2	13.6	111 23.6	6.5	18 56.4	0.2	58.8
D 12	0 13.3	N11 14.5	125 49.1	6.5	S18 56.6	0.1	58.8
A 13	15 13.4	15.4	140 14.6	6.5	18 56.7	0.1	58.8
Y 14	30 13.6	16.2	154 40.1	6.5	18 56.6	0.2	58.8
15	45 13.7	.. 17.1	169 05.6	6.5	18 56.4	0.3	58.8
16	60 13.8	18.0	183 31.1	6.4	18 56.1	0.5	58.9
17	75 14.0	18.8	197 56.5	6.5	18 55.6	0.5	58.9
18	90 14.1	N11 19.7	212 22.0	6.4	S18 55.1	0.7	58.9
19	105 14.2	20.5	226 47.4	6.5	18 54.4	0.8	58.9
20	120 14.4	21.4	241 12.9	6.4	18 53.6	1.0	58.9
21	135 14.5	.. 22.3	255 38.3	6.4	18 52.6	1.0	58.9
22	150 14.6	23.1	270 03.7	6.4	18 51.6	1.2	58.9
23	165 14.8	24.0	284 29.1	6.5	18 50.4	1.3	58.9
20 00	180 14.9	N11 24.8	298 54.6	6.4	S18 49.1	1.4	58.9
01	195 15.0	25.7	313 20.0	6.4	18 47.7	1.5	58.9
02	210 15.2	26.6	327 45.4	6.5	18 46.2	1.7	59.0
03	225 15.3	.. 27.4	342 10.9	6.4	18 44.5	1.8	59.0
04	240 15.4	28.3	356 36.3	6.4	18 42.7	1.9	59.0
05	255 15.6	29.1	11 01.7	6.5	18 40.8	2.0	59.0
06	270 15.7	N11 30.0	25 27.2	6.4	S18 38.8	2.2	59.0
S 07	285 15.8	30.8	39 52.6	6.5	18 36.6	2.2	59.0
U 08	300 16.0	31.7	54 18.1	6.4	18 34.4	2.4	59.0
N 09	315 16.1	.. 32.6	68 43.5	6.5	18 32.0	2.5	59.0
D 10	330 16.2	33.4	83 09.0	6.5	18 29.5	2.7	59.0
A 11	345 16.3	34.3	97 34.5	6.5	18 26.8	2.7	59.0
Y 12	0 16.5	N11 35.1	112 00.0	6.5	S18 24.1	2.9	59.0
13	15 16.6	36.0	126 25.5	6.5	18 21.2	3.0	59.1
14	30 16.7	36.8	140 51.0	6.5	18 18.2	3.1	59.1
15	45 16.9	.. 37.7	155 16.5	6.6	18 15.1	3.2	59.1
16	60 17.0	38.5	169 42.1	6.5	18 11.9	3.4	59.1
17	75 17.1	39.4	184 07.6	6.6	18 08.5	3.4	59.1
18	90 17.3	N11 40.3	198 33.2	6.6	S18 05.1	3.6	59.1
19	105 17.4	41.1	212 58.8	6.6	18 01.5	3.7	59.1
20	120 17.5	42.0	227 24.4	6.6	17 57.8	3.8	59.1
21	135 17.6	.. 42.8	241 50.0	6.7	17 54.0	4.0	59.1
22	150 17.8	43.7	256 15.7	6.7	17 50.0	4.0	59.1
23	165 17.9	44.5	270 41.4	6.7	17 46.0	4.2	59.1
21 00	180 18.0	N11 45.4	285 07.1	6.7	S17 41.8	4.2	59.1
01	195 18.2	46.2	299 32.8	6.7	17 37.6	4.4	59.1
02	210 18.3	47.1	313 58.5	6.8	17 33.2	4.5	59.2
03	225 18.4	.. 47.9	328 24.3	6.7	17 28.7	4.7	59.2
04	240 18.5	48.8	342 50.0	6.9	17 24.0	4.7	59.2
05	255 18.7	49.6	357 15.9	6.8	17 19.3	4.8	59.2
06	270 18.8	N11 50.5	11 41.7	6.9	S17 14.5	5.0	59.2
M 07	285 18.9	51.3	26 07.6	6.8	17 09.5	5.1	59.2
O 08	300 19.1	52.2	40 33.4	7.0	17 04.4	5.1	59.2
N 09	315 19.2	.. 53.0	54 59.4	6.9	16 59.3	5.3	59.2
D 10	330 19.3	53.9	69 25.3	7.0	16 54.0	5.4	59.2
A 11	345 19.4	54.7	83 51.3	7.0	16 48.6	5.5	59.2
Y 12	0 19.6	N11 55.6	98 17.3	7.0	S16 43.1	5.6	59.2
13	15 19.7	56.4	112 43.3	7.1	16 37.5	5.7	59.2
14	30 19.8	57.3	127 09.4	7.1	16 31.8	5.8	59.2
15	45 19.9	.. 58.1	141 35.5	7.1	16 26.0	6.0	59.2
16	60 20.1	58.9	156 01.6	7.2	16 20.0	6.0	59.2
17	75 20.2	11 59.8	170 27.8	7.2	16 14.0	6.1	59.2
18	90 20.3	N12 00.6	184 54.0	7.2	S16 07.9	6.3	59.2
19	105 20.4	01.5	199 20.2	7.2	16 01.6	6.3	59.2
20	120 20.6	02.3	213 46.4	7.3	15 55.3	6.4	59.2
21	135 20.7	.. 03.2	228 12.7	7.3	15 48.9	6.6	59.2
22	150 20.8	04.0	242 39.1	7.3	15 42.3	6.6	59.3
23	165 20.9	04.9	257 05.4	7.4	S15 35.7	6.7	59.3
	SD 15.9	d 0.9	SD 16.0		16.1		16.1

Twilight / Sunrise / Moonrise

Lat.	Naut.	Civil	Sunrise	Moonrise 19	20	21	22
N 72	////	00 58	03 10	■■		04 15	03 49
N 70	////	01 58	03 31	01 57	02 51	03 10	03 15
68	////	02 32	03 48	01 04	02 01	02 33	02 51
66	00 50	02 56	04 01	00 32	01 29	02 08	02 32
64	01 43	03 14	04 12	00 08	01 06	01 47	02 16
62	02 14	03 29	04 21	24 47	00 47	01 31	02 03
60	02 36	03 41	04 29	24 32	00 32	01 17	01 52
N 58	02 53	03 52	04 36	24 19	00 19	01 06	01 43
56	03 08	04 01	04 42	24 07	00 07	00 55	01 34
54	03 20	04 09	04 48	23 57	24 46	00 46	01 27
52	03 30	04 16	04 53	23 49	24 38	00 38	01 20
50	03 39	04 23	04 57	23 41	24 31	00 31	01 14
45	03 58	04 36	05 07	23 24	24 15	00 15	01 01
N 40	04 13	04 47	05 15	23 10	24 03	00 03	00 50
35	04 24	04 56	05 22	22 58	23 52	24 41	00 41
30	04 34	05 03	05 28	22 48	23 42	24 32	00 32
20	04 49	05 16	05 38	22 30	23 26	24 18	00 18
N 10	05 01	05 26	05 47	22 15	23 11	24 06	00 06
0	05 10	05 34	05 56	22 00	22 58	23 54	24 49
S 10	05 18	05 42	06 04	21 46	22 44	23 43	24 40
20	05 24	05 50	06 12	21 31	22 30	23 30	24 31
30	05 30	05 58	06 22	21 13	22 13	23 16	24 19
35	05 32	06 02	06 28	21 03	22 04	23 08	24 13
40	05 35	06 06	06 34	20 51	21 53	22 58	24 06
45	05 37	06 11	06 41	20 38	21 40	22 47	23 57
S 50	05 39	06 17	06 50	20 21	21 24	22 34	23 47
52	05 40	06 19	06 54	20 13	21 17	22 27	23 42
54	05 40	06 22	06 58	20 04	21 09	22 20	23 37
56	05 41	06 24	07 03	19 54	21 00	22 13	23 31
58	05 42	06 28	07 08	19 43	20 49	22 04	23 24
S 60	05 42	06 31	07 14	19 30	20 37	21 54	23 17

Sunset / Twilight / Moonset

Lat.	Sunset	Civil	Naut.	Moonset 19	20	21	22
N 72	20 52	23 20	////	■■		06 17	08 40
N 70	20 30	22 07	////	04 35	05 40	07 21	09 13
68	20 13	21 31	////	05 27	06 30	07 57	09 36
66	19 59	21 06	23 25	06 00	07 02	08 22	09 55
64	19 48	20 47	22 21	06 24	07 25	08 42	10 09
62	19 38	20 31	21 49	06 42	07 44	08 58	10 22
60	19 30	20 18	21 25	06 56	07 59	09 11	10 32
N 58	19 23	20 08	21 07	07 11	08 12	09 23	10 41
56	19 17	19 58	20 52	07 23	08 23	09 33	10 49
54	19 11	19 50	20 40	07 33	08 33	09 41	10 56
52	19 06	19 43	20 29	07 42	08 42	09 49	11 02
50	19 01	19 36	20 20	07 50	08 49	09 56	11 08
45	18 52	19 23	20 01	08 07	09 06	10 11	11 20
N 40	18 43	19 12	19 46	08 21	09 20	10 23	11 30
35	18 36	19 03	19 34	08 32	09 31	10 34	11 39
30	18 30	18 55	19 24	08 43	09 41	10 43	11 46
20	18 20	18 42	19 09	09 01	09 59	10 59	11 59
N 10	18 11	18 32	18 57	09 16	10 14	11 12	12 10
0	18 02	18 23	18 48	09 30	10 28	11 25	12 21
S 10	17 54	18 15	18 40	09 45	10 42	11 38	12 31
20	17 45	18 08	18 34	10 00	10 57	11 51	12 42
30	17 35	18 00	18 28	10 18	11 14	12 06	12 55
35	17 30	17 56	18 25	10 28	11 24	12 15	13 02
40	17 23	17 51	18 23	10 40	11 35	12 25	13 10
45	17 16	17 46	18 20	10 54	11 48	12 37	13 20
S 50	17 07	17 40	18 18	11 10	12 05	12 51	13 31
52	17 03	17 38	18 17	11 18	12 12	12 58	13 36
54	16 59	17 35	18 16	11 27	12 20	13 05	13 42
56	16 54	17 32	18 16	11 37	12 30	13 13	13 49
58	16 49	17 29	18 15	11 48	12 41	13 23	13 56
S 60	16 42	17 26	18 14	12 01	12 53	13 33	14 04

SUN / MOON

Day	Eqn. of Time 00h	12h	Mer. Pass.	Mer. Pass. Upper	Lower	Age	Phase
	m s	m s	h m	h m	h m	d	%
19	00 46	00 53	11 59	03 17	15 45	20	80
20	00 59	01 06	11 59	04 14	16 43	21	70
21	01 12	01 18	11 59	05 11	17 40	22	60

Fig 10.4 *A 'daily page' from* The Nautical Almanac.

12ᵐ

m/s 12	SUN PLANETS	ARIES	MOON	v or d / Corrⁿ	v or d / Corrⁿ	v or d / Corrⁿ
00	3 00.0	3 00.5	2 51.8	0.0 0.0	6.0 1.3	12.0 2.5
01	3 00.3	3 00.7	2 52.0	0.1 0.0	6.1 1.3	12.1 2.5
02	3 00.5	3 01.0	2 52.3	0.2 0.0	6.2 1.3	12.2 2.5
03	3 00.8	3 01.2	2 52.5	0.3 0.1	6.3 1.3	12.3 2.6
04	3 01.0	3 01.5	2 52.8	0.4 0.1	6.4 1.3	12.4 2.6
05	3 01.3	3 01.7	2 53.0	0.5 0.1	6.5 1.4	12.5 2.6
06	3 01.5	3 02.0	2 53.2	0.6 0.1	6.6 1.4	12.6 2.6
07	3 01.8	3 02.2	2 53.5	0.7 0.1	6.7 1.4	12.7 2.6
08	3 02.0	3 02.5	2 53.7	0.8 0.2	6.8 1.4	12.8 2.7
09	3 02.3	3 02.7	2 53.9	0.9 0.2	6.9 1.4	12.9 2.7
10	3 02.5	3 03.0	2 54.2	1.0 0.2	7.0 1.5	13.0 2.7
11	3 02.8	3 03.3	2 54.4	1.1 0.2	7.1 1.5	13.1 2.7
12	3 03.0	3 03.5	2 54.7	1.2 0.3	7.2 1.5	13.2 2.8
13	3 03.3	3 03.8	2 54.9	1.3 0.3	7.3 1.5	13.3 2.8
14	3 03.5	3 04.0	2 55.1	1.4 0.3	7.4 1.5	13.4 2.8
15	3 03.8	3 04.3	2 55.4	1.5 0.3	7.5 1.6	13.5 2.8
16	3 04.0	3 04.5	2 55.6	1.6 0.3	7.6 1.6	13.6 2.8
17	3 04.3	3 04.8	2 55.9	1.7 0.4	7.7 1.6	13.7 2.9
18	3 04.5	3 05.0	2 56.1	1.8 0.4	7.8 1.6	13.8 2.9
19	3 04.8	3 05.3	2 56.3	1.9 0.4	7.9 1.6	13.9 2.9
20	3 05.0	3 05.5	2 56.6	2.0 0.4	8.0 1.7	14.0 2.9
21	3 05.3	3 05.8	2 56.8	2.1 0.4	8.1 1.7	14.1 2.9
22	3 05.5	3 06.0	2 57.0	2.2 0.5	8.2 1.7	14.2 3.0
23	3 05.8	3 06.3	2 57.3	2.3 0.5	8.3 1.7	14.3 3.0
24	3 06.0	3 06.5	2 57.5	2.4 0.5	8.4 1.8	14.4 3.0
25	3 06.3	3 06.8	2 57.8	2.5 0.5	8.5 1.8	14.5 3.0
26	3 06.5	3 07.0	2 58.0	2.6 0.5	8.6 1.8	14.6 3.0
27	3 06.8	3 07.3	2 58.2	2.7 0.6	8.7 1.8	14.7 3.1
28	3 07.0	3 07.5	2 58.5	2.8 0.6	8.8 1.8	14.8 3.1
29	3 07.3	3 07.8	2 58.7	2.9 0.6	8.9 1.9	14.9 3.1
30	3 07.5	3 08.0	2 59.0	3.0 0.6	9.0 1.9	15.0 3.1
31	3 07.8	3 08.3	2 59.2	3.1 0.6	9.1 1.9	15.1 3.1
32	3 08.0	3 08.5	2 59.4	3.2 0.7	9.2 1.9	15.2 3.2
33	3 08.3	3 08.8	2 59.7	3.3 0.7	9.3 1.9	15.3 3.2
34	3 08.5	3 09.0	2 59.9	3.4 0.7	9.4 2.0	15.4 3.2
35	3 08.8	3 09.3	3 00.2	3.5 0.7	9.5 2.0	15.5 3.2
36	3 09.0	3 09.5	3 00.4	3.6 0.8	9.6 2.0	15.6 3.3
37	3 09.3	3 09.8	3 00.6	3.7 0.8	9.7 2.0	15.7 3.3
38	3 09.5	3 10.0	3 00.9	3.8 0.8	9.8 2.0	15.8 3.3
39	3 09.8	3 10.3	3 01.1	3.9 0.8	9.9 2.1	15.9 3.3
40	3 10.0	3 10.5	3 01.3	4.0 0.8	10.0 2.1	16.0 3.3
41	3 10.3	3 10.8	3 01.6	4.1 0.9	10.1 2.1	16.1 3.4
42	3 10.5	3 11.0	3 01.8	4.2 0.9	10.2 2.1	16.2 3.4
43	3 10.8	3 11.3	3 02.1	4.3 0.9	10.3 2.1	16.3 3.4
44	3 11.0	3 11.5	3 02.3	4.4 0.9	10.4 2.2	16.4 3.4
45	3 11.3	3 11.8	3 02.5	4.5 0.9	10.5 2.2	16.5 3.4
46	3 11.5	3 12.0	3 02.8	4.6 1.0	10.6 2.2	16.6 3.5
47	3 11.8	3 12.3	3 03.0	4.7 1.0	10.7 2.2	16.7 3.5
48	3 12.0	3 12.5	3 03.3	4.8 1.0	10.8 2.3	16.8 3.5
49	3 12.3	3 12.8	3 03.5	4.9 1.0	10.9 2.3	16.9 3.5
50	3 12.5	3 13.0	3 03.7	5.0 1.0	11.0 2.3	17.0 3.5
51	3 12.8	3 13.3	3 04.0	5.1 1.1	11.1 2.3	17.1 3.6
52	3 13.0	3 13.5	3 04.2	5.2 1.1	11.2 2.3	17.2 3.6
53	3 13.3	3 13.8	3 04.4	5.3 1.1	11.3 2.4	17.3 3.6
54	3 13.5	3 14.0	3 04.7	5.4 1.1	11.4 2.4	17.4 3.6
55	3 13.8	3 14.3	3 04.9	5.5 1.1	11.5 2.4	17.5 3.6
56	3 14.0	3 14.5	3 05.2	5.6 1.2	11.6 2.4	17.6 3.7
57	3 14.3	3 14.8	3 05.4	5.7 1.2	11.7 2.4	17.7 3.7
58	3 14.5	3 15.0	3 05.6	5.8 1.2	11.8 2.5	17.8 3.7
59	3 14.8	3 15.3	3 05.9	5.9 1.2	11.9 2.5	17.9 3.7
60	3 15.0	3 15.5	3 06.1	6.0 1.3	12.0 2.5	18.0 3.8

13ᵐ

m/s 13	SUN PLANETS	ARIES	MOON	v or d / Corrⁿ	v or d / Corrⁿ	v or d / Corrⁿ
00	3 15.0	3 15.5	3 06.1	0.0 0.0	6.0 1.4	12.0 2.7
01	3 15.3	3 15.8	3 06.4	0.1 0.0	6.1 1.4	12.1 2.7
02	3 15.5	3 16.0	3 06.6	0.2 0.0	6.2 1.4	12.2 2.7
03	3 15.8	3 16.3	3 06.8	0.3 0.1	6.3 1.4	12.3 2.8
04	3 16.0	3 16.5	3 07.1	0.4 0.1	6.4 1.4	12.4 2.8
05	3 16.3	3 16.8	3 07.3	0.5 0.1	6.5 1.5	12.5 2.8
06	3 16.5	3 17.0	3 07.5	0.6 0.1	6.6 1.5	12.6 2.8
07	3 16.8	3 17.3	3 07.8	0.7 0.2	6.7 1.5	12.7 2.9
08	3 17.0	3 17.5	3 08.0	0.8 0.2	6.8 1.5	12.8 2.9
09	3 17.3	3 17.8	3 08.3	0.9 0.2	6.9 1.6	12.9 2.9
10	3 17.5	3 18.0	3 08.5	1.0 0.2	7.0 1.6	13.0 2.9
11	3 17.8	3 18.3	3 08.7	1.1 0.2	7.1 1.6	13.1 2.9
12	3 18.0	3 18.5	3 09.0	1.2 0.3	7.2 1.6	13.2 3.0
13	3 18.3	3 18.8	3 09.2	1.3 0.3	7.3 1.6	13.3 3.0
14	3 18.5	3 19.0	3 09.5	1.4 0.3	7.4 1.7	13.4 3.0
15	3 18.8	3 19.3	3 09.7	1.5 0.3	7.5 1.7	13.5 3.0
16	3 19.0	3 19.5	3 09.9	1.6 0.4	7.6 1.7	13.6 3.1
17	3 19.3	3 19.8	3 10.2	1.7 0.4	7.7 1.7	13.7 3.1
18	3 19.5	3 20.0	3 10.4	1.8 0.4	7.8 1.8	13.8 3.1
19	3 19.8	3 20.3	3 10.7	1.9 0.4	7.9 1.8	13.9 3.1
20	3 20.0	3 20.5	3 10.9	2.0 0.5	8.0 1.8	14.0 3.2
21	3 20.3	3 20.8	3 11.1	2.1 0.5	8.1 1.8	14.1 3.2
22	3 20.5	3 21.0	3 11.4	2.2 0.5	8.2 1.8	14.2 3.2
23	3 20.8	3 21.3	3 11.6	2.3 0.5	8.3 1.9	14.3 3.2
24	3 21.0	3 21.6	3 11.8	2.4 0.5	8.4 1.9	14.4 3.2
25	3 21.3	3 21.8	3 12.1	2.5 0.6	8.5 1.9	14.5 3.3
26	3 21.5	3 22.1	3 12.3	2.6 0.6	8.6 1.9	14.6 3.3
27	3 21.8	3 22.3	3 12.6	2.7 0.6	8.7 2.0	14.7 3.3
28	3 22.0	3 22.6	3 12.8	2.8 0.6	8.8 2.0	14.8 3.3
29	3 22.3	3 22.8	3 13.0	2.9 0.7	8.9 2.0	14.9 3.4
30	3 22.5	3 23.1	3 13.3	3.0 0.7	9.0 2.0	15.0 3.4
31	3 22.8	3 23.3	3 13.5	3.1 0.7	9.1 2.0	15.1 3.4
32	3 23.0	3 23.6	3 13.8	3.2 0.7	9.2 2.1	15.2 3.4
33	3 23.3	3 23.8	3 14.0	3.3 0.7	9.3 2.1	15.3 3.4
34	3 23.5	3 24.1	3 14.2	3.4 0.8	9.4 2.1	15.4 3.5
35	3 23.8	3 24.3	3 14.5	3.5 0.8	9.5 2.1	15.5 3.5
36	3 24.0	3 24.6	3 14.7	3.6 0.8	9.6 2.2	15.6 3.5
37	3 24.3	3 24.8	3 14.9	3.7 0.8	9.7 2.2	15.7 3.5
38	3 24.5	3 25.1	3 15.2	3.8 0.9	9.8 2.2	15.8 3.6
39	3 24.8	3 25.3	3 15.4	3.9 0.9	9.9 2.2	15.9 3.6
40	3 25.0	3 25.6	3 15.7	4.0 0.9	10.0 2.3	16.0 3.6
41	3 25.3	3 25.8	3 15.9	4.1 0.9	10.1 2.3	16.1 3.6
42	3 25.5	3 26.1	3 16.1	4.2 0.9	10.2 2.3	16.2 3.6
43	3 25.8	3 26.3	3 16.4	4.3 1.0	10.3 2.3	16.3 3.7
44	3 26.0	3 26.6	3 16.6	4.4 1.0	10.4 2.3	16.4 3.7
45	3 26.3	3 26.8	3 16.9	4.5 1.0	10.5 2.4	16.5 3.7
46	3 26.5	3 27.1	3 17.1	4.6 1.0	10.6 2.4	16.6 3.7
47	3 26.8	3 27.3	3 17.3	4.7 1.1	10.7 2.4	16.7 3.8
48	3 27.0	3 27.6	3 17.6	4.8 1.1	10.8 2.4	16.8 3.8
49	3 27.3	3 27.8	3 17.8	4.9 1.1	10.9 2.5	16.9 3.8
50	3 27.5	3 28.1	3 18.0	5.0 1.1	11.0 2.5	17.0 3.8
51	3 27.8	3 28.3	3 18.3	5.1 1.1	11.1 2.5	17.1 3.8
52	3 28.0	3 28.6	3 18.5	5.2 1.2	11.2 2.5	17.2 3.9
53	3 28.3	3 28.8	3 18.8	5.3 1.2	11.3 2.5	17.3 3.9
54	3 28.5	3 29.1	3 19.0	5.4 1.2	11.4 2.6	17.4 3.9
55	3 28.8	3 29.3	3 19.2	5.5 1.2	11.5 2.6	17.5 3.9
56	3 29.0	3 29.6	3 19.5	5.6 1.3	11.6 2.6	17.6 4.0
57	3 29.3	3 29.8	3 19.7	5.7 1.3	11.7 2.6	17.7 4.0
58	3 29.5	3 30.1	3 20.0	5.8 1.3	11.8 2.7	17.8 4.0
59	3 29.8	3 30.3	3 20.2	5.9 1.3	11.9 2.7	17.9 4.0
60	3 30.0	3 30.6	3 20.4	6.0 1.4	12.0 2.7	18.0 4.1

Fig 10.5 An 'Increments and Corrections' page from the back of **The Nautical Almanac.**

Celestial longitude: Greenwich Hour Angle

The *celestial zero meridian* is the projection of the terrestrial zero (Greenwich) meridian. Terrestrial longitude is measured from the Greenwich Meridian in degrees east or west around the world to 180°. Because the Earth keeps on turning in one direction, celestial longitude, known as Greenwich Hour Angle (GHA), doesn't work like this. Instead, it is measured directly westward from 0° to 359°. The phrase 'Greenwich Hour Angle' might sound like gobbledygook. It isn't. It is merely a useful way of expressing celestial longitude.

Fig 10.6 shows that 70°W longitude is the equivalent of GHA 70° on the celestial sphere and that 135°E longitude marries up with GHA 225°. A second glance shows that if 135°E were

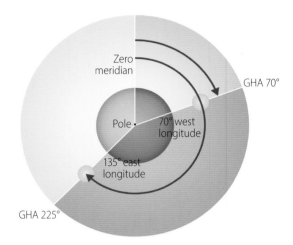

Fig 10.6 *View of the Earth and the celestial sphere from the north elevated pole. Greenwich Hour Angle (GHA) compared with longitude.*

expressed in a 0° to 360° notation, beginning at Greenwich and working westward, it would represent a longitude of 225°. It is just a question of convention. To convert east longitude to 360° notation and tie it to the corresponding GHA, subtract it from 360°.

The almanac

The sun's GHA is found in *The Nautical Almanac* NP 314 from HMSO. Data for astro navigation are called the *Nautical Ephemeris*. The ephemeris is available elsewhere, but NP 314 and its USNO clone are by far the easiest to use. Fig 10.4 (page 128) is an example of the 'daily page' for 19–21 April in 2014. The left column refers to hours of GMT and the next column gives the GHA of the sun for the hour. The incremental change needed for minutes and seconds is found in the 'Increments and Corrections' tables in the back pages (see Fig 10.5, page 129).

Each long box refers to a single minute. The seconds are numbered off down the left-hand side. Read across to the 'Sun' column and away you go.

Note that since the sun is always moving westward and the GHA increases all the way to 360° after which it starts again, the minutes and seconds increments are always added to the hourly value of the GHA.

Example

What is the GHA of the sun at 09h 13m 47s GMT on 20 April?

GHA 09h	315°	16′.1
+ Increment for 13m 47s	003°	26′.8
GHA sun	318°	42′.9

Celestial latitude or declination

The celestial equivalent of terrestrial latitude is *declination*. Declination is angular distance north or south of the celestial equator. Like latitude, and unlike the 360-degree GHA, it is named north or south. A body with a declination of 30°N will, at some time in the 24-hour period, pass directly over the head of an observer in 30°N latitude.

The sun's declination changes with time and is given in the almanac. Look again at the daily pages illustration (Fig 10.4). The sun column gives the declination immediately to the right of the GHA.

At the bottom of this column is a small letter 'd' with a numerical value beside it – in this case, 0.9. This is the rate of change per hour. You can see by inspection of the adjacent hours whether the change is to be added, or subtracted, for increasing or decreasing declination.

Now check the increments columns in Fig 10.5 headed 'v or d correction' for each minute. Ignore seconds. They have nothing to do with this. Read off the increment and adjust the hourly declination as appropriate. In practice, this correction can often be applied in the head by simple mental arithmetic.

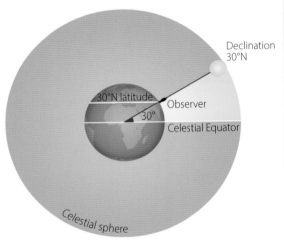

Example of increments for declination

If you are 12 minutes into the hour with a 'd' value of 0.9, go down the column for 12 minutes as far as 'd' 0.9 and read off the value, which is 0.2. The seconds' column is irrelevant. The figures in the column are for minutes only, which is quite accurate enough. If the day were 19 April, declination value is rising, so 0.2 is added to the hourly figure on the daily page.

Fig 10.7 *Left: Earth and the celestial sphere from the equator. Latitude compared with declination.*

■ Zenith and nadir

An observer's *zenith* is his terrestrial position projected from the centre of the Earth on to the celestial sphere. Standing on level ground, it's the point directly above his head. The declination of his zenith is the same as his latitude. The GHA of his zenith is the same as his longitude, adjusted for east longitude if necessary by subtracting it from 360°.

A celestial position delightfully termed the *nadir* is found by projecting a line from the zenith through the observer to the centre of the Earth and on until it cuts the celestial sphere on the other side. From the subjective

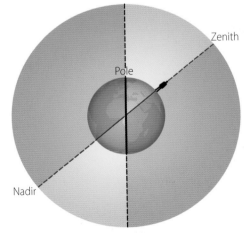

Fig 10.8 *Zenith and nadir viewed from the celestial equator.*

viewpoint of a terrestrial observer, things don't get much lower than this.

Local Hour Angle

In the majority of the calculations involved in celestial navigation, the Local Hour Angle (LHA) is of more concern than the GHA. Just as the GHA of the sun at a given time is its angular distance west of the Greenwich Meridian, so the LHA is its angular distance to the west of the observer's meridian.

Given that you have lifted the sun's GHA from the almanac and have some idea of your longitude, working out the approximate LHA is straightforward.

Figures 10.9 to 10.12 are four examples of the most common LHA calculations. It is vital that these are understood. Without a grasp of the concept of Local Hour Angle, the rest of this chapter may as well be written in Hottentot for all the sense it will make.

■ West longitude: GHA of sun greater than observer's longitude

LHA = GHA – longitude west

Note in the example below that 48° 23'.7 minus 14° 55' equals 33° 28'.7. Sixty minutes, not 100 minutes, make one degree. If you are using the old-fashioned arithmetic carrying digits and decimals, you must remember that moving from minutes to degrees, one 'borrows' six, not ten, for the 60 minutes.

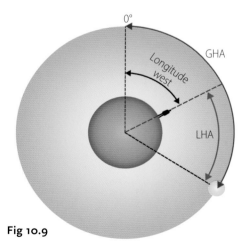

Fig 10.9

Example

What is the LHA of the sun at 15h 12m 27s GMT on 20 April? Your longitude is 14° 55'W.

GHA 15h	45°	16'.9
+ Increment 12m 27s	03°	06'.8
GHA sun	48°	23'.7
–Longitude west	14°	55'.0
LHA	33°	28'.7

A different example might be to add 2° 45' to 5° 30'. The answer would be 8° 15' because 45 + 30 = 75. Sixty makes up the degree to carry over and 15 is left in the minutes column. This anomaly in the decimal system generates many an error, so watch out for it.

■ West longitude: GHA less than observer's longitude

LHA = GHA + 360 – longitude west

Fig 10.10 shows that to find LHA here, you must chase all the way round the clock, as it were, until you finally catch up with the sun, which has been just a few degrees behind you all the time. This does look awkward, but help is at hand. By far the easiest way to deal with it is to add the GHA to 360, then subtract the west longitude. The answer, as the man in the fairground said, is 'every one a coconut'.

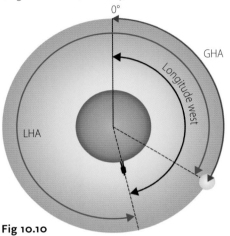

Fig 10.10

Example

What is the LHA of the sun at 14h 12m 18s GMT on 21 April 21? Your longitude is 38° 43'W.

GHA 14h	30°	19'.8
+ Increment 12m 18s	3°	04'.5
GHA sun	33°	24'.3
+ 360	360°	
GHA + 360	393°	24'.3
Longitude west	038°	43'.0
LHA	354	41'.3

In both the above examples, LHA = GHA minus longitude west. If longitude west happens to be greater than GHA the sun will be a nonsense, so just add a quick 360° to the GHA and all will be well.

■ East longitude: GHA a smaller value than the longitude

LHA = GHA + longitude east

A glance at Fig 10.11 makes this one obvious. Just remember that LHA is the angular distance of the body from the observer, moving to the westward (clockwise on the diagram) and the answer is clear.

Fig 10.11

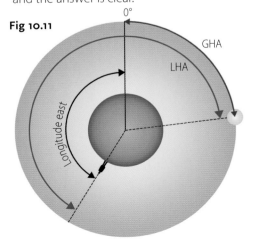

Example

What is the LHA of the sun at 15h 12m 22s on 19 April? Your longitude is 151° 13'E.

GHA 15h	45°	13'.7
+ Increment 12m 22s	3°	05'.5
GHA sun	48°	19'.2
+Longitude east	151°	13'.0
LHA	199°	32'.2

■ East longitude: GHA a greater value than longitude (expressed in 360° notation)

LHA = (GHA + longitude east) − 360°

This is easier than a first glance at Fig 10.12 implies. Don't forget that LHA is the angular distance to the westward between you and the sun. The easiest answer is to add up the GHA and the longitude expressed as degrees east of Greenwich. The sum is going to be greater than 360°, so all that is needed now is to subtract 360° from the result, and that's the LHA.

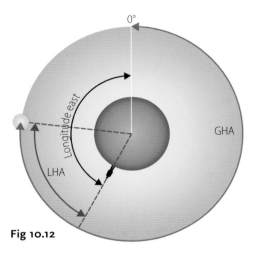

Fig 10.12

Example

What is the LHA of the sun at 02h 13m 48s on 21 April? Your longitude is 172° 15′E.

GHA 02h	210°	18′.3
+ Increment 13m 48s	3°	27′.0
GHA sun	213°	45′.3
+ Longitude east	172°	15′.0
	386°	00′.3
−360	360°	
LHA sun	26°	00′.3

GENERAL RULES

What all this boils down to is:

- **In west longitude** LHA = GHA minus longitude.
  If GHA is a smaller figure than longitude west, just add 360° to it and you're in business.
- **In east longitude** LHA = GHA plus longitude east.
  If this makes the LHA more than 360°, subtract the magic number 360 and all is well.

The horizon

Every schoolboy fancies he knows what the horizon is. It's where the sky meets the sea, isn't it? To a poet, this may be true. For the navigator, there's a little more to it. The sun's altitude can only be observed as the angle between the heavenly body and the observer's horizon. However, navigation tables assume that the observer is at the centre of the terrestrial sphere rather than on the Earth's surface. Because the Earth has a measurable size, at least in comparison with the distance to the sun, this discrepancy leads to an error between what we are actually seeing (the terrestrial or 'corrected' visual horizon) and what the tables would have us see. This error is called *horizontal parallax*. It is only a fraction of a minute for the sun and is easily dealt with. All such considerations defer to infinity when you start dealing with stars, but that is another book. Parallax is with us for solar calculations.

To enter the tables, we need the angle between the celestial horizon and the sun, measured at the centre of the Earth. The celestial horizon sits on a plane that makes a right angle with a line dropped from the position of the observer to the centre of the Earth. The observer cannot see this horizon, but, with a few small adjustments, he can see the *terrestrial horizon* that is parallel to it. This lies at a tangent to the Earth's surface at right angles to the line joining the observer, his zenith and the centre of the Earth.

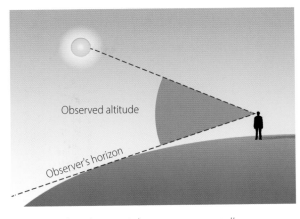

Fig 10.13 *The observer's horizon is materially different from the celestial horizon.*

Because the observer's eye will be above the surface of the Earth by six feet in a small yacht and a hundred or more in a container ship, he actually sees 'over the edge', beyond the terrestrial horizon to his own visual horizon. The angular inaccuracy that results is called *dip* and is subject to a corrective factor given in the almanac.

Horizons and parallax sound intimidating, but relax. All the hard work has been done already by the great minds that put the almanacs together. What's left for us is a couple of easy addition or subtraction sums.

The author shoots the sun with his 1942 Husun sextant, a treasured possession he plans to hand on to his grandchildren.

The sextant in practice

True altitude and sextant altitude

Having set up your sextant in Chapter 9, you can be confident that it is reading accurately, given perhaps a minor correction for index error, which must be checked as a matter of course before taking a sight. Unless you bounce it, it should remain true for years without further attention. Just check it over once in a while.

In order to transform the altitude measured with the sextant (H_S) into the angle the sun is making with the *celestial* horizon (its 'true', or 'observed altitude' – H_O), a few corrections must be applied, on paper, not to the instrument this time.

■ Dip

This compensates for the fact that your height of eye enables you to see beyond the theoretical terrestrial horizon. In the front of *The Nautical Almanac* and on the cardboard bookmark (*see* Fig 10.14) is a group of tables for correcting sextant altitude (H_S). The dip section is at the right-hand side. If you estimate your height of eye to be, for example, 10ft or 3 metres, the dip correction – which is always subtractive – is minus 3.1 minutes.

■ Wave height

Exactly what effect wave height has on a sight is a moot point. Specific advice is thin on the ground from any major authority, including the great Captain Lecky who has solutions to most anomalies tucked away in his *Wrinkles in Practical Navigation* (my copy dated 1888). The best conclusion seems to be that if you're up on a big wave, the horizon you're seeing is probably the crest of a far-off equivalent lump of water. In a heavy sea, you'll certainly be waiting for a few moments until the boat rises to a hefty one to see the horizon at all, so wave height can safely be ignored.

For some reason I've never understood, the movement of a boat in a rough sea bothers a sextant far less than it troubles the sailor struggling to find a steady reading with a hand-bearing compass. The sun sits solidly on the horizon in those mirrors as the boat turns herself inside out, so you can rest easy on that score.

Sun's total altitude correction

On the same bookmark as the dip table is a more significant section entitled *Altitude Correction Tables* (opposite). This is a 'package correction' which, in addition to parallax, includes semidiameter and refraction, described on page 138. The point of entry for the table is *apparent altitude* (App Alt), which is sextant altitude corrected for index error (if any) and dip. The value worked up after applying the Total Altitude Correction to App Alt is the number from which all sight reductions are made. It is called the 'Observed Altitude' (H_O).

■ Semidiameter

All sun sights are theoretically based on the centre of the sun as well as the centre of the Earth.

ALTITUDE CORRECTION TABLES 10°–90°—SUN, STARS, PLANETS

OCT.–MAR. **SUN** APR.–SEPT.						**STARS AND PLANETS**				**DIP**					
App. Alt.	Lower Limb	Upper Limb	App. Alt.	Lower Limb	Upper Limb	App Alt.	Corrⁿ	App. Alt.	Additional Corrⁿ	Ht. of Eye	Corrⁿ	Ht. of Eye	Corrⁿ	Ht. of Eye	Corrⁿ
° ′	′	′	° ′	′	′	° ′	′	**2014**		m	′	ft.	′	m	′
9 33	+10·8	−21·5	9 39	+10·6	−21·2	9 55	−5·3	**VENUS**		2·4	−2·8	8·0		1·0	−1·8
9 45	+10·9	−21·4	9 50	+10·7	−21·1	10 07	−5·2	Jan. 1–Jan. 9		2·6	−2·9	8·6		1·5	−2·2
9 56	+11·0	−21·3	10 02	+10·8	−21·0	10 20	−5·1	Jan. 13–Jan. 31		2·8	−3·0	9·2		2·0	−2·5
10 08	+11·1	−21·2	10 14	+10·9	−20·9	10 32	−5·0			3·0	−3·1	9·8		2·5	−2·8
10 20	+11·2	−21·1	10 27	+11·0	−20·8	10 46	−4·9	° ′		3·2	−3·2	10·5		3·0	−3·0
10 33	+11·3	−21·0	10 40	+11·1	−20·7	10 59	−4·8	26 +0·5		3·4	−3·3	11·2			
10 46	+11·4	−20·9	10 53	+11·2	−20·6	11 14	−4·7	46 +0·4		3·6	−3·4	11·9		See table	
11 00	+11·5	−20·8	11 07	+11·3	−20·5	11 29	−4·6	60 +0·3		3·8	−3·5	12·6		←	
11 15	+11·6	−20·7	11 22	+11·4	−20·4	11 44	−4·5	73 +0·2		4·0	−3·6	13·3			
11 30	+11·7	−20·6	11 37	+11·5	−20·3	12 00	−4·4	84 +0·1		4·3	−3·7	14·1		m	′
11 45	+11·8	−20·5	11 53	+11·6	−20·2	12 17	−4·3	Jan. 10–Jan. 12		4·5	−3·8	14·9		20 −7·9
12 01	+11·9	−20·4	12 10	+11·7	−20·1	12 35	−4·2			4·7	−3·9	15·7		22 −8·3
12 18	+12·0	−20·3	12 27	+11·8	−20·0	12 53	−4·1	° ′		5·0	−4·0	16·5		24 −8·6
12 36	+12·1	−20·2	12 45	+11·9	−19·9	13 12	−4·0	24 +0·6		5·2	−4·1	17·4		26 −9·0
12 54	+12·2	−20·1	13 04	+12·0	−19·8	13 32	−3·9	41 +0·5		5·5	−4·2	18·3		28 −9·3
13 14	+12·3	−20·0	13 24	+12·1	−19·7	13 53	−3·8	54 +0·4		5·8	−4·3	19·1		
13 34	+12·4	−19·9	13 44	+12·2	−19·6	14 16	−3·7	65 +0·3		6·1	−4·4	20·1		30 −9·6
13 55	+12·5	−19·8	14 06	+12·3	−19·5	14 39	−3·6	76 +0·2		6·3	−4·5	21·0		32 −10·0
14 17	+12·6	−19·7	14 29	+12·4	−19·4	15 03	−3·5	85 +0·1		6·6	−4·6	22·0		34 −10·3
14 41	+12·7	−19·6	14 53	+12·5	−19·3	15 29	−3·4	Feb. 1–Feb. 16		6·9	−4·7	22·9		36 −10·6
15 05	+12·8	−19·5	15 18	+12·6	−19·2	15 56	−3·3			7·2	−4·8	23·9		38 −10·8
15 31	+12·9	−19·4	15 45	+12·7	−19·1	16 25	−3·2	° ′		7·5	−4·9	24·9		
15 59	+13·0	−19·3	16 13	+12·8	−19·0	16 55	−3·1	29 +0·4		7·9	−5·0	26·0		40 −11·1
16 27	+13·1	−19·2	16 43	+12·9	−18·9	17 27	−3·0	51 +0·3		8·2	−5·1	27·1		42 −11·4
16 58	+13·2	−19·1	17 14	+13·0	−18·8	18 01	−2·9	68 +0·2		8·5	−5·2	28·1		44 −11·7
17 30	+13·3	−19·0	17 47	+13·1	−18·7	18 37	−2·8	83 +0·1		8·8	−5·3	29·2		46 −11·9
18 05	+13·4	−18·9	18 23	+13·2	−18·6	19 16	−2·7	Feb. 17–Mar. 10		9·2	−5·4	30·4		48 −12·2
18 41	+13·5	−18·8	19 00	+13·3	−18·5	19 56	−2·6			9·5	−5·5	31·5		
19 20	+13·6	−18·7	19 41	+13·4	−18·4	20 40	−2·5	° ′		9·9	−5·6	32·7		ft. ′
20 02	+13·7	−18·6	20 24	+13·5	−18·3	21 27	−2·4	34 +0·3		10·3	−5·7	33·9		2 −1·4
20 46	+13·8	−18·5	21 10	+13·6	−18·2	22 17	−2·3	60 +0·2		10·6	−5·8	35·1		4 −1·9
21 34	+13·9	−18·4	21 59	+13·7	−18·1	23 11	−2·2	80 +0·1		11·0	−5·9	36·3		6 −2·4
22 25	+14·0	−18·3	22 52	+13·8	−18·0	24 09	−2·1	Mar. 11–Apr. 30		11·4	−6·0	37·6		8 −2·7
23 20	+14·1	−18·2	23 49	+13·9	−17·9	25 12	−2·0			11·8	−6·1	38·9		10 −3·1
24 20	+14·2	−18·1	24 51	+14·0	−17·8	26 20	−1·9	° ′		12·2	−6·2	40·1		
25 24	+14·3	−18·0	25 58	+14·1	−17·7	27 34	−1·8	41 +0·2		12·6	−6·3	41·5		See table
26 34	+14·4	−17·9	27 11	+14·2	−17·6	28 54	−1·7	76 +0·1		13·0	−6·4	42·8		←
27 50	+14·5	−17·8	28 31	+14·3	−17·5	30 22	−1·6	May 1–Dec. 31		13·4	−6·5	45·5		ft. ′
29 13	+14·6	−17·7	29 58	+14·4	−17·4	31 58	−1·5			13·8	−6·6	45·5		70 −8·1
30 44	+14·7	−17·6	31 33	+14·5	−17·3	33 43	−1·4	° ′		14·2	−6·7	46·9		75 −8·4
32 24	+14·8	−17·5	33 18	+14·6	−17·2	35 38	−1·3	60 +0·1		14·7	−6·8	48·4		80 −8·7
34 15	+14·9	−17·4	35 15	+14·7	−17·1	37 45	−1·2	**MARS**		15·1	−6·9	49·8		85 −8·9
36 17	+15·0	−17·3	37 24	+14·8	−17·0	40 06	−1·1	Jan. 1–Feb. 9		15·5	−6·9	51·3		90 −9·2
38 34	+15·1	−17·2	39 48	+14·9	−16·9	42 42	−1·0	June 30–Dec. 31		16·0	−7·0	52·8		95 −9·5
41 06	+15·2	−17·1	42 28	+15·0	−16·8	45 34	−0·9	° ′		16·5	−7·1	54·3		100 −9·7
43 56	+15·3	−17·0	45 29	+15·1	−16·7	48 45	−0·8	60 +0·1		16·9	−7·2	55·8		105 −9·9
47 07	+15·4	−16·9	48 52	+15·2	−16·6	52 16	−0·7	Feb. 10–June 29		17·4	−7·3	57·4		110 −10·2
50 43	+15·5	−16·8	52 41	+15·3	−16·5	56 09	−0·6			17·9	−7·4	58·9		115 −10·4
54 46	+15·6	−16·7	56 59	+15·4	−16·4	60 26	−0·5	° ′		18·4	−7·5	60·5		120 −10·6
59 21	+15·7	−16·6	61 50	+15·5	−16·3	65 06	−0·4	41 +0·2		18·8	−7·6	62·1		125 −10·8
64 28	+15·8	−16·5	67 15	+15·6	−16·2	70 09	−0·3	76 +0·1		19·3	−7·7	63·8		130 −11·1
70 10	+15·9	−16·4	73 14	+15·7	−16·1	75 32	−0·2			19·8	−7·8	65·4		135 −11·3
76 24	+16·0	−16·3	79 42	+15·8	−16·0	81 12	−0·1			20·4	−7·9	67·1		140 −11·5
83 05	+16·1	−16·2	86 31	+15·9	−15·9	87 03	−0·1			20·9	−8·0	68·8		145 −11·7
90 00			90 00			90 00	0·0			21·4	−8·1	70·5		150 −11·9
														155 −12·1

App. Alt. = Apparent altitude = Sextant altitude corrected for index error and dip.

Fig 10.14 *The Correction Table bookmark from* The Nautical Almanac. *If your copy has no bookmark, the table is at the front of the book.*

This can't be guessed with any accuracy through a sextant, so the upper or lower 'limb' is placed on the horizon instead.

The lower limb is a lot easier to use, but once in a while only the upper presents itself so the correction is there if need be.

Note that the Altitude Correction Table has two columns: one for northern summer and one for winter, both with the lower limb in bolder type face.

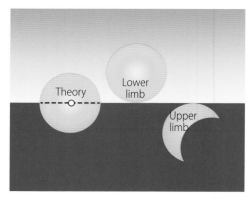

Fig 10.15

■ **Parallax**

Parallax is interesting in that everything in the solar system – even relatively tiny Venus – is, to a larger or smaller extent, affected by it. We are concerned only with the sun here, whose parallax is handled by the ever-useful Altitude Correction Table.

■ **Refraction**

Sunlight is bent as it passes through the atmosphere, so a correction for refraction is also added to the pudding mix of altitude. This is included in the table along with parallax and semidiameter.

Low-altitude sights

If the sun must be observed at altitudes below 10 degrees, refraction increases rapidly. This leads to an unpromising picture, so such sights are best avoided. If there seems no option, a special set of correction tables will be found in the front of *The Nautical Almanac* before the title page. An extra table allows the main event to be additionally adjusted for unusual atmospheric pressure and temperature. All these are negligible at normal altitudes, but when the object is unusually low down they begin to bite, so take care.

Example of a sextant altitude correction

Sextant altitude (Hs)	42° 35'.5
Index error (IE) 2.4' on the arc	−2.4'
Dip (height of eye 8ft)	−2.8'
Apparent altitude (App alt)	42° 30'.3
Altitude correction (April–Sept)	+15'
Observed altitude (Ho)	42° 45'.3

■ **Practice**

If you are ever to be more than marginally competent, you must be at home with the sextant. Load it into the car, drive down to the nearest south-facing beach and run off a forenoon sight. Then slide off to the pub, have a pint and wait for noon when the sun is on the meridian and you can pull it down. Go home, plot the sights on a real chart and see if the beach is where you thought it was. You ought to be within a few miles.

USING THE SEXTANT

Assuming that your sextant is adjusted correctly and any index error noted, here's the procedure for shooting the sun:

- First, carefully take the lanyard you should by now have spliced to the instrument and place it around your neck. Then, holding the sextant by the frame in your left hand, lift it from its box. Never grasp it by the index bar or the scale.

- Now take the handle in your right hand and find a comfortable position with a clear view of sun and horizon. On a large, stable boat in fair weather this might be standing on deck, but sitting is usually easier. Both hands are needed for the sextant, so take care that you are proof against being thrown about.

- Set the instrument to zero, check index error using the horizon and make sure the telescope is focused.

- Still at zero, drop a shade or two over the index mirror and one over the horizon mirror for safety. Look directly up at the sun through the telescope. It's critical to shade the horizon mirror as well in case you glimpse the sun through plain glass. On no account look at the sun without a shade in place.

- Open the clamp on the index bar with your left hand. Sweep the instrument down towards the horizon with your right hand, 'following' the image of the sun by moving your left hand carefully away from you. When the sun's image is somewhere near the horizon, flip up the shade from the horizon mirror before transferring the left hand to the micrometer to work the sun's image firmly on to the line of the horizon. This is tricky at first, but it comes with practice.

- It's important that the sextant is exactly vertical. Once the sun is approximately in place, twist your right wrist from side to side to rock the sextant. The image of the sun will look like the bob of a pendulum swinging across the horizon. When it is at its lowest point, the sextant is vertical and it is to this point that you work the micrometer. When you are satisfied with the observation, unless you are taking a noon sight, note the exact time. These days this is best done with a wristwatch.

- At ten o'clock on a midsummer morning, the sun's rate of climb can be surprising. Around noon it more or less stops still. Be ready for either state or anything in between.

Only you can teach yourself how to do this, but you'll soon find you no longer need to start with the sextant at zero and look directly up at the sun. Instead, you'll guess its height, set the sextant and search in its general direction. When the sun pops into view it'll be somewhere near the horizon, ready for the micrometer.

■ Quality of horizon

The ideal horizon is the one served up by the trade-wind skies; a perfect blue line. From this high point, horizons deteriorate steadily until finally, in poor visibility, you can't see far enough to discern where the sky meets the sea at all. Sometimes, what seems a good day can throw up a false horizon, in the form of a line of haze a few miles away, barely visible. If results on a day seem to be three or four miles out, don't despair. It may be that you have a duff horizon. Only time and experience can teach how to spot this.

Noon sight for latitude

A noon sight for latitude is taken when the sun is on your meridian. When the sun bears exactly due south or due north of you on its daily journey from east to west, or once in a lifetime is right over your head (at your zenith), its celestial meridian, which is also its GHA at that moment, will correspond to your longitude.

Because the sun is very much in evidence at noon and finding latitude has always been half the navigator's battle, the noon sight has always been the cornerstone of the navigator's day.

Local noon

The 'Greenwich' time of noon varies with longitude as the sun appears to travel round the Earth. You can tell when the sun is on the meridian because it stops rising as you observe it through the sextant, but you have more to do with your day than spend half the morning waiting for it, so it helps to work out the approximate time of local noon.

Preparing to work the sight. Note the important feature that the sextant box is open and the instrument is still showing the reading as taken. Discount any sextant that has to be set at a certain angle to fit in its box.

The sun completes its apparent journey once every 24 hours. During that time, it traverses 360 degrees. It follows, then, that in one hour it will move through 15 degrees, or one degree every four minutes. The sun is proceeding west from Greenwich, so in west longitude local noon is later than Greenwich. In east longitude, it is earlier. To determine how much earlier or later, multiply the number of degrees you are east or west of Greenwich by four to find how many minutes local noon will vary from Greenwich.

At the bottom right-hand corner of the daily page from the almanac (see Fig 10.4, page 128) is a box labelled SUN and MOON. The column headed 'Mer Pass' gives the time that the sun will cross the Greenwich meridian on that day. The difference between this and 1200 is called the *Equation of Time*. Because of the Earth's elliptical orbit around the sun, this may vary by ten minutes or more.

However unsure of your position you may be, you can always take a stab at a DR longitude for the time of local noon. Go for a whole degree and make sure you err on the 'early' side so as not to miss it.

If you are within a few degrees of the Date Line, a query may arise as to what day it is. Refer to the section in this chapter headed 'Time' (page 144).

Example 1

What is the GMT of local noon in DR longitude 4°W on 19 April?

Mer pass at Greenwich	11h 59m
4W @ 4 minutes per degree late	+16m
Local noon	12h 15m GMT

Example 2

What is the GMT of local noon in DR longitude 73°E on 21 April?

Mer pass at Greenwich	11h 59m
73E @ 4 minutes per degree early	4h 52m
Local noon	07h 07m GMT

Taking the sight

Once you know the approximate time of local noon, it pays to be on deck 10 minutes early and start shooting the sun. It should still be rising. As it approaches the meridian you'll be racking it down ever more slowly until, finally, it stands still for a minute or two. The sextant is now reading the noon altitude. Be careful not to start winding the sun back up again as it begins to fall. Wait until the lower limb bites positively into the horizon without altering the sextant and you know you're there. Noon is past and gone for another day. Note the log; read the sextant, put it away, then work out your latitude.

The theory

Fig 10.16 shows the noon sight setup when viewed from the celestial elevated pole. Fig 10.17 is the same shown from the celestial equator. Note how the celestial horizon makes a right angle with the line dropped from the observer's zenith, through his geographic position to the centre of the Earth. *Zenith Distance* (ZD) is the only new concept involved in this calculation and it's easy. It is the angular distance in degrees between the observer's zenith and the position of the sun on the celestial sphere. Because the sun is on the meridian, it runs vertically and is therefore a straight-shot angle. Since the line from the observer's zenith meets the celestial horizon at 90 degrees, the zenith distance must equal 90 degrees minus the sun's altitude:

ZD = 90° – Altitude

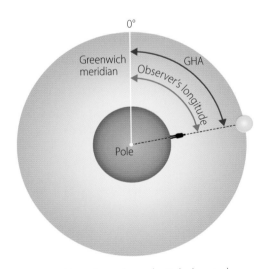

Fig 10.16 *View from the celestial elevated pole. Local noon, for the observer, occurs when the sun crosses his meridian of longitude. At this point the GHA of the sun is the same as the observer's longitude.*

Case 1

In Fig 10.17, latitude is the same angle on the terrestrial sphere as ZD + declination is on the celestial. Declination can be found in the almanac, and you can easily work out ZD. Add them together, and that's the latitude.

Given that your latitude is greater than the sun's declination, and of the same 'name' (i.e. north or south): Lat = ZD + dec.

Depending on the season and where you are, latitude and declination may have different names and relative values, so two other cases may arise:

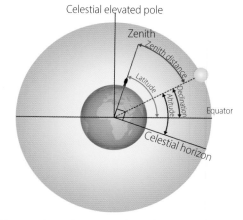

Fig 10.17 *Latitude at noon. Latitude greater than declination, same name (e.g. both north).*

Case 2

In Fig 10.18, the latitude has the opposite 'name' to the declination and you can see that: Lat = ZD – dec.

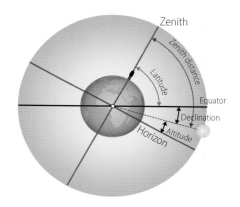

Fig 10.18 *Latitude and declination with different names.*

Case 3

Fig 10.19 shows a situation commonly met in the tropics, where the latitude may be the same name as the declination, but could well be a lower value (e.g. latitude 13°N, sun's declination 19°N). Here, Lat = dec – ZD.

All this boils down to three simple rules:
Latitude GREATER than declination, same name: Lat = ZD + dec
Latitude OPPOSITE name to declination: Lat = ZD – dec
Latitude LESS than declination, same name: Lat = dec – ZD

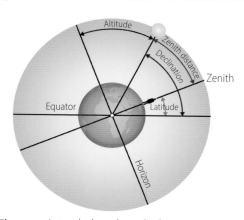

Fig 10.19 *Latitude less than declination, same name.*

In practice, unless your voyage passes 'under' the sun or takes place during an equinox when the sun's declination changes name, the decision as to which is your case must only be made once per trip. The answer is then the same every day.

Example

19 April: Your DR is 48°N 07'W. Mer pass is at 1159 (from the daily pages of the almanac – see Fig 10.4, page 128). Local noon is therefore 1227 GMT. This enables you to obtain the declination of the sun from the almanac. Using the sextant, you find that the sun's *corrected* altitude (Ho) at noon is 52° 38'.4. What is your latitude?

Note that to facilitate the arithmetic, I have designated 90° as 89° 60'. This may not suit you, but it helps me as it lessens the need to 'carry', or 'borrow' tens and sixes.

This is Case 1: **Lat = ZD + dec**

Dec 12h	N 11° 14'.5
+27m ('d' = +0.9), so by inspection	+ 00'.4
Dec 1225	N 11° 14'.9

	90	89° 60'
	− Ho	52° 38'.4
	= ZD	37° 21.6
	+ dec	11° 14'.9
Latitude =		**N 48° 36'.5**

Maximum altitudes

In theory, this system for determining latitude only works perfectly from a stationary vessel, or one travelling exactly east or west. This is because if you are in the northern hemisphere and sailing southwards towards the sun (your latitude being greater than its declination), your changing latitude causes it to go on rising even after it has passed your meridian. The converse holds true sailing north.

For a big ocean racer logging 20 knots or more due north or south, the errors thus generated can be at least five minutes of arc. Aboard a cruising boat struggling to maintain six knots it is rarely a factor to consider, but with a significant north/south component in the course it should not be forgotten because your latitude from a meridian sight may not be quite as accurate as you might otherwise hope.

Time

While considering the Greenwich time of local noon for a given longitude, we found the basic relationship of arc and time to be:

One day	= 360°	
One hour	= 360° :	24 = 15°
Four minutes =	1°	

However, while a degree is clearly 1/360 of a circle, the definition of a day is not so clear-cut. Among other things, the Earth is travelling in an elliptical orbit at the same time as it revolves, and 'real-time' orbits can be less regular than the ideal model.

Mean time

A suitable definition of a day might be the time taken for the sun to proceed from our nadir (midnight) through sunrise, across our meridian, down through sunset and back to the nadir once more. Unfortunately, when measured in hours rather than angles, this does not take exactly the same amount of time on every occasion. To make life tolerable for everyone who uses a watch and measures appointments in hours and minutes, an average must be taken. It was decided long ago to refer the celestial co-ordinates for every day to an average time and to tabulate them accordingly in a single almanac. The averaged-out time was referred to as mean time measured at the Greenwich Observatory, which gave us Greenwich Mean Time (GMT). This excellent institution served us all well until computers and those whose politics did not include London as the fount of this data – which it undoubtedly was – demanded the name be dropped in favour of *Universal Time* (UT).

The only area in which the difference between mean time and actual time need interest us at this stage is that it causes the anomalies in the time of noon we call the equation of time (see the bottom right of Fig 10.4, page 128).

Zone time

Navigators and astronomers may be content to live their lives by UT, but the rest of the world insists on lunching at 1300 hours, no matter where they are, and expecting the sun to rise at 0600. Since their inception, clocks have been set essentially to coincide with the sun, so 'working time' alters around the globe. The time of sunrise varies with every step you take east or west. A century or two ago, each town and village worked to its own time, setting the church clock to noon when the sun stood due south, but since the arrival of the railways, nobody wants to do that any more. To simplify matters, the world is divided into 24 time zones 15 degrees of longitude across. Each meridian divisible by 15 is a *zone meridian* and its time zone spreads out 7½ degrees to either side of it.

■ Naming the zones '+' or '−'

Since the sun rises in the east and proceeds to the west, it must rise later in 90°W than it does at Greenwich. Actually, it will rise 90 divided by 15, or six hours later. So when the sun is rising at 0600 at Greenwich, it is midnight (0000 hours) on Lake Superior at 90°W. Six hours later, when the sun does rise over the lake, the navigational time there will be, conveniently, 0600 hours. By then it will be 1200 (noon) at Greenwich and they'll be setting tables for lunch.

If your watch were set to Lake Superior's Zone Time (not the US's EST which, for administrative purposes, is used on the lake) and you were on an aeroplane to London, you'd have to add six hours to make it right as you land. The time zone is therefore said to be 'Zone +6'. In the same way, all the western time zones, right round to the International Date Line, are named 'plus'.

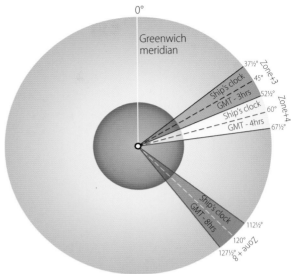

Fig 10.20 *Zone time.*

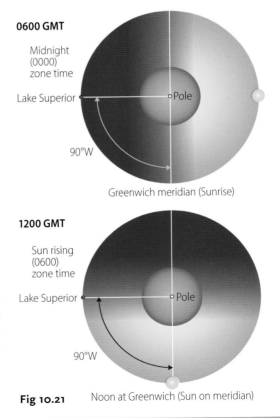

0600 GMT

Midnight (0000) zone time

Lake Superior

Pole

90°W

Greenwich meridian (Sunrise)

1200 GMT

Sun rising (0600) zone time

Lake Superior

Pole

90°W

Fig 10.21 Noon at Greenwich (Sun on meridian)

The eastern time zones are named 'minus' because the sun rises in Moscow before it does at Greenwich. Zone time at Moscow is therefore later than Greenwich and you'll have to subtract the relevant number of hours to reduce Moscow time to Greenwich time.

For political convenience, the zone divisions don't always fall exactly halfway between the zone meridians concerned. France, for example, in order to fit in with the rest of continental Europe, has placed itself in 'Zone –1', although most of its land mass falls plumb into the Greenwich time zone. Even Spain, well into west longitude, lines up with Germany. The UK maintains its independence in this and, like Portugal, very sensibly, will have none of it.

None of this need affect your ship's working clock in mid-ocean, but it pays to be aware of it. Tide tables, for example, are usually issued in the official zone time of the country concerned, regardless of its longitude. A useful aide-memoire for deciding whether to add or subtract is:

Longitude east, Greenwich time least.
Longitude west, Greenwich time best (biggest).

Change of date and the International Date Line

This can be a brain-twister, but as long as you tackle it logically it shouldn't present any problems. Let us assume you are in Zone +8. It is 1830 zone time (ZT) on 25 March. What is UT? If you are in Zone +8, you will add eight hours to 1830 ZT and come up with 2630 UT on 25 March, which is more sensibly expressed as 0230 UT on 26 March.

The *International Date Line* runs north–south from pole to pole around the 180th meridian, but it advances the date on the basis of ease of administration, diverting from the meridian here and there to keep the lid on. The kink in the line between Alaska and Siberia is an obvious example, as are a number of diversions made to group Pacific island nations together.

Standard time

Most Western countries add an hour or more to their zone time during the summer in order to extend daylight into the evenings. These arrangements have no relevance to the astro navigator, but if you are putting out on a voyage from a country operating such an arrangement, I recommend setting your ship's clock to something more sensible as soon as the local thought police have turned their backs.

It's also important to be aware of standard time when you arrive or you may be caught out by that greatest of disasters – to step ashore after crossing an ocean only to discover that the pubs have shut.

The navigation clock

It pays to keep your ship's chronometer – the official navigation clock to which you refer your sights – set on UT. Even if you physically time your sights with a quartz wristwatch, as I do, you should always have a backup clock somewhere on board, unless you propose to offend the gods by checking your watch against a handy GPS receiver. Personally, I keep my watch on zone time, which, on my boat, is usually ship's time. If my mind blows a time fuse when I'm dog tired, I can refer to the navigation clock to check up on GMT.

■ Rating the clock

Few watches or clocks keep time to a second per month. In reality, it doesn't matter if your navigation clock loses or gains 15 seconds or more. As long as you are aware of its habits and they are regular, you can *rate* it. Mine used to gain four seconds a week, so I knew that after ten days I'd have to subtract six seconds to find UT, and so on. Perfection is very jolly, but applied knowledge runs it close.

Position lines and plotting

As with coastal navigation, an astro fix is plotted on a chart using position lines (PLs). Instead of being straight, however, these are theoretically circular. Most traditional sources of PL for coastal navigation produce straight lines, but not all. Consider the 'rising or dipping' lighthouse for 'distance off'. If you still use this in the GPS age, you'll be aware that tables in the coastal almanacs tell us that, with a certain height of eye, we will see a light of a given height 'rise' at a defined distance. Let's say this is 12 miles. When the light stops 'looming' and finally pops up, we take a magnetic bearing and plot our position 12 miles out along the bearing. If we had no compass we would still know we were on a circle around the light of 12 miles radius. This would be a circular position line.

Apart from meridian sights, which are a special case, all sun-derived PLs are parts of a circle scribed around the terrestrial position of the sun at the instant of the sight. The circles are so huge, however, that a usable section is, to all intents and purposes, a straight line.

Azimuth and intercept

For such a huge circle to be usable we must know which sector to plot, so a line is constructed along the sun's bearing from your rough position in degrees true. The PL is plotted at right angles to this. The 'bearing line' is called an *azimuth* (Zn – pronounced 'azzmuth') and is defined as 'the horizontal direction of a celestial point from a terrestrial point'.

The first step in working up a PL is to calculate the altitude and azimuth of the sun at the time of your sight from a convenient assumed position (AP). This is not actually the DR but, as we shall see, is as close to this as we can sensibly make it within the rules. The AP is selected to fit data taken from the almanac and sight reduction tables. All is revealed in the following section of this chapter.

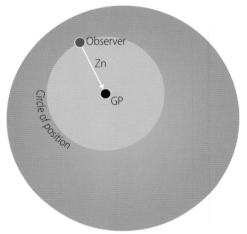

If you know your distance from a lighthouse but have no compass, you know that you are somewhere on a circular position line.

If you know the altitude of the sun you can locate yourself on a circle of position because the altitude of the sun will be the same from any point on the circle. The azimuth (Zn) is a bearing to the geographical position (GP) that tells you which part of the circle to use.

Fig 10.22

Because of the colossal distances from both DR and AP to the geographic position of the sun, the azimuth from either can be considered to be the same. The altitude observed on the sextant, however, will be different from the one calculated from the assumed position. This difference, measured in minutes of arc, is called the *intercept*. It is expressed on the chart as minutes of latitude, or sea miles. In effect, the AP is no more than an arbitrary datum point. The intercept gives the distance from this to the position line.

Practical plotting

The point at which the PL crosses the azimuth is *not* a fix. It is merely a reference point from which to construct a PL, which is no different from the sort of PL you might plot on a compass bearing from a lighthouse. For a fix, you're going to need at least one more PL. Typically, with sun navigation, this will be supplied by a meridian sight at noon.

INTERCEPTS

If the observed altitude from the actual position (H_o) is greater than the calculated altitude at the assumed position (H_c), then the PL will be nearer to the geographic position (GP) of the body. If the H_o is less than the H_c, the PL will be further away. Because the assumed position is effectively on the same azimuth as the DR, the precise GP of the body is irrelevant.

It's enough to draw a short section of the azimuth through the assumed position on your chart. Then, if the H_o is *greater* than the H_c, mark the intercept at the calculated distance *in the direction* of the sun. Where the H_o is less than the H_c, scribe the distance on the azimuth *away* from it. The PL passes through the intercept at right angles to the azimuth.

The rule for the direction of intercepts is:

- Calculated (**Tabulated**) altitude (H_c) less (**Tinier**) than observed altitude: intercept Towards the body – **Tabulated Tinier Towards** or **TTT**
- When the H_o is less than the H_c the reverse will apply.
- Intercepts are always labelled 'towards' or 'away'.

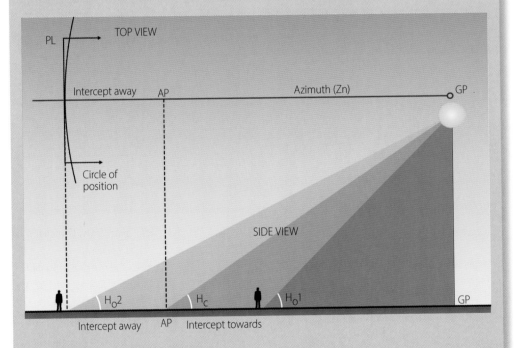

Fig 10.23 *The side view shows how the difference between observed altitude (H_O) and calculated altitude (H_C) is used to find the direction of the intercept from the assumed position (AP). If H_O is less than H_C, for example, the intercept is away from the celestial body, as shown in the top view. Notice that the PL is actually at a tangent to the circle of position.*

■ Plotting sheets

In coastal waters, sights can be plotted directly on to the working chart, as long as the scale is suitable. On ocean charts, the width of the pencil line becomes a significant factor and accurate plotting is impossible. Plotting sheets take up the slack. Once a position is fixed on the sheet it can be expressed as latitude and longitude, logged and transferred to the ocean chart.

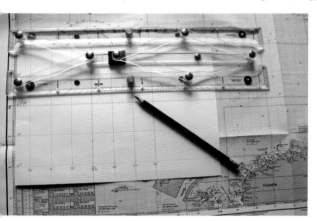

A cheap plotting sheet can be made by lifting the scale from a suitable chart to a blank sheet of paper.

You can make plotting sheets by offering up a sheet of plain paper to the corner of any old coastal chart of similar latitude to the one concerned. Crib the lat/long grid and there's your plotting sheet at a popular price. The scale may well be more useful than that of a 'bought one'. The downside for Americans is that it won't have a compass rose so, if you still use the parallel rulers popular on the west side of the Atlantic, you'll have to brass up for 'official' sheets.

Published plotting sheets can be downloaded free, but good ones are so cheap to buy that, unless you are on short commons, you may feel it's worth investing in a sheaf before setting sail. As long as your

---

HOW TO USE A PLOTTING SHEET

To use a plotting sheet, one of the transverse lines – usually the middle one – is designated the assumed latitude. Measurements for assumed longitude are lifted from the appropriate latitude on the scale at the bottom right-hand corner. All further measurements of intercept etc. use the latitude scale down the middle of the sheet.

The compass rose is for the convenience of those plotting with parallel rulers.

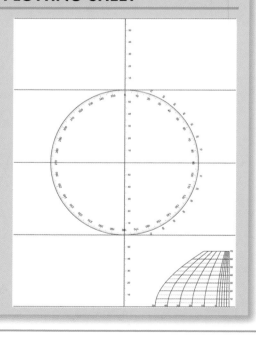

Fig 10.24 *A blank plotting sheet.*

plotting kit includes a quality eraser and a sharp 2B pencil, they are recyclable. They come on robust paper, so don't worry about having enough to last the voyage. I prefer the ones issued by the United States Defense Mapping Agency. The scale is smaller than UKHO's offerings, but they are a lot cheaper and, with care, a whole day's run can be fitted on to one chart.

Forenoon and afternoon sun sights

Sun-run-sun fix

This is the guts of the whole business. One sight is taken during the forenoon or afternoon. The forenoon is favoured so as to produce a fix at noon. When the forenoon position line is 'run up' along the course line to the noon latitude, the running fix delivers the position. Failing this, or in addition to it for further confirmation, the PLs can be advanced to an afternoon sight. The afternoon PL can also be transferred back to the noon latitude to check the noon position.

The sun-run-sun can be operated effectively in quite poor conditions. A good navigator needs only a glimpse of the sun to achieve an altitude, but the limitations are obvious. All traditional navigators know the inaccuracies of the running fix from their efforts along the coast. You can only have one noon fix per 24-hour day and, while it is possible to transfer a single sun PL up to another taken quite soon afterwards, the small change in angle means that the resulting 'cut' of the PLs will be poor.

In general, a forenoon sight should be taken not less than 90 minutes before noon. How much earlier you take it becomes a trade-off. The earlier the better for the cut, balanced by a longer run-up for the transferred position line to the noon latitude. The longer the run,

FORENOON SIGHT

Here's the procedure for plotting a forenoon sight taken at 0940:

- Plot the assumed position (AP).
- Decide whether the intercept is towards or away from the body. This one is towards. The Zn is 135°, so the azimuth is drawn from the AP accordingly.
- Measure off the intercept and plot the PL at right angles to the azimuth. The PL is marked as a straight line with arrowheads at each end pointing towards the body.

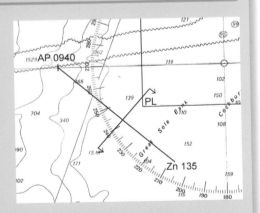

Fig 10.25 A standard paper chart with a forenoon sight position line plotted on it.

the bigger the potential running-fix error, particularly if the current is in doubt. Despite these reservations, a good sun fix can, in the right hands and conditions, deliver a position that is good to within a couple of miles.

Sight reduction

When considering plotting earlier in this chapter, it was noted that, to plot any sight other than a meridian altitude, the required data were an assumed position, an azimuth and an intercept. These are worked up from the raw sextant altitude and accurate time by means of *sight reduction*.

■ Tables

Unless you subscribe to sight reduction computer programs, this apparent mystery is taken care of by sight reduction tables. The handiest are those produced for aviators (*AP 3270* in the UK, or *Pub. No.249* in the US). Volume 1 deals with stars, while volumes 2 (Latitudes 0°–39°) and 3 (Latitudes 40°–89°) handle all celestial bodies with a declination of less than 30°. This encompasses everything in the solar system including, needless to say, the sun.

■ Calculators and computer programs

It is possible to buy sight reduction programs loaded with almanac information as well as complete sight reduction data. For surprisingly modest money, this remarkable software will deliver azimuth and intercept from an altitude plus a DR or an assumed position. The simple and effective *Navigator Light 32* is a good example.

The advantages are obvious, but it is recommended that before relying on electronics as a primary astro tool, the book form is mastered. It would be madness to go to sea without an almanac and a set of sight reduction tables lest all else should fail. To find oneself unable to use them would be a sorry state of affairs.

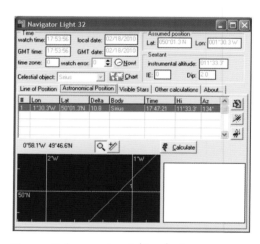

Fig 10.26 *A computer sight reduction program.*

The assumed position

The tables are entered using an assumed latitude, the real declination and an assumed LHA.

■ Assumed latitude

Sight reduction tables work their altitudes and azimuths from positions whose latitudes are *whole numbers*. The first step to an assumed position, then, is to shift your DR latitude north or south to the nearest whole degree. This is now called the *assumed latitude*.

Assumed longitude

The next job is to massage your DR longitude so that the LHA of the sun for the time of your sight also turns into a whole number. Just as with assumed latitude, the tables will not tolerate fractions of degrees of LHA.

West longitude

Look up the sun's GHA at the instant of the sight, then juggle your AP so that the degrees, minutes and decimals are the same as those of the sun's GHA. You'll recall that to find LHA in west longitude, you subtract longitude from GHA. When you subtract this new assumed longitude from the real GHA, all fractions disappear, leaving you with the whole number of degrees required.

Example 1

DR longitude 17° 46'W

Sun's GHA at 04h 12m 07s	242°	57'	.3
– Assumed longitude west	17°	57'	.3
LHA	225°		

Example 2

DR longitude 27° 49'E

Sun's GHA at 04h 12m 07s	242°	57'	.3
+ Assumed longitude east	28°	02'	.7
LHA	271°		

East longitude

Adjust the minutes of longitude so that, when added to the minutes and seconds of the sun's GHA, they add up to a whole number to create the AP. It's as simple as that.

Sight reduction tables

To choose the right page in the sight reduction tables (see Fig 10.27, page 154), you need the declination of the sun and an assumed latitude.

On the extreme left and right of the page are columns for LHA. Choose the value you have calculated and enter the table from it by moving across until you reach the correct declination, as shown in the boxes at top and bottom. Three figures are given: 'H_c', 'd' and 'Z'.

Azimuth

'Z' is the figure from which the sun's azimuth (Zn) is determined. The formulae are in the left-hand corners of the page – north latitudes at the top, and south latitudes at the bottom, as follows:

N. Lat	LHA greater than 180°	Zn = Z
	LHA less than 180°	Zn = 360 − Z
S. Lat	LHA greater than 180°	Zn = 180 − Z
	LHA less than 180°	Zn = 180 + Z

Azimuths are expressed in degrees true.

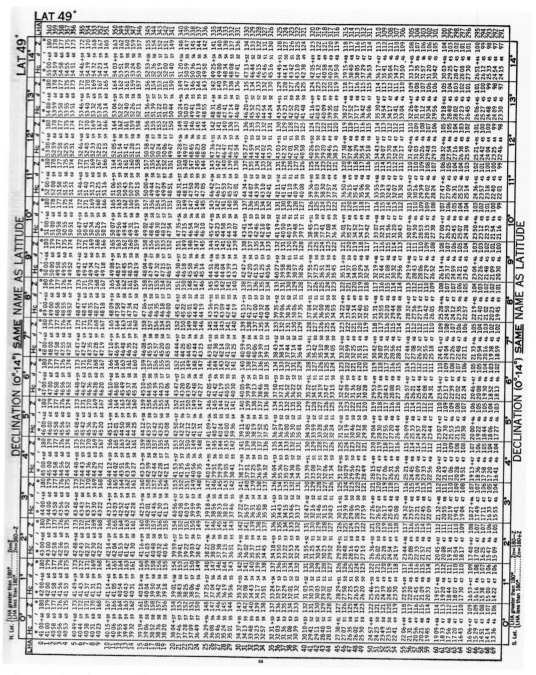

Fig 10.27 A working page from Volume 3 of **AP 3270**. The top right-hand corner gives the latitude of 49°. Each latitude (40°–89° for this volume) carries its own group of pages. The label at the top decides which page of the group to use. This one is 'Declination (0°–14°) SAME name as latitude'.

TABLE 5—CORRECTION TO TABULATED ALTITUDE FOR MINUTES OF DECLINATION

d / ′	1	2	3	4	5	6	7	8	9	10	11	12	13	14	15	16	17	18	19	20	21	22	23	24	25	26	27	28	29	30
0	0	0	0	0	0	0	0	0	0	0	0	0	0	0	0	0	0	0	0	0	0	0	0	0	0	0	0	0	0	0
1	0	0	0	0	0	0	0	0	0	0	0	0	0	0	0	0	0	0	0	0	0	0	0	0	0	0	0	0	0	0
2	0	0	0	0	0	0	0	0	0	0	0	0	0	0	0	1	1	1	1	1	1	1	1	1	1	1	1	1	1	1
3	0	0	0	0	0	0	0	0	0	0	1	1	1	1	1	1	1	1	1	1	1	1	1	1	1	1	1	1	1	2
4	0	0	0	0	0	0	0	1	1	1	1	1	1	1	1	1	1	1	1	1	1	1	2	2	2	2	2	2	2	2
5	0	0	0	0	0	0	1	1	1	1	1	1	1	1	1	1	1	2	2	2	2	2	2	2	2	2	2	2	2	2
6	0	0	0	0	0	1	1	1	1	1	1	1	1	1	2	2	2	2	2	2	2	2	2	2	2	3	3	3	3	3
7	0	0	0	0	1	1	1	1	1	1	1	1	2	2	2	2	2	2	2	2	2	3	3	3	3	3	3	3	3	4
8	0	0	0	1	1	1	1	1	1	1	1	2	2	2	2	2	2	2	3	3	3	3	3	3	3	3	4	4	4	4
9	0	0	0	1	1	1	1	1	1	2	2	2	2	2	2	2	3	3	3	3	3	3	3	4	4	4	4	4	4	4
10	0	0	0	1	1	1	1	1	2	2	2	2	2	2	2	3	3	3	3	3	4	4	4	4	4	4	4	5	5	5
11	0	0	1	1	1	1	1	1	2	2	2	2	2	3	3	3	3	3	3	4	4	4	4	4	5	5	5	5	5	6
12	0	0	1	1	1	1	1	2	2	2	2	2	3	3	3	3	3	4	4	4	4	4	5	5	5	5	5	6	6	6
13	0	0	1	1	1	1	2	2	2	2	2	3	3	3	3	3	4	4	4	4	5	5	5	5	5	6	6	6	6	6
14	0	0	1	1	1	1	2	2	2	2	3	3	3	3	4	4	4	4	4	5	5	5	5	6	6	6	6	7	7	7
15	0	0	1	1	1	2	2	2	2	2	3	3	3	4	4	4	4	4	5	5	5	6	6	6	6	6	7	7	7	8
16	0	1	1	1	1	2	2	2	2	3	3	3	3	4	4	4	5	5	5	5	6	6	6	6	7	7	7	7	8	8
17	0	1	1	1	1	2	2	2	3	3	3	3	4	4	4	5	5	5	5	6	6	6	7	7	7	7	8	8	8	8
18	0	1	1	1	2	2	2	2	3	3	3	4	4	4	4	5	5	5	6	6	6	7	7	7	8	8	8	8	9	9
19	0	1	1	1	2	2	2	3	3	3	3	4	4	4	5	5	5	6	6	6	7	7	7	8	8	8	9	9	9	10
20	0	1	1	1	2	2	2	3	3	3	4	4	4	5	5	5	6	6	6	7	7	7	8	8	8	9	9	9	10	10
21	0	1	1	1	2	2	2	3	3	4	4	4	5	5	5	6	6	6	7	7	7	8	8	8	9	9	9	10	10	10
22	0	1	1	1	2	2	3	3	3	4	4	4	5	5	6	6	6	7	7	7	8	8	8	9	9	10	10	10	11	11
23	0	1	1	2	2	2	3	3	3	4	4	5	5	5	6	6	7	7	7	8	8	8	9	9	10	10	10	11	11	12
24	0	1	1	2	2	2	3	3	4	4	4	5	5	6	6	6	7	7	8	8	8	9	9	10	10	10	11	11	12	12
25	0	1	1	2	2	2	3	3	4	4	5	5	5	6	6	7	7	8	8	8	9	9	10	10	10	11	11	12	12	12
26	0	1	1	2	2	3	3	3	4	4	5	5	6	6	6	7	7	8	8	9	9	10	10	10	11	11	12	12	13	13
27	0	1	1	2	2	3	3	4	4	4	5	5	6	6	7	7	8	8	9	9	9	10	10	11	11	12	12	13	13	14
28	0	1	1	2	2	3	3	4	4	5	5	6	6	7	7	7	8	8	9	9	10	10	11	11	12	12	13	13	14	14
29	0	1	1	2	2	3	3	4	4	5	5	6	6	7	7	8	8	9	9	10	10	11	11	12	12	13	13	14	14	14
30	0	1	2	2	2	3	4	4	4	5	6	6	6	7	8	8	8	9	10	10	10	11	12	12	12	13	14	14	14	15
31	1	1	2	2	3	3	4	4	5	5	6	6	7	7	8	8	9	9	10	10	11	11	12	12	13	13	14	14	15	16
32	1	1	2	2	3	3	4	4	5	5	6	6	7	7	8	9	9	10	10	11	11	12	12	13	13	14	14	15	15	16
33	1	1	2	2	3	3	4	4	5	6	6	7	7	8	8	9	9	10	10	11	12	12	13	13	14	14	15	15	16	16
34	1	1	2	2	3	3	4	5	5	6	6	7	7	8	8	9	10	10	11	11	12	12	13	14	14	15	15	16	16	17
35	1	1	2	2	3	4	4	5	5	6	6	7	8	8	9	9	10	10	11	12	12	13	13	14	15	15	16	16	17	18
36	1	1	2	2	3	4	4	5	5	6	7	7	8	8	9	10	10	11	11	12	13	13	14	14	15	16	16	17	17	18
37	1	1	2	2	3	4	4	5	6	6	7	7	8	9	9	10	10	11	12	12	13	14	14	15	15	16	17	17	18	18
38	1	1	2	3	3	4	4	5	6	6	7	8	8	9	10	10	11	11	12	13	13	14	15	15	16	16	17	18	18	19
39	1	1	2	3	3	4	5	5	6	6	7	8	8	9	10	10	11	12	12	13	14	14	15	16	16	17	18	18	19	20
40	1	1	2	3	3	4	5	5	6	7	7	8	9	9	10	11	11	12	13	13	14	15	15	16	17	17	18	19	19	20
41	1	1	2	3	3	4	5	5	6	7	8	8	9	10	10	11	12	12	13	14	14	15	16	16	17	18	18	19	20	20
42	1	1	2	3	4	4	5	6	6	7	8	8	9	10	10	11	12	13	13	14	15	15	16	17	18	18	19	20	20	21
43	1	1	2	3	4	4	5	6	6	7	8	9	9	10	11	11	12	13	14	14	15	16	16	17	18	19	19	20	21	22
44	1	1	2	3	4	4	5	6	7	7	8	9	10	10	11	12	12	13	14	15	15	16	17	18	18	19	20	21	21	22
45	1	2	2	3	4	4	5	6	7	8	8	9	10	10	11	12	13	14	14	15	16	16	17	18	19	20	20	21	22	22
46	1	2	2	3	4	5	5	6	7	8	8	9	10	11	12	12	13	14	15	15	16	17	18	18	19	20	21	21	22	23
47	1	2	2	3	4	5	5	6	7	8	9	9	10	11	12	13	13	14	15	16	16	17	18	19	20	20	21	22	23	24
48	1	2	2	3	4	5	6	6	7	8	9	10	10	11	12	13	14	14	15	16	17	18	18	19	20	21	22	22	23	24
49	1	2	2	3	4	5	6	7	7	8	9	10	11	11	12	13	14	15	16	16	17	18	19	20	20	21	22	23	24	24
50	1	2	2	3	4	5	6	7	8	8	9	10	11	12	12	13	14	15	16	17	18	18	19	20	21	22	22	23	24	25
51	1	2	3	3	4	5	6	7	8	8	9	10	11	12	13	14	14	15	16	17	18	19	20	20	21	22	23	24	25	26
52	1	2	3	3	4	5	6	7	8	9	10	10	11	12	13	14	15	16	16	17	18	19	20	21	22	23	23	24	25	26
53	1	2	3	4	4	5	6	7	8	9	10	11	11	12	13	14	15	16	17	18	19	19	20	21	22	23	24	25	26	26
54	1	2	3	4	4	5	6	7	8	9	10	11	12	13	14	14	15	16	17	18	19	20	21	22	22	23	24	25	26	27
55	1	2	3	4	5	6	6	7	8	9	10	11	12	13	14	15	16	16	17	18	19	20	21	22	23	24	25	26	27	28
56	1	2	3	4	5	6	7	7	8	9	10	11	12	13	14	15	16	17	18	19	20	21	21	22	23	24	25	26	27	28
57	1	2	3	4	5	6	7	8	9	10	10	11	12	13	14	15	16	17	18	19	20	21	22	23	24	25	26	27	28	28
58	1	2	3	4	5	6	7	8	9	10	11	12	13	14	14	15	16	17	18	19	20	21	22	23	24	25	26	27	28	29
59	1	2	3	4	5	6	7	8	9	10	11	12	13	14	15	16	17	18	19	20	21	22	23	24	25	26	27	28	29	30

d / ′	31	32	33	34	35	36	37	38	39	40	41	42	43	44	45	46	47	48	49	50	51	52	53	54	55	56	57	58	59	60	d / ′
0	0	0	0	0	0	0	0	0	0	0	0	0	0	0	0	0	0	0	0	0	0	0	0	0	0	0	0	0	0	0	0
1	1	1	1	1	1	1	1	1	1	1	1	1	1	1	1	1	1	1	1	1	1	1	1	1	1	1	1	1	1	1	1
2	1	1	1	1	1	1	1	1	1	1	1	1	1	1	2	2	2	2	2	2	2	2	2	2	2	2	2	2	2	2	2
3	2	2	2	2	2	2	2	2	2	2	2	2	2	2	2	2	2	2	2	2	3	3	3	3	3	3	3	3	3	3	3
4	2	2	2	2	2	2	2	3	3	3	3	3	3	3	3	3	3	3	3	3	3	3	4	4	4	4	4	4	4	4	4
5	3	3	3	3	3	3	3	3	3	3	3	4	4	4	4	4	4	4	4	4	4	4	4	4	5	5	5	5	5	5	5
6	3	3	3	3	4	4	4	4	4	4	4	4	4	4	4	5	5	5	5	5	5	5	5	5	6	6	6	6	6	6	6
7	4	4	4	4	4	4	4	4	5	5	5	5	5	5	5	5	5	6	6	6	6	6	6	6	6	7	7	7	7	7	7
8	4	4	4	5	5	5	5	5	5	5	5	6	6	6	6	6	6	6	7	7	7	7	7	7	7	7	8	8	8	8	8
9	5	5	5	5	5	5	6	6	6	6	6	6	6	7	7	7	7	7	7	8	8	8	8	8	8	8	9	9	9	9	9
10	5	5	6	6	6	6	6	6	6	7	7	7	7	7	8	8	8	8	8	8	8	9	9	9	9	9	10	10	10	10	10
11	6	6	6	6	6	7	7	7	7	7	8	8	8	8	8	8	9	9	9	9	9	10	10	10	10	10	10	11	11	11	11
12	6	6	7	7	7	7	7	8	8	8	8	8	9	9	9	9	9	10	10	10	10	10	11	11	11	11	11	12	12	12	12
13	7	7	7	7	7	8	8	8	8	9	9	9	9	10	10	10	10	10	11	11	11	11	11	12	12	12	12	13	13	13	13
14	7	7	8	8	8	8	9	9	9	9	10	10	10	10	10	11	11	11	11	12	12	12	12	13	13	13	13	14	14	14	14
15	8	8	8	8	9	9	9	10	10	10	10	10	11	11	11	12	12	12	12	12	13	13	13	14	14	14	14	14	15	15	15
16	8	9	9	9	9	10	10	10	10	11	11	11	11	12	12	12	13	13	13	13	14	14	14	14	15	15	15	15	16	16	16
17	9	9	9	10	10	10	10	11	11	11	12	12	12	12	13	13	13	14	14	14	14	15	15	15	16	16	16	16	17	17	17
18	9	10	10	10	10	11	11	11	12	12	12	13	13	13	14	14	14	14	15	15	15	16	16	16	16	17	17	17	18	18	18
19	10	10	10	11	11	11	12	12	12	13	13	13	14	14	14	15	15	15	16	16	16	16	17	17	17	18	18	18	19	19	19
20	10	11	11	11	12	12	12	13	13	13	14	14	14	15	15	15	16	16	16	17	17	17	18	18	18	19	19	19	20	20	20
21	11	11	12	12	12	13	13	13	14	14	14	15	15	15	16	16	16	17	17	18	18	18	19	19	19	20	20	20	21	21	21
22	11	12	12	12	13	13	14	14	14	15	15	15	16	16	16	17	17	18	18	18	19	19	19	20	20	21	21	21	22	22	22
23	12	12	13	13	13	14	14	15	15	15	16	16	16	17	17	18	18	18	19	19	20	20	20	21	21	21	22	22	23	23	23
24	12	13	13	14	14	14	15	15	16	16	16	17	17	18	18	18	19	19	20	20	20	21	21	22	22	22	23	23	24	24	24
25	13	13	14	14	15	15	15	16	16	17	17	18	18	18	19	19	20	20	20	21	21	22	22	22	23	23	24	24	25	25	25
26	13	14	14	15	15	16	16	16	17	17	18	18	19	19	20	20	20	21	21	22	22	23	23	23	24	24	25	25	26	26	26
27	14	14	15	15	16	16	17	17	18	18	18	19	19	20	20	21	21	22	22	22	23	23	24	24	25	25	26	26	27	27	27
28	14	15	15	16	16	17	17	18	18	19	19	20	20	21	21	21	22	22	23	23	24	24	25	25	26	26	27	27	28	28	28
29	15	15	16	16	17	17	18	18	19	19	20	20	21	21	22	22	23	23	24	24	25	25	26	26	27	27	28	28	29	29	29
30	16	16	16	17	18	18	18	19	20	20	20	21	22	22	22	23	24	24	24	25	26	26	26	27	28	28	28	29	30	30	30
31	16	17	17	18	18	19	19	20	20	21	21	22	22	23	23	24	24	25	25	26	26	27	27	28	28	29	29	30	30	31	31
32	17	17	18	18	19	19	20	20	21	21	22	22	23	23	24	25	25	26	26	27	27	28	28	29	29	30	30	31	31	32	32
33	17	18	18	19	19	20	20	21	21	22	23	23	24	24	25	25	26	26	27	28	28	29	29	30	30	31	31	32	32	33	33
34	18	18	19	19	20	20	21	22	22	23	23	24	24	25	26	26	27	27	28	28	29	29	30	31	31	32	32	33	33	34	34
35	18	19	19	20	20	21	22	22	23	23	24	24	25	26	26	27	27	28	29	29	30	30	31	32	32	33	33	34	34	35	35
36	19	19	20	20	21	22	22	23	23	24	25	25	26	26	27	28	28	29	29	30	31	31	32	32	33	34	34	35	35	36	36
37	19	20	20	21	22	22	23	23	24	25	25	26	27	27	28	28	29	30	30	31	31	32	33	33	34	35	35	36	36	37	37
38	20	20	21	22	22	23	23	24	25	25	26	27	27	28	28	29	30	30	31	32	32	33	34	34	35	35	36	37	37	38	38
39	20	21	21	22	23	23	24	25	25	26	27	27	28	29	29	30	31	31	32	32	33	34	34	35	36	36	37	38	38	39	39
40	21	21	22	23	23	24	25	25	26	27	27	28	29	29	30	31	31	32	33	33	34	35	35	36	37	37	38	39	39	40	40
41	21	22	23	23	24	25	25	26	27	27	28	29	29	30	31	31	32	33	33	34	35	36	36	37	38	38	39	40	40	41	41
42	22	22	23	24	24	25	26	27	27	28	29	29	30	31	32	32	33	34	34	35	36	36	37	38	38	39	40	41	41	42	42
43	22	23	24	24	25	26	27	27	28	29	29	30	31	32	32	33	34	34	35	36	37	37	38	39	39	40	41	42	42	43	43
44	23	23	24	25	26	26	27	28	29	29	30	31	32	32	33	34	34	35	36	37	37	38	39	40	40	41	42	43	43	44	44
45	23	24	25	26	26	27	28	28	29	30	31	32	32	33	34	34	35	36	37	38	38	39	40	40	41	42	43	44	44	45	45
46	24	25	25	26	27	28	28	29	30	31	31	32	33	34	34	35	36	37	38	38	39	40	41	41	42	43	44	44	45	46	46
47	24	25	26	27	27	28	29	30	31	31	32	33	34	34	35	36	37	38	38	39	40	41	42	42	43	44	45	45	46	47	47
48	25	26	26	27	28	29	30	30	31	32	33	34	34	35	36	37	38	38	39	40	41	42	42	43	44	45	46	46	47	48	48
49	25	26	27	28	29	29	30	31	32	33	33	34	35	36	37	38	38	39	40	41	42	42	43	44	45	46	47	47	48	49	49
50	26	27	28	28	29	30	31	32	32	33	34	35	36	37	38	38	39	40	41	42	42	43	44	45	46	47	48	48	49	50	50
51	26	27	28	29	30	31	31	32	33	34	35	36	37	37	38	39	40	41	42	42	43	44	45	46	47	48	48	49	50	51	51
52	27	28	29	29	30	31	32	33	34	35	36	36	37	38	39	40	41	42	42	43	44	45	46	47	48	49	49	50	51	52	52
53	27	28	29	30	31	32	33	34	34	35	36	37	38	39	40	41	42	42	43	44	45	46	47	48	49	49	50	51	52	53	53
54	28	29	30	31	32	32	33	34	35	36	37	38	39	40	40	41	42	43	44	45	46	47	48	49	50	50	51	52	53	54	54
55	28	29	30	31	32	33	34	35	36	37	38	38	39	40	41	42	43	44	45	46	47	48	49	50	50	51	52	53	54	55	55
56	29	30	31	32	33	34	35	35	36	37	38	39	40	41	42	43	44	45	46	47	48	49	49	50	51	52	53	54	55	56	56
57	29	30	31	32	33	34	35	36	37	38	39	40	41	42	43	44	45	46	47	48	48	49	50	51	52	53	54	55	56	57	57
58	30	31	32	33	34	35	36	37	38	39	40	41	42	43	44	44	45	46	47	48	49	50	51	52	53	54	55	56	57	58	58
59	30	31	32	33	34	35	36	37	38	39	40	41	42	43	44	45	46	47	48	49	50	51	52	53	54	55	56	57	58	59	59

Fig 10.28 *Table 5 from AP 3270. In older editions this is issued as a useful bookmark. To correct tabulated altitude, enter with minutes of declination (top line) and the 'd' number down the sides.*

■ Calculated altitude

'H$_C$' is the calculated altitude for the *whole* degree of declination. To apply the minutes of declination, note the figure given under 'd' and enter 'Table 5' in *AP 3270* (see Fig 10.28, page 155). In older volumes this comes on a useful bookmark. With 'd' as one argument, and 'minutes of declination' as the other, extract the relevant value and apply it to the main figure for H$_C$. Notice that 'd' is labelled + or −. You now have a calculated altitude.

Example

Find the calculated altitude and azimuth for the sun with declination at 10° 19'. The LHA is 315° and the assumed latitude is 49° N.

- Find the LHA (on the right-hand side of Fig 10.27) and move across to the column marked 10°. This gives you the following:

H$_c$ 36 01	d + 49	Z 121

- Since you are in northern latitudes and the LHA is greater than 180°, Zn = Z. So the azimuth (Zn) is 109°.
- For the calculated altitude, go to the 'bookmark' Table 5 (Fig 10.28). Find 49 in the 'd' column down the side, and move across

to the figure in the column beneath the figure 19 (remember that the declination is 24° 19'). This gives you 16, and since the 'd' figure is *plus* 44 the resulting increment is +16.

H$_c$	36° 01'
d + 44	+ 16
H$_c$	36° 17'

- You now have an *assumed position* and an *azimuth*. By finding the difference between the calculated altitude above and your observed (corrected sextant) altitude, you have an *intercept* as well.

REDUCING A SUN SIGHT

- Lay a pro-forma out on the chart table.
- Go up on deck, take a sun sight, note the time, then read the log. Don't forget that every four seconds gives an error of up to one mile, so check that watch.
- Fill in 'watch time' in the pro-forma.
- Correct for UT if a rating correction is called for.
- Note the sun's GHA and declination for the hour concerned from the almanac and enter these as well.
- Work up the actual declination for the minute of the sight. Round any decimals up or down.

PRO FORMA FOR SUN SIGHT

Date		Watch time
		Correction
		GMT

GHA (hrs)		
+Correction (mins/secs)		
GHA		
Assumed Long		Assumed Lat
LHA		

Hc		z	Declination (hrs)
d		180/360	d difference
Hc		Zn	Declination

Hs	
Index Error	
Dip	
Apparent Alt	
Main Correction	
Ho	
Hc	
Intercept	TOWARDS/AWAY

Fig 10.29

- Find the minutes and seconds of GHA in the increments pages of the almanac and enter these in the pro-forma. Add them up to find the sun's GHA.
- Decide on an assumed longitude to supply an LHA for the sun as a whole number of degrees. While you are about it, choose an assumed latitude and enter them both. This is the assumed position (AP).
- Open the sight reduction tables (*AP 3270*) at the page for your assumed latitude, making sure you've chosen the one with the correct name for declination ('same name as' or 'contrary name to' latitude).
- Extract 'H$_c$', 'd' and 'Z' and enter them on the pro-forma. Note whether 'd' is '+' or '−'.
- While *AP 3270* is open, look at the notes about what to do with 'Z', which is not an azimuth, to convert it to 'Zn', which emphatically is. These are at the top and bottom of the pages in a corner. Enter the Zn into the pro-forma.
- Consult the 'bookmark' page or Table 5 in *AP 3270* to deal with the minutes of declination, then work up the final, corrected, calculated altitude (H$_c$).
- Enter sextant altitude in the pro-forma. Next comes any index error and the dip to determine the apparent altitude. Enter the Altitude Correction from the 'bookmark' of *The Nautical Almanac* in order to find the true altitude (H$_o$).
- The difference between H$_o$ and H$_c$ is the intercept. Label it towards or away (TTT), and you can plot your sight.

NOW TRY WORKING THIS EXAMPLE

20 April. You take a forenoon sight at 10h 12m 43s watch time. The sextant altitude was 43° 37'.5 and the log read 238.5. Your height of eye was estimated at 8ft, your watch was 6 seconds fast and your sextant has no index error. The DR position was 48° 59'N 5° 16'W. At noon the log reads 249.9 and you observe the latitude to be 48° 45'.4. You have been steering '092°T, the tide has self-cancelled by turning and you are making about 6 knots.

See pages 128–9 to find *The Nautical Almanac* data for GHA, etc. Sight reduction tables for Hc, Z, etc. are on pages 154–5. Use these to work out what you need to plot a fix, then check pages 158–9 to see how you've done.

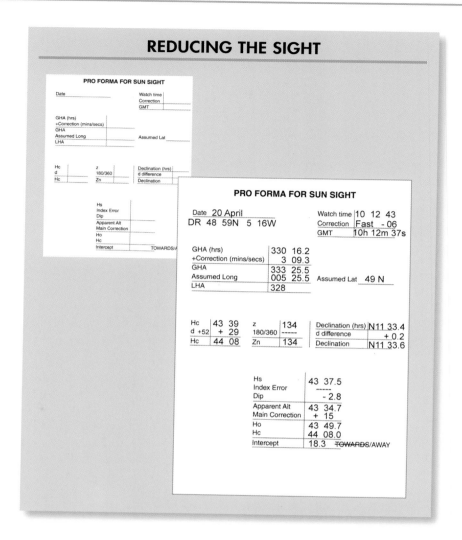

PRO FORMA FOR SUN SIGHT

Date		Watch time	
		Correction	
		GMT	

GHA (hrs)			
+Correction (mins/secs)			
GHA			
Assumed Long		Assumed Lat	
LHA			

Hc		z		Declination (hrs)	
d		180/360		d difference	
Hc		Zn		Declination	

Hs	
Index Error	
Dip	
Apparent Alt	
Main Correction	
Ho	
Hc	
Intercept	TOWARDS/A

PRO FORMA FOR SUN SIGHT

Date 20 April		Watch time	10 12 43
DR 48 59N 5 16W		Correction	Fast - 06
		GMT	10h 12m 37s

GHA (hrs)	330 16.2	
+Correction (mins/secs)	3 09.3	
GHA	333 25.5	
Assumed Long	005 25.5	Assumed Lat 49 N
LHA	328	

Hc	43 39	z	134	Declination (hrs)	N11 33.4
d +52	+ 29	180/360	-----	d difference	+ 0.2
Hc	44 08	Zn	134	Declination	N11 33.6

Hs	43 37.5
Index Error	-----
Dip	- 2.8
Apparent Alt	43 34.7
Main Correction	+ 15
Ho	43 49.7
Hc	44 08.0
Intercept	18.3 ~~TOWARDS~~/AWAY

Plotting the sight

Fig 10.30 shows a forenoon sight (designated 'AM' here) taken at around 0930 local time and run up to the noon latitude to deliver a fix at the point where the transferred position line cuts the latitude.

The lower diagram shows how this has been checked by taking another observation in the afternoon between 1500 and 1600 local time, then running the PL back. Alternatively, the noon position could have been run forward. The result can be evaluated by inspecting the cocked hat. In good conditions you can expect an area of probable position two to four miles across. You may do better, but remember: Even in an ideal world this is only a running fix subject to inevitable uncertainties.

PLOTTING THE SIGHT

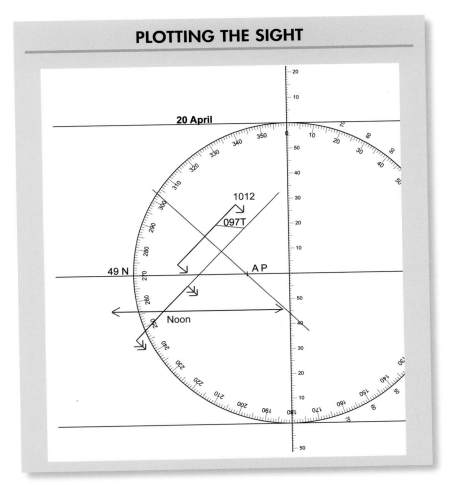

Fig 10.30

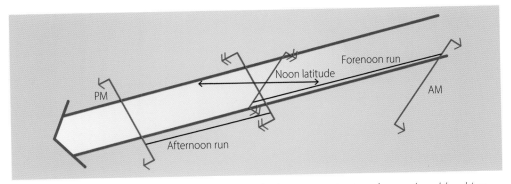

A classic sun-run-sun noon fix, with forenoon and afternoon sights 'run forward and back' to the noon latitude with transferred position lines delineated by two arrowheads. The result is a cocked-hat fix at noon. Note that the afternoon sight is a luxury. A forenoon sight followed by a noon sight creates a legitimate fix. The third position line is a bonus.

Sorting the good from the bad

The more experienced you are, the easier it is to assess the quality of a particular sight. If in doubt about the standard of an important one, and if conditions permit, take a series of observations (five or seven is customary) and graph the results with 'time' against 'altitude'. The better sights should produce a reasonably straight line. Any duffers can be thrown out, and a time and altitude average taken for those that remain. Some make this a daily practice. I rarely bother because I have confidence in my ability to assess a sight for quality. I advise going for one good sight from the start and only graphing if results seem arbitrarily erratic.

Most difficulties and errors arise from carelessness in looking things up or in reading the sextant. Proceed carefully, one step at a time, and every sight will be a winner.

Compass checking on the ocean

When you are steering a heading that may, wind permitting, stay more or less constant for days or even weeks, it's important to know that your deviation card is up to date. The only way of checking it in mid-ocean without resorting to electronics is to use the signs in the sky.

Sunset and sunrise tables

A proprietary nautical almanac, such as *Reeds*, should have a page giving the true bearing of the sun at sunrise and sunset in various latitudes and for all declinations. This doesn't change with longitude. It's only 'lat' and 'dec' that matter.

The difference between this and the setting sun's bearing, observed via the steering compass with the ship on her heading, will be the total compass error. Chapter 9 deals with the mechanics of how these bearings can be taken.

Compass error in mid-ocean is the sum of variation and deviation, just as it is on the coast. Variation in a given area is known from the pilot charts used for ocean passage planning. Once this has been applied to the true bearing from the tables, any error remaining can only be deviation.

It's worth noting that while pilot charts will last a lifetime in terms of wind and current, the variation curves they give alter with the years. The arrival of GPS receivers has removed any requirement to replace the charts on this basis alone. Most GPS sets can read out courses and bearings in degrees true or degrees magnetic, corrected for zone and annual changes. Comparing the two gives an instant variation reading.

Semidiameter and the method

Because of refraction, the sun is technically 'rising' or 'setting' when it is one semidiameter above the horizon, so that's the time to take its bearing.

On east–west passages, the sun often rises or sets close to ahead or astern. If this is so, a small course alteration to bring it right on the course line will give you its bearing from the lubber line on the steering compass. The difference in deviation between this heading and the course is unlikely to be significant.

When the sun sets and rises a long way from your heading, you've no option but to measure its bearing relative to the ship's head. By applying that to the compass heading, you can deduce its bearing on the steering compass. The best way of taking the bearing of the setting or rising sun is by sighting it directly across the steering compass. This is often possible where the instrument is mounted on a binnacle. If the horizon is obscured from the compass, the bearing can only be taken 'relative to the ship's head' by means of a pelorus (see Chapter 9).

If sea conditions permit, I generally check my compass every time I'm able to observe the sunrise or the sunset. I enter the results in the back of my log book and maintain a running check on my ship's deviation card. Any new errors are noticed straightaway.

Fig 10.31 *Refraction places the rising and setting sun one semi-diameter above the horizon.*

Example

Ship's head by steering compass	235°C
Relative bearing of setting sun	052°
∴ compass bearing of sun	287°C
Bearing from amplitude tables	283°T
∴ total compass error	4°W
But variation (from pilot chart or GPS)	7°W
∴ deviation on this heading	3°E

Recommended further study

Page space, and the modern perspective on the importance of astro-navigation, have dictated that this subject has been handled here in the perspective of the whole portfolio of the ocean skipper's skills. This chapter therefore gives little more than the bones of a basic sun fix. To more fully understand this fascinating subject, the author recommends his book *Celestial Navigation*, published by Fernhurst. Careful study of this modest, but best-selling paperback will reward you with all you need to navigate by the sun, moon, planets and stars.

11 PASSAGE PLANNING

Any sailor with basic coastal qualifications and experience will be aware of the importance of passage planning. Poor planning on tides, weather and distances to run can leave the coastal navigator with what should have been a six-hour jolly turning into a twelve-hour epic of wretchedness. The same is even more true for ocean passages where the effects of successful or inadequate planning are multiplied by the mileage.

Ocean passage planning is all about strategy. Some elements are obvious. Others less so. For example, nobody brought up in Scotland or the Eastern Provinces of Canada would dream of crossing the North Atlantic in February aboard anything short of a container ship. The same would be true for a Russian yachtsman from Vladivostok contemplating a trip to Vancouver. Everyone knows it'll be freezing cold, blowing like the clappers and that a successful outcome is by no means guaranteed. The question of when the voyage might become relatively safe is a matter of passage planning.

For an inexperienced sailor from higher latitudes, things in the tropics may seem less obvious, but the concept that life is a series of pleasant zephyrs wafting the mariner gently from one paradise island to the next is seriously flawed. Those who have had the experience will chuckle up their oilskin sleeves at such naivety. Misreading the reversing monsoons of the Indian Ocean would be like running up the 'down' escalator at Waterloo underground station on crutches.

Within certain broad parameters, global wind systems are predictable, but planning doesn't end with considerations of the breeze. Currents affect passage times and morale, fog is creepy even 100 miles from the coast if you venture on to the Grand Banks of Newfoundland, and free icebergs in otherwise clear northern and southern seas will crank up stress levels dramatically, even if they don't bring the passage to an untimely end. More recently, considerations of piracy, demands for cash bonds in exchange for permits to cruise certain areas and other human factors have also impinged on the sailor's freedom to roam the seas at will.

All the questions involving natural forces can be answered by readily available publications. Information on the elements imposed by man, whether with official clipboards or unofficial Kalashnikovs, is often best discovered by keeping an ear to the boardwalk.

Round voyage or one-way passage

Anyone sitting an Ocean Yachtmaster examination in Britain is likely to be asked about planning a one-shot passage – typically from the UK to the Caribbean. Given a good understanding of modern cartography and the issues discussed in this chapter, such passages rarely involve a high challenge level. Things start to get interesting when longer voyages are considered. Planning a circumnavigation, unless it is to be undertaken on an entirely casual, gypsy-ride sort of basis, is a major logistical effort.

As a case study, an Atlantic circuit from northern Europe to the Caribbean and home again in the same year needs careful thought. The questions are many, each with its own flow diagram of options:

VOYAGE PLANNING

- Assuming you plan to cross from the Canary Islands, how quickly do you head down there? Is that part of the trip a two-week 'rugby club' dash or a cruise in itself? The answer may depend on what time you feel is the latest you're prepared to leave the latitude of Gibraltar or it may be governed by when you can get off work or even the date of your daughter's wedding.

- Do you call at Cape Verde or just go for it? Either way, this will affect the date you opt to leave for the crossing.

- Should you cross at the earliest possible time that offers a good chance of avoiding hurricanes? This would see you over there nicely by Christmas. Or do you leave after Christmas and be sure of strong trade winds and no hurricanes?

- Where do you plan to make landfall: Barbados, to be strategically placed to windward of everything; Grenada, to be handy for Trinidad, then to cruise steadily north; St Lucia, because lots of people do, etc.?

- How will you return? Via the US, Canada and the North Atlantic? Very interesting, but with an almost-certain dusting near the end. Or straight back via the Azores? Tough to start with, hacking full and by in the trades, but it comes out progressively easier as you work north and east. Or detour via Bermuda? Lovely place, a bit expensive, but an easier ride all round. It'll take a week or so longer.

- And, of course, when do you leave home?

A good voyage plan leaves lots to think about, but if you like charts it can be almost as much fun as the real thing.

Publications

Charts

Like any passage plan, an ocean strategy begins with the charts. From them, distance to run is drawn. This gives some idea of time. Latitudes suggest likely wind, weather, temperatures and the rest, while any land masses or islands to be visited or avoided are immediately obvious. Or they should be. There is nothing more to say about charts here, other than to read Chapter 9 carefully. Passage planning on a vector ENC alone is to be avoided like a rotten oyster. By all means look at it, but study in-date paper and/or raster charts as well, because only they are foolproof and will never let you down. Don't forget the issue of the Great Circle where it is appropriate. Either pull out your gnomonic chart, or set your raster chart plotter to read off courses and bearings as Great Circles rather than rhumb lines, so there is no mistake.

Pilot charts

By far the most important aids to ocean voyaging are the month-by-month 'pilot charts' issued by the British Admiralty and the American Defense Mapping authorities. Sometimes known as 'routeing' charts, these comprehensive documents have been produced from countless sightings, observations and readings taken by ships on passage. The information was originally correlated in the 19th century by Lieutenant Maury, US Navy, whose early results were in high demand among clipper-ship captains. Today they can be purchased in paper form or bound in books. They can also be downloaded for free from a number of sites, including the excellent and ever-useful passageweather.com.

A pilot chart is a Mercator projection featuring all the general information a mariner could require for a particular ocean and a given month. This is presented in a graphic form that makes reading it intuitive, with high-frequency gale probability and zones of reliable trade winds being recognisable at a glance.

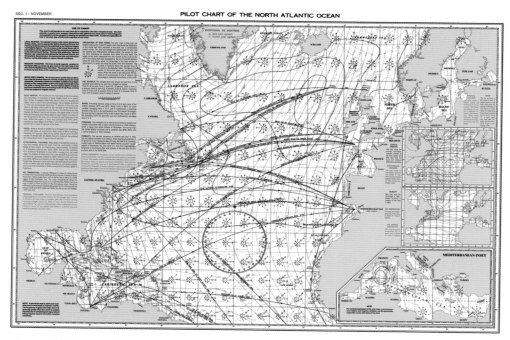

Fig 11.1 *A US pilot chart. These charts are the critical basis of all ocean passage planning. Published for each month, they last a lifetime.*

In addition to data on wind direction and strength, these admirable charts also depict magnetic variation (for the year of their issue), currents, typical and specific tracks of tropical revolving storms and mid-latitude depressions, wave heights, fog probabilities, water and air temperatures, as well as mean and extreme ice limits. They even plot the main Great Circle tracks and note their distances. However important the books described here may be, planning a voyage without pilot charts is simply unthinkable.

■ Wind roses

Pilot charts provide the concise wind predictions vital for any sailing craft in the form of closely spaced 'wind roses'. The British Admiralty wind roses are more comprehensive than the American ones. At their centre they contain figures indicating the number of observations their data are based on, which is, of course, as effective a measure of probable reliability as the survey data on a raster or paper chart. Beneath this

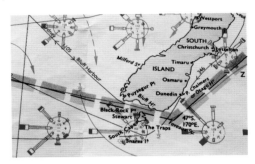

Fig 11.2 *Detail from a UKHO pilot chart.*

is another small figure indicating the percentage of variable winds and a third enumerating calms. Arranged around each rose's periphery are arrows that fly with the wind. Their length indicates the percentage of airflow from that direction. The nature of the arrow shows the wind strength, broken up into the proportions that have been observed. The Brits do this on arrow length, the Americans with little boxes on the shaft, but these give only average wind force and no indication of the number of observations upon which data are based.

Use these wind roses for planning a route on the expected month of your passage, but note what is happening on the months either side as well. Weather is notorious for failure to conform to man's best predictions, so a good guess about what will happen if either you or the developing meteorological pattern is late can avoid too much disappointment.

■ Ocean currents

Half a knot of current may not sound much, but if it's favourable it means a shove of 12 nautical miles per day, 85 per week and more than 300 in a month. For a yacht averaging six knots, that's a seven or eight per cent saving in passage time. Double the figure if you're unlucky enough to blunder into a counter-current, and you are looking at a significant factor.

Some currents are very reliable indeed, such as the North Atlantic Drift, once it has swirled away from the Gulf Stream 'eddies' off the American continent. Others can be far less so. Once, long before GPS could have given me an instant SOG (speed over ground) reading, I was off the mouth of the Amazon when I noted a day's run through the water of 140 miles. The pilot chart placed me at dead centre of the 100-mile-wide westbound South Equatorial Current that swishes along at up to two knots, so I took my sights anticipating the unusual joy of 200 miles between observations. Infuriatingly, my sights revealed a dismal day's run between observations of a mere 95 miles. As I sat watching seas that looked like wind against tide in the

A counter-current, such as the Equatorial, running against a trade wind kicks up an unmistakable sea. The navigator knows his day's run is going to be short long before he plots the noon sight.

English Channel, it was obvious that I was in fact experiencing the South Equatorial Counter-Current. I took my frustrations out on the log book, as one does, and determined to write to their Lordships of the Admiralty, but thought better of it back in port. No doubt even they are subject to the vagaries of nature.

The bottom line is not to be too disappointed if winds and currents fail to work out as you'd hoped. If you've used the pilot charts and considered the further information here you can do no more, as the West Indian caulker observed stepping ankle-deep from the deck of the sinking schooner.

■ Ice

The possibility of meeting ice at sea is not restricted to those who venture into the polar regions. In certain areas, currents carry bergs into surprisingly low latitudes. Labrador and the Grand Banks of Newfoundland are a case in point. Any yacht sailing from the US to northern Europe must take into account the fact that if she leaves in May or June, the danger zone inside the ice limit lies athwart her track. This is clearly marked on the pilot chart. If your track leads inside the maximum ice limit you must take the greatest care to look out and plan a detour if possible. You would be well advised to keep clear of the mean limit.

For any yacht equipped with radar, the problem with ice is not so much the dramatic possibility of crashing into a berg like a latter-day *Titanic*, but rather that of running into a growler or a bergy bit. These comparatively small chunks of ice (see Chapter 8) are plenty big enough to send you to Davey Jones' locker, yet they are all too easily missed by a casual lookout policy, even in daylight and good visibility, let alone in fog and darkness. Ice is often associated with fog, so if you find yourself plunging onward through dense mist across the

A mid-ocean trade-wind sea typically runs at 8ft or so.

wrong part of the pilot chart, look out as if your life depended upon it. It could well do just that. Take ice seriously, even if it's not supposed to be part of your trip.

■ Magnetic variation

An unexpected spin-off of universal GPS navigation is that, should you choose to ask for it, the instrument will deliver the course in degrees 'magnetic' or 'true', with the former corrected up to the minute. This is a far more satisfactory answer to the ever-varying compass than making a guesstimate from the incremental changes data on a 20-year-old pilot chart.

Books

Ocean Passages for the World

This Admiralty publication (NP 136) used to be the gold standard when it came to beefing up the data on the pilot charts. Second-hand editions like mine carry an open-sided cardboard sleeve containing a number of useful chartlets. In newer editions these are 'bound in'. Among them, the 'World Climatic Charts' (nos. 5301/2) give large-scale generalised information for the winter and summer months. While not specific enough to replace the pilot charts, these show wind direction, fog, gale frequency, ice etc. and can be of considerable value when planning a circumnavigation, or for general reference.

Also in the pack is chart no. 5308 of the 'World's Sailing Ship Routes'. This is now somewhat anachronistic, being designed for engineless square riggers, but contemplating its advice in light of the contrasting performance of a modern yacht remains time well spent. Completing the package is chart no. 5310, 'The World: General Surface Current Distribution'.

The text of the volume, like chart no. 5308, appears at first to be more relevant to square riggers than to modern yachts, but it would be arrogant to conclude that it can therefore be disregarded. A flat-floored, fin-keeled 40-footer might slice the wind at 40 degrees in flat water, but once in the big waves off soundings, her crew will be no keener to point high than the hands aboard a four-masted barque who did not have the option. When the sailing instructions for a trip to Rio from Europe advise us to pass over 100 miles to windward of Cabo Sao Roque, they mean what they say. A yachtsman who heeds their advice will have a far more comfortable ride than one who vainly imagines he can sail to windward for 1,000 miles and have any friends left on board at the end of it.

On the other hand, in close waters such as leaving the English Channel bound far to the south and ultimately west across the ocean, the stern advice to work out hundreds of miles to the west before turning south is usually irrelevant for any yacht with weather forecasting, an engine and a sensibly determined crew. So long as Ushant is weathered and a favourable forecast is secured, it is generally safe to steer direct towards Finisterre. If the weather fails to develop as you'd hoped, you can always bear away and hide in northern Spain to await an improvement.

In the southern hemisphere, particularly in reversing monsoon territory, *Ocean Passages* is useful in general terms, together with its chartlets described above. If nothing else, it will sketch out the big picture and give you a better-than-evens chance of not making any avoidable mistakes.

World Cruising Routes

It might seem odd that Jimmy Cornell's comprehensive book carries less column space in this work than that dedicated to *Ocean Passages for the World*. The reason is simple. This is a very different kettle of fish from *Ocean Passages* and in today's world it is a far more important book. However, it is so easy to work with and needs so little explanation that I need trouble readers little with my comments.

Geared specifically to the requirements of the cruising sailor, it recommends optimum times for every route you can think of and plenty you can't, up to a remarkable total of more than 1,000. Its chapters do not concentrate entirely on mainstream, blue-water destinations; it also covers the Antarctic and even deals with Spitzbergen for those gallant spirits not seduced by the promise of everlasting sunshine in lower latitudes. It is so highly recommended that it's hard to imagine a serious long-term cruising yacht not carrying a well-thumbed copy.

■ Specific passage guides

Such works are generally comprehensive beyond the bare needs of the navigation plan. Typically, they contain advice on suitable craft, living with the climate, likely provisioning problems and port information, in addition to comprehensive studies of the various crossing options. *The Atlantic Crossing Guide* by Anne Hammick is an excellent example.

■ Admiralty pilots and other official sailing directions

These contain more information than you might imagine about likely wind and weather patterns. It is always worth shipping one for your chosen area, and it will certainly help with your landfall in the unlikely event of GPS failure. The descriptions of the world's headlands, cliffs, cities and lighthouses were written for sailors before the electronic age and are remarkable in their detail. They have helped me decide where I was on many a precarious morning in time to save my face before the hands began asking awkward questions. They also contain genuinely useful data on ocean currents, sea temperatures, meteorology and much more that you are unlikely to find elsewhere.

The Mariner's Handbook

You can probably manage without this remarkable and surprisingly well illustrated UKHO publication unless you are planning to visit the frozen extremities of the oceans. If that is your intention, buy a copy tomorrow. It is required reading. If it doesn't put you off, you are the person for the job.

Anecdotal evidence

This is often the only assistance available about such matters as piracy, which over the decades rears its head in different parts of the world. At the time of writing, the African side of the Indian Ocean has a serious problem for ships of all sizes, let alone short-handed yachts. If unwelcome boarders are a possibility along part of your route, talk to those who may have been on hand, hit the radio nets, get the buzz, then, if violence seems on the cards, treat pirates like hurricanes and go somewhere else.

It's a long way around the Cape of Good Hope, but the Red Sea isn't a cakewalk either, and many a yacht bound for Europe from the Antipodes has left Africa to starboard after Indonesia and come north via St Helena and Ascension. If it's the Med you're headed for, there's no law against entering from Gibraltar and you may feel the extra 4,000 miles is a more honourable and economical answer to a horrible situation than putting the yacht on a ship and carrying her as deck cargo through Suez to Marseilles.

12 GREAT CIRCLE SAILING AND PASSAGE EXECUTION

One of the shortfalls in the lives of sailors who, centuries ago, might have subscribed to the Flat Earth Society was that by imagining their world on a sort of giant Mercator projection, they always ran their passages as rhumb lines. Looking at a world atlas, children in school still walk away with the impression that Greenland is substantially larger than India and that the Antarctic continent is a long strip at the bottom of the map. A standard ocean chart can give a similar impression because it is struggling to depict a section of a spherical object on a flat medium. The Mercator projection achieves this by stretching the latitude as the numbers increase while prising the meridians of longitude apart as the poles approach, thus creating the distortions of scale.

The overriding benefit of this arrangement, as readers will be well aware, is that a course to steer plotted from A to B retains a constant compass bearing throughout its length. Thus, using a Mercator projection, a yacht can sail across the Gulf of Maine or from Scotland to Norway maintaining the same course the whole way within the vagaries of wind and weather. Because it is a straight line, the rhumb-line course also represents the least mileage. However, this convenient arrangement only works where its length is insignificant compared with the size of the Earth. At ocean scales, the system breaks down to a greater or lesser extent. Operating on an unadorned Mercator projection can have a noticeable effect on a yacht's routeing.

Great Circle sailing

The easiest way to illustrate the business of sailing on a sphere is to imagine a large orange. If we draw a line with a marker pen exactly around its middle, halfway between its stalk end and the opposite 'pole', that will be its 'equator'. Measure its surface between any two points along this line and you won't find a shorter distance between them than by running directly along it. This is because, if we were now to slice the orange in half, using the line we've drawn to guide the knife, the cut would pass directly through the centre of the orange. If we now take a box of identical oranges and cut lots of them in half all sorts of ways while making sure each time that the cut passes through the centre of the fruit, the same rule will apply. Measuring around the outside of the surface along the cut, each cut will be of identical length and the distance between any two points on the cut will be the shortest it can be on the orange's surface. These cuts passing through the centre of a sphere are called 'Great Circles'.

If we now cut an orange halfway from its equator to its stalk, keeping the cut parallel to the equator instead of passing through the centre of the orange, the line between any two points on the cut will be longer than if we had 'up-ended' the cut to make it pass through the centre.

The cut running parallel to the orange's equator represents a parallel of latitude. Unless it is the equator itself which, Q.E.D., passes through the centre of the Earth, it is not a Great Circle, so to run along it for any serious distance is to add miles. The parallel of latitude is called a 'Small Circle'. Any straight line plotted on a Mercator projection is another of them. If it's only one or two hundred miles long, it won't make any measurable difference, but at oceanic scale the variance becomes significant, sometimes to the tune of 100 miles or more.

The shortest distance between two points on the surface of any sphere is always the track of the Great Circle on which both are situated. When deciding which course to steer from one side of an ocean to the other, it must be considered.

Precisely how much a Small Circle departs from the great in terms of course and distance depends on how closely the course approaches due east or due west and how far it is from the equator. In high latitudes, on east–west headings, the rhumb line diverges substantially from the Great Circle route. On similar headings on the Great Circle of the equator they are one and the same. In any latitude a heading of due north or south is, by definition, a Great Circle, because each meridian represents a cut through the centre of the orange. As your headings swing away from this, the differences begin to compound.

A track from Australia to Durban in South Africa (Fig 12.1) is a case in point. The rhumb-line yacht will, in theory, steer 272° all the way. The Great Circle yacht will start out on a heading of 248° and sail into Durban on 295°, having sailed 130 miles less – not a big saving, you might think, but, as the Scotsman observed, 'many a mickle makes a muckle' and every little helps.

Crossing the Atlantic or the Pacific in the trade-wind belts nearer the equator, any savings on the Great Circle track will be much smaller – as little as 15 miles on a run from the Canary Islands to Antigua – and will certainly be overshadowed by other considerations.

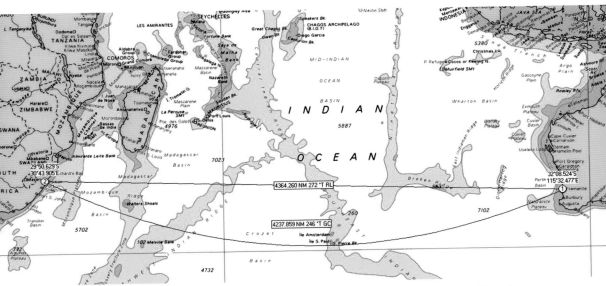

Fig 12.1 *Great Circle – if you can sail it, it will save 130 miles on this passage, although in practice, it doesn't always work out.*

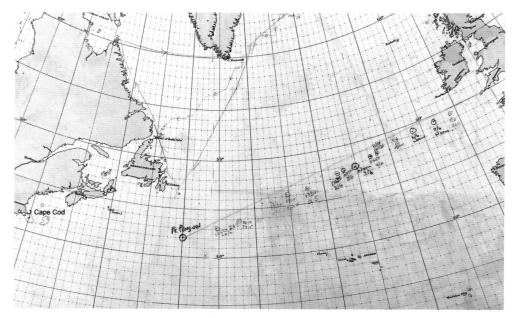

Fig 12.2 *A section from a gnomonic chart I used on a North Atlantic passage in pre-chart plotter days. We had run the parallel west–east from Cape Cod in order to reach an arbitrary position I called 'Point Penguin'. This avoided the ice and fog of the Grand Banks. Thereafter, we struck out more or less up the Great Circle towards the Bishop Rock. The daily positions were transferred from astro plotting sheets sheets and it looks as though my pencil needs sharpening over the first week or so.*

Working the Great Circle

Fortunately for the non-mathematical ocean navigator, gnomonic projection charts covering all major routes are available on which a straight line is, in fact, a Great Circle. The meridians converge towards the poles; by some geometric magic, to determine the Great Circle course at any position, the chart protractor can be used to measure the angle between the track and the nearest meridian. If you're lucky enough to steer the course you want all the time – a theoretical Nirvana rarely achieved in real life, the ideal would be to use this system, altering course every five degrees or so of longitude, proceeding in a series of rhumb lines from one Great Circle point to the next.

For planning purposes, motor-yacht skippers are advised to lift a series of points from their gnomonic chart and pre-plot them on to a Mercator projection. The results may look eccentric, but they work. On a sailing craft, it doesn't seem to matter how carefully you plan a Great Circle route, it's not going to happen once the wind gets up to its tricks. A hundred miles out you'll experience a head wind or, if you're in the trades, you'll find yourself on the dreaded dead run. Either will blow the Great Circle to bits.

The best bet is to use GPS to give you a Great Circle course as you set out and steer this with hope in your heart, while sailing your ship for the longed-for compromise of speed and comfort. Soon you'll be miles from your hoped-for track, but if there's any choice in the matter, err towards the Great Circle. As you wander around and need a new course, make sure you ask the plotter or any other GPS receiver for a Great Circle rather than a rhumb line. You will feel at least a degree of benefit.

Composite tracks

As latitudes rack up, the Great Circle option becomes increasingly important, especially on long-haul runs in the Southern Ocean and the North Pacific. There can be various reasons why a pure Great Circle may take you to unacceptable places. It could be the iceberg menace near the poles; perhaps it's unlit isolated dangers or a too-high a gale frequency for your taste. The usual solution is to follow the Great Circle track until you arrive at a parallel of latitude that delimits the danger, run along this until the Great Circle re-emerges from the danger area, then rejoin it.

Sticking to the principles outlined here in the real world of wind and weather may seem unrealistic. It often is, yet by doing so, as far as can sensibly be managed, an average yacht can sometimes save a day or two on passage time across an ocean. Our days on Earth are numbered and, as the great John William Norie pointed out more than a century ago, a good captain conducts his ship not only with 'the greatest safety', but also 'in the shortest time possible'.

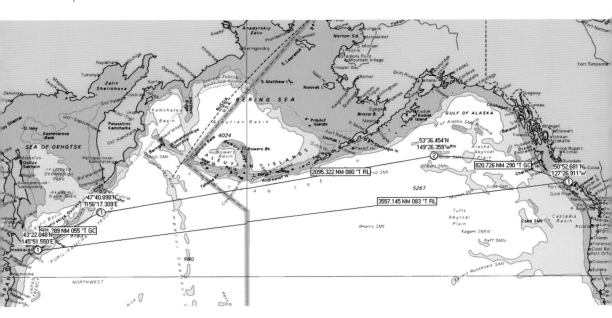

Fig 12.3 *Composite Great Circle. On a passage from Hokkaido to Vancouver, the Great Circle saves a whopping 250 miles – not to be sniffed at – but it passes north of the Aleutian islands. A composite Great Circle south of these still saves 160 miles, always assuming the weather permits its use.*

Passage execution

Setting sail to cross an ocean for the first time can be a daunting prospect, yet the statistics tell us that life aboard a well-found, properly crewed yacht is probably safer than in a motor car on the London orbital motorway. As long as the vessel has been selected on the criteria of real seafaring, not some misguided advertiser's flight of fancy, and sensible precautions are taken in the way of spares, tools, victuals and equipment, passage-making should be an adventure, not a nightmare. Part of the adventure is navigating. Here, then, is a résumé of the navigator's duties.

A time to leave

The skipper/navigator can generally ensure that the first few days at sea are trouble-free by keeping his or her nerve and refusing to leave until the weather looks like delivering an even break. This isn't always easy. Not only will the crew be anxious to be gone, they will be met regularly on the dock by stay-at-homes quipping along the lines of: 'What! You still here, then?'

This is enough to drive anyone to drink and makes the task of maintaining crew morale even harder, but if you're in charge you simply must take it on the chin. The last thing anyone wants is to begin a 3,000-mile passage with a beat. Sixty miles made good per day and a drubbing in the bargain is going to be even worse for the troops than the frustration of waiting for a break in the head winds.

Once the chance comes, I try to leave at a sensible hour of the morning or early afternoon. This gives everyone plenty of daylight to settle down to the motion and the rule of the compass. It's easier that way. With a full crew, I encourage a casual lookout and steering rota until after dinner, then start watches. If it's just the two of us, we take it easy through the day before sliding into our watch routine after supper.

Keeping the course

As you sail along your track, be it a theoretical Great Circle or low-latitude rhumb line, it's highly unlikely that you will benefit from a perfect breeze. The wind may come from too close ahead, too near dead aft or too strong on the beam. From time to time you get lucky, but often you'll prefer to modify your ideal heading to take conditions into account. If you end up close-hauled, for example, don't try to stuff the boat up into the seas at 45 degrees from the true wind. Crack off to 55 or 60 degrees. The breeze won't stay foul for ever and, when it changes, the ground you lost will vaporise like morning dew.

The same holds good for the dreaded dead run. Come up a bit and make it into a genuine broad reach, or at least a comfortable 'boomed-out' course. Don't be afraid, either, to bear away ten or fifteen degrees to put a steep sea a touch abaft the beam. The wind will change sooner or later and you'll make up the distance in due course. Comfort is worth a great deal when you've a long way to go.

The downside of wandering with the wind is that you often end up miles from the planned track. I once entered the Irish Sea south-about around Ireland, homeward bound to Liverpool

Bashing into a head sea is a mug's game on a long passage. Bear away a bit. The wind will change sooner or later.

from North America, when I had intended to leave Ireland to starboard, but the weather kept on stuffing me further and further south. It was all the same in the end. I discovered an excellent transport café in Kinsale and was much the better for a good breakfast. We came in around Anglesey instead of the Isle of Man a week or so later. The secret is to keep the GPS set to the Great Circle, so that at least every new course it serves up is the best available.

Ship's time

In most areas of the globe, while the time selected by the local authorities for the people living ashore gives them the long summer evenings landsmen love, it doesn't stack up with real time as set by the sun. This means it is normal to start a passage with the ship's domestic clock keeping the local daylight-saving time. I prefer my life on the ocean to comply with 'sun time'. It works well for any number of reasons, including the noon sight and the night watch system.

Once a vessel is on sun time, the question arises as to when this is to be altered as she reels off her longitude. Common sense

Ship's clock set to ship's time. My super-accurate watch on UTC for celestial sights.

should prevail here for a private yacht. A sail training vessel may have to be more formal and alter her clocks at the first midnight after entering her next time zone (at 7½ degrees either side of the zone meridians of 0°, 15°, 30° etc. – see Chapter 10 for details of this important subject), though it is more humane to do it at 1800. This is the turn of the old dogwatch when the traditional four-hour rota changed sequence with a pair of two-hour 'dogs' between 1600 and 2000. Few yachts today stick with the traditional system, but six o'clock is still 'happy hour' for many of us. A glass of the right stuff will compensate the unfortunate watch that must either bear an extra 60 minutes if sailing one way or miss the benefit of losing an hour's duty the other.

The navigator's day

■ Traditional mode

For the classical yacht navigator, what has always been called 'the day's work' involves a forenoon sight of the sun, together with a log reading, followed by a noon sight and a transferred position line to provide a fix. This is logged and the distance run from yesterday's position calculated, to the joy or despair of all hands.

If the sky is clear in the evening or morning, you might run off a series of stars and/or planets. In deep, reef-free waters, this is executed largely for practice, but when the yacht is in the vicinity of an unlit archipelago, a mid-ocean shoal, or is coming up to her ultimate landfall, the time spent rehearsing pays off. Then, the simultaneous position lines offered by the stars become an important tool, offering the best possible position fix. Far from land and in no special danger, most 'analogue' navigators will be content with the two-mile accuracy an experienced operator can realistically expect from sun and chronometer on a good day.

And so for centuries forenoon preceded afternoon, the dogwatches led to the first watch, the dead men turned out at midnight for the middle watch, to be replaced by sleepy-eyed shipmates for the grey morning hours. The skipper appeared in his slippers early in the forenoon. The noon position preceded dinner yet again. One day followed another until finally the excitement built towards landfall. Would you see the light or pile up on some iron-bound coast? Was that smudge on the horizon really the low-lying shore of a treeless island or was it a cloud bank coming up to spoil your supper?

Questions such as these plagued us all before GPS arrived to give us a good night's sleep, but electronics cannot replace the satisfaction felt when what might have been a rising star begins to blink 'Group Flash 3 every 15 seconds'. Life will never be the same again.

■ New age ocean navigators

Now that for most people astro navigation is no longer required except for fun or practice against the remote contingency of electronic failure, the natural rhythm of the navigator's day has disappeared. We can have a fix any time we want one. I've even caught my crew peeking at how far the ship has to run to Bishop Rock a mere week out from Cape Cod – and doing so before breakfast. Whatever next?

Like it or not, the truth is that the navigator's job is vastly simplified. There have always been two facets to navigation, either on the coast or far offshore. The first is working out where you are; the second is sorting out how to sail from there to your destination. The former problem has ceased to exist and the latter was always largely common sense anyway. What remains is a question of reading the pilot chart in the light of what is actually happening, interpreting the weather reports and considering the sea area into which you have strayed while hunting for a broad reach. In zones where islands, atolls and reefs might be found, perhaps the most important task is to make certain that the twin pitfalls of vector chart navigation – the datum shift and the layering-out of dangers – are being avoided.

■ The noon position

Traditionally, the pivotal moment of the navigator's – and the ship's – day was noon. In sailing ships before radio communication and universal time, local noon was preferred as the gold standard for ship's time. The captain, having agreed with his mates, sailing master or midshipmen that the sun was on the meridian, ordered: 'Make it so.' The hourglass was turned, eight bells were struck and a new day began from time set by the sun, not by any human pretender. Whatever else was or was not ascertained, it was the noon position that was recorded and a series of noon plots that marked the ship's progress across the immensity of the ocean chart.

Those of us at sea in yachts before electronic navigation changed everything did the same, although we no longer used local noon to reset our working ship's clocks every day. In the new world of instant fixes available 24/7, it might be good for discipline (even self-discipline) to ration fixes to one a day, and to make it noon. This gives all hands something to look forward to, focuses their minds on one of the ancient heartbeats of seafaring and keeps them in the dark for at least some of the time, a policy favoured by successful pilots from the days of the Yankee clipper to some of the more prudent race navigators of my acquaintance.

Enjoy GPS and the freedom from care that it has brought, but spare a thought for how recently our brotherhood sailed the misty seas in uncertainty, rejoicing in the beauty of the sextant and the wonder of the constellations to which it tied us, while remembering every day the motto from the jacket of the old Air Almanac: 'Man is not lost.'

13 DAY-TO-DAY SEAMANSHIP

I believe that seamanship is the art of making everything done on a boat look easy. A secondary definition could be that seamanship is looking for trouble before it happens and making sure it doesn't.

The seamanship of day-to-day deep-sea passage-making in non-extreme weather differs very little from coastal sailing in theory, and no new techniques are to be mastered. In practice, however, once far out at sea with thousands of miles ahead in what the French so colourfully call *le grand large*, areas of expertise where I, for one, have regularly taken liberties on a one- or two-day trip can no longer be ignored. Much of this comes down to living for weeks on end with rough water. The 'painted ship upon a painted ocean' mentioned by Coleridge's Ancient Mariner is an extraordinary rarity. The ocean never gives up. One of the most significant comments I have found in my early log books is a remark entered casually when I arrived in Rio four weeks out from the Canary Islands. 'There is no motion,' it records joyfully. That says it all. The constant heaving, rolling, pitching and general mayhem of the sea are wearing on the crew. They drive some as far as homicide, and they do horrible things to the ship if left unchecked.

Reaching or sailing upwind (perish the thought) lays no additional demands on seamanship, beyond watching for chafe and perhaps setting up an intermediate running backstay to stabilise the mast as it is wrenched for the ten-thousandth time by yet another five-foot wave. Off the wind, it's a different story.

In-mast reefing is far from ideal for long-distance cruising, but vertical battens help, so long as they do not break.

It's perfectly possible to dead-run up Long Island Sound or the Solent with a sloop's genoa casually goose-winged. Offshore, the eternal waves give this arrangement no chance at all. Making a 50-mile passage in rougher water you might settle for clipping the booming-out pole on to the mast, setting a topping lift, passing the bight of the working sheet through the bayonet fitting on the outer end, then heaving in on it until the sail sets. This will just about do for a quick run across the English Channel, but it won't cut the mustard on a trade-wind passage. In this chapter I have flagged up some areas where rough water over a prolonged period will take its toll if we offer it a shadow of a chance.

Sail handling on a downwind passage

Reefing the mainsail

We aren't talking handling systems here because, on passage, the sail is hoisted and likely to stay up, barring extreme weather, until you arrive. Dealing with a boomed sail on a run or near-run will be considered later in the chapter, but we can take it that for much of the time out there a boom preventer will be rigged. This raises questions about reefing.

On the face of things, any mainsail is happier being reefed or unreefed at an angle to the breeze that allows it to spill wind. This does not mean 'head to wind', and if you are suffering a system that demands this, the only thing to do is get rid of it now. Fortunately, despite strange lessons taught in mysterious covens of ignorance, few arrangements really do ask for this. If the sail-handling gear is any good at all, reefing should be easily dealt with by coming on to a reach close enough to set the apparent wind forward of the beam, easing the sheet and letting things flog for a few seconds while you deal with the heave-ho part of the operation.

Close-reaching or beating, there's no problem. Just let the sheet off, reef and heave it in again. If the apparent wind is just abaft the beam, it won't be a big deal to luff 20 or 30 degrees to let things flap.

The trouble starts when the boat is so far off the wind that the main boom is restrained by a preventer, and a booming-out pole is rigged on the windward side. If the preventer is rigged in a seamanlike manner, easing this before luffing will be easy. The problem is the headsail. Coming up far enough to flog the main will almost certainly cause it to lie aback against its pole, which puts ghastly strains on things, renders the boat 'not under command' and is generally unacceptable. Rolling it away is a solution of sorts, but who wants to do that? If the pole is rigged properly, the sheet can be eased away and the sail taken up on the lee sheet for a short while, but it's a messy answer. By far the most satisfactory solution is to reef the main while sailing downwind.

It is true that with some mainsail systems the sail simply must spill wind to hoist, shorten or drop, but anybody who's ever tried to stuff a running boat into half a gale, in a big sea, will never want to do it again. The technique described here works well on a slab-reefing main, although not on a single-line reefing version, because with this the clew cannot be properly controlled at all times. If your system can't maintain a restrained clew tension while reefing, you'll just have to pay the price and luff up somehow. If yours can, you might be agreeably surprised. Here's how it works with a conventional slab-reefing mainsail:

- Don't top up the boom, but take its full weight by heaving up the topping lift against the vang or kicker, which you have emphatically not let off.
- Don't slack away on any preventers. Leave the sheet where it is and the boom is now held, rock-solid, in all directions.

- Ease the halyard carefully while pulling the tack down. The sail will now try to sag against the shrouds and spreaders, making it impossible to drag it any further. To negate this tendency, pull hard but carefully on the clew pennant as the sail descends.
- Snug the tack down tightly, then winch in the last of the pennant, making sure to flatten the foot fully.
- If you have aft-swept spreaders you may find it helps to ease away the preventer a few feet and heave in the sheet, so as to get the sail off the worst of the friction bonanza offered by the standing rigging.

So far, so good, but what about other handling systems? Fortunately, although it is often not advocated as an easy option, I've known people with in-mast systems on modest-sized yachts who assure me they can reef downwind. Sadly, in my experience the same cannot be said for in-boom. The further out the boom is, the more of a hammering the universal joint in the rolling mechanism is taking, while the friction in the luff tape with the sail full and drawing militates against anything approaching a seamanlike roll. There is no help for it. With in-boom reefing, the sail must be allowed to spill wind to reef successfully.

Being able to reef the main without rounding up is an inestimable benefit. The number of times I have been sitting at dinner in the trade winds only to be turned out to reef for the sunset squall, as I am about to rip into the treacle pudding and custard, is nobody's business. You won't want to be taking in poles and putting the seas abeam at a time like that.

Headsails

It's assumed that the vast majority of voyaging yachts now have roller-furling headsails. I'd suggest that if there's any choice in the matter these should be on the small, rather than the big size, with clews well up off the deck. High-clewed sails roll better than deck-scrapers, you can see under them and they never even look like touching the water on an extreme roll. There is, however, a school of thought that high clews encourage rolling. There may well be something in this, so, as they say, the choice is yours.

Reefing a headsail is always easier if it can be sheeted into the shadow of the mainsail. On a reach, therefore, it pays to run off briefly while reefing. Wait until the genoa falls, windless, into the main's lee, then roll it in.

On my 44-footer I can reef the sail readily without reverting to a winch as long as I can let it flog or shadow it. If you can't roll it in without power assistance on any boat under that size, you'd be well advised to ask yourself why not. The usual reason is a bad lead on the furling line. When I bought my boat, this was led to the cockpit via a nasty, cheap block that turned it through 120°. The block sheave was worn almost flat. A predecessor had bought a small reefing winch and cluttered up my nice clean cockpit coaming with it, rather than binning a block worth £10. With that block out of the system, the line led sweetly all the way.

By perching on the pushpit quarter seat I can now heave in the whole sail in 25 knots of wind. The winch is redundant, unless the sail is poled out with wind in it and I don't feel inclined to gybe the main to give it some lee. Then I must winch it in as I ease the sheet, but the reefing winch is so small that I generally lead the line to a spare primary instead. It'll be on eBay next winter, so if you've a bad lead and are thinking about a dedicated winch, stand by for a bargain.

I remember not so long ago heading southwards over 400 miles-worth of the Bay of Biscay with a 38ft sloop in a northeast wind. We started in force 4 with the boom securely prevented and the genoa poled out. By the time we were halfway across, the breeze had piped up to a good force 6. We had two reefs in the main and several rolls in the headsail. Approaching Finisterre, true to form, the wind rose to gale force. All we had to do was drag down the third reef, roll in the genoa to a few feet short of nothing and press on. We never touched the pole's guys, the boom preventer or even the main boom vang, all the way across. The boat had no special gear and the passage was a classic manifestation of the success of well-organised downwind reefing.

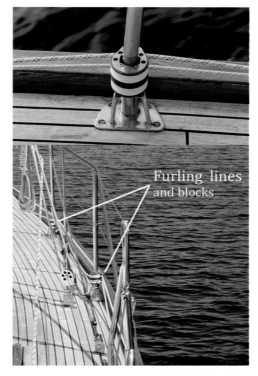

Furling lines and blocks

The furling lines on the author's 44ft cutter. The blocks are of such quality and the lead is so fair that a reasonably fit adult can furl the genoa in F5 without using the winch.

Chafe

Sailing downwind in the sort of sea one encounters in the ocean trades, boats roll. Some worse than others, and modern beamy cruisers with their high initial stability are less trying than their forebears, which were narrower and relied more on ballast. However, roll they all do. Rolling, especially in light or moderate airs when the sails snatch from time to time, creates chafe, and chafe is the bogeyman of the ocean sailor. It eats sails, it worries away at fittings and it saws through expensive ropes. A genoa sheet being quietly sandpapered by even a slightly unsympathetic pole end-fitting can let go in a single night.

The best solution to chafe is an unstayed rig, such as an Aerorig (see Chapter 2), which, apart from any minor issues of halyard blocks and reefing gear, has zero chafe. A Freedom rig is also pretty good in this respect. If, like most of us, you haven't come around to either of these and so are the victim of shrouds, backstays and spreaders, you are stuck with chafe. In an ideal world, things are all re-led until it stops happening, but there are some areas that can never be cured. One of these is the mainsail of a yacht with swept-back spreaders. It must be said that these rigs are not recommended by this author for world cruising, but many such craft make transatlantic passages.

To sail properly and maintain helm balance on a run, it just won't do to pull in the mainsheet until the sail is off the rig. Contact has to be accepted and dealt with. The best solution is to have the sailmaker stitch in chafe panels in way of the spreaders for the full main, plus reefs one and two, but in the real world this rarely happens. Fortunately, you can make your own chafe patches from stick-on sailcloth sold in 4-inch rolls, or sail repair tape – somewhat narrower. They are reported to work well.

Chafe is the ever-present enemy of the downwind sailor. Here's one nobody noticed until it was too late.

I carry a bag of old bits of leather I've begged, borrowed or stolen over the years for dealing with chafe hot spots for which I can find no better cure. The hide used to be a major lifeline when I voyaged in traditional gaff-rigged craft. These could be real chafe monsters, and my leather saw a lot of action. Things are quieter with my modern rig, but I'm shaping up a patch right now to stick on the lower surface of my spring kicker. The upper purchase block bashes away at it even when it's set up and it's doing neither block nor kicker any good.

Most yachts on short passages allow headsail sheets to cross the guardrails with the pole up and take any resulting chafe on the chin. On longer legs, this is no good. For running, many boats must re-lead the sheets through quarter blocks, so make sure you have plenty of spare blocks to experiment with, a choice of suitable securing points well aft and a pair of sheets that are good and long.

FRESHEN THE NIP

Probably the best advice is to follow the old square-rigged seaman's policy of freshening the nip daily. This is simply a matter of easing or hardening a rope an inch or two so that any unseen flash points are moved around. This is especially worthwhile with the control lines of any sail that is set flying, such as a cruising chute, or one with known propensity to chafe – a poled-out genoa sheet being the usual culprit.

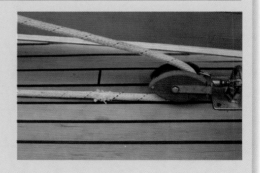

Downwind rig options

I'm not going to try to describe all the possible rigs people use for ocean cruising. Many of these are highly specific and their owners are generally specialists as well. Schooners of all descriptions will often run wing and wing. Ketches and yawls, if they can keep to a broad reach, are able to set useful mizzen staysails with remarkably little fuss. Gaff cutters make their own arrangements (I could write a book about them, and I have...), while Aerorigs simply ease the sheet and blast off. This section will deal with what we might term 'mainstream rigs', mostly Bermudan sloops and cutters.

The big question to be answered is whether to go with what the builder gave you, which is almost certainly a squared-off mainsail and a headsail poled out on the other side, or to think hard about different ways to run.

The mainsail option

On any boat, and especially one with aft-swept spreaders, keeping the main up on a run is going to involve the sail in some degree of chafe. If the sheet is eased far enough for the sail to set properly without creating unnecessary heeling, slowing the boat and causing steering problems, chafe is inevitable. With in-line cap shrouds, as long as the boom is held absolutely rigid by preventer, sheet and vang, the effects can be minimised, but there will usually be at least some stitching to attend to at the end of a passage. With aft-swept spreaders, the only hope of salvation is chafe pieces glued or stitched to the sail at chafe hot spots. This being accepted, the main thing is the preventer. The rest of the gear is already in place.

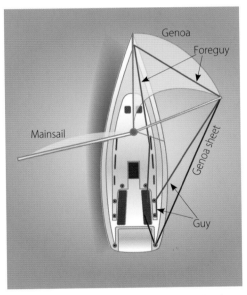

Fig 13.1 *A standard 'boomed-out headsail' downwind rig. The main boom preventer has been omitted, but many skippers will choose to rig one.*

■ Preventers

Materials

I once presided over the breaking of the main boom on a 70ft ketch. We were running in high latitudes. It was heavy weather with fog tossed in as a bonus. The preventer was cow-hitched halfway along the wooden boom, under the loose foot of the gaff mainsail. This was a while ago and we had no radar. AIS was unheard of. When a ship hove in sight crossing from the lee bow, I was alone at the helm and had little choice but to bear away and pray. My supplications went unanswered. When we gybed, the boom snapped like a carrot at the cow hitch. The sheet pulled one way and the preventer the other, while the gooseneck – the perfect fulcrum – held fast. What the skipper said when he came on deck to view the shambles is best left unprinted, but in my defence I was only a gash hand and had had no executive part in the siting of that dreadful rope.

For reasons that will now be obvious, a preventer should be secured to the boom in way of the mainsheet. I keep mine permanently on the boom for instant deployment, made fast ready at the sheet end and coiled neatly at the gooseneck where I can reach it. It's Dyneema, light and immensely strong.

Some hold that a preventer should have some give in it to absorb shock loading in a gybe, or if the boom rolls into the sea at 7 knots and loads up the gooseneck beyond its safe limits. This approach would recommend nylon. It makes a good deal of sense and I wouldn't argue about it. My boom is fairly high and has never yet rolled in, unlike a 28ft one on an earlier boat that seemed to submarine as much as it was out in the air on a rough day. On balance, then, I'd go for the non-stretch option, but owners of boats whose booms 'drag' from time to time would be well advised to consider the alternative. Some race boats go so far as to rig 'fuses' in their preventer lines. These are sections of lighter line that will break if loads become too high during a drag. It protects the potentially vulnerable gooseneck, but leaves the crew exposed to danger in a gybe.

Lead

If it can be arranged, it makes sense to lead a preventer so that it can instantly be released or adjusted from the cockpit. The ideal setup, if there's a spare winch, is to lead it from the boom end through a block well forward, then bring it aft, via whatever it takes, to the winch. If a block cannot be organised, some boats, notably Scandinavian yachts, have useful bow cleats through which a rope can be passed free of chafe. This works equally well, and such cleats are often sited outboard, giving a lovely lead off the boom end and a better run down the side decks to a winch on the cockpit coaming.

Where no winch offers itself, this is no cause for tears. None of my gaffers had any winches at all, and we managed fine. The job proceeds as described but, instead of a winch, the preventer is secured to a conventional cleat, **not** a jammer. The sheet is eased further than you want it, often so far as to let the boom sag against the shrouds for a few seconds. Once the preventer is made up as tightly as you can get it, the sheet is hove in. It has sufficient purchase to manage most of what a winch can do, so the boom should now be off the shrouds with everything good and tight.

The reason that using a jammer is a bad plan is this: if the boat should crash-gybe, the preventer will be so heavily loaded that, unless there is a winch to relieve it, the jammer will be stuck shut. A boat with her mainsail aback, heeling heavily the wrong way, will need to ease the preventer carefully once all crew are safe. A jammer alone doesn't allow this. A cleat does.

If you can't lead the preventer aft for any reason, it will just have to be secured up forward. In light of what's been said so far, you'll understand why this is undesirable, but, if needs must, then so be it.

Running under headsails

■ Downwind strategy

It's unusual to find oneself on an absolutely dead square run and, even if the shortest distance between two points seems to demand it, experienced voyagers don't often give in to the temptation, preferring to broad-reach on one tack or the other. This is not the same thing as tacking downwind. A fast, lightweight yacht or a sporty multihull can crank up its apparent wind speed by sailing a broad reach rather than a run. After a given mileage she will gybe and reach back to the rhumb line, saving time while adding distance. She will also give her crew a less stressful ride, for no boat likes a run, not even a square rigger. For most real-world cruising yachts, this policy doesn't work well enough. To gain a significant boat-speed advantage, the yacht must steer a long way wide of the run and the distance accumulated is rarely worth the candle.

In order to remove the danger of gybing and the worst of the dead-run rolling, you don't have to come many degrees off dead downwind, and it almost always pays on an ocean passage to make the boat comfortable while going in the right general direction, rather than sticking slavishly to the course demanded by a GPS waypoint on some far distant shore. Things have a way of evening out in the end and skippers equipped with the wherewithal to download seven-day forecasts can increase their chances by seeing into the future.

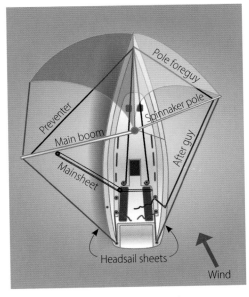

Fig 13.2 *Twin headsails (on two forestays).*

Running with main and genoa offers a reasonably well-balanced rig, but it doesn't quite have the self-steering benefits conferred by the 'front-wheel drive' approach of two headsails. Traditionally, it was understood that boats running under what used to be called 'twins' rolled their crews' heads off their shoulders. As yachts have gained in beam and the initial stability that goes with it, this tendency has eased back so that many circumnavigators now favour some sort of combination of headsails for long downwind passages, perhaps with a mainsail set as well.

■ Double headsail rigs

Organising two headsails on a mainstream cruising yacht is usually approached in one of three ways. The straightforward cutter carries a genoa or a high-clewed yankee on the outer forestay and a smaller staysail on a secondary stay lower down the mast. The staysail is rarely big enough to work as a 'twin' downwind, although it can be useful in heavy weather.

Stowing the light-weather preventer. This is left permanently attached to the outboard end of the boom so that it can be quickly deployed if the boom is snatching in a seaway. This one is Dyneema. For heavy weather, a beefier nylon version is preferred.

The second option is to set a large genoa, of up to 150 per cent, from an outer forestay and a blade jib of full hoist on a second forestay just inside it. Short-tacking with the genoa is a non-starter but works well with the blade. The pair make possibly the ideal combination for downwind work.

A third possibility is to fly a genoa or yankee from the headfoil and carry an extra sail that can be hoisted on its own halyard in the second groove in the headfoil. This can be whizzed up on a run and sheeted accordingly. If overpowered, it can be allowed to gybe and lie inside the genoa on the other side. There, it can await the passing of the squall or be dropped in comparative ease if the going looks like continuing rough.

The windward side

On a downwind passage, a boat has a nominal windward side for most of the time. This is where the smaller of two headsails will be set, poled out to windward. The pole should be held solidly with a fore guy or downhaul, an after guy and a topping lift. Some voyagers rig the guys as a permanently made-up bridle with three snap shackles, one to set up forward, one aft and one on the pole. The whole lot is tensioned when the topping lift raises it up. The only problem with this is that the pole is permanently in one position. As a reach sharpens, you may well want to ease the pole forward with the sheet, so having the guys adjustable is an advantage.

When a pole is triangulated like this, the headsail can be gybed in an emergency and the pole simply left where it is, with the sheet running through its end. Setting the sail is also easy

Even on quite large boats, a skilfully handled snuffer makes foredeck work a singlehanded job.

because it can be kept rolled while the pole is being put in position. When all is in place, it is unrolled and sheeted out through the end of the pole.

A pole should be at least as long as the foredeck between the mast and the outer forestay. Depending on the foot length of the sail it may well want to be longer because, ideally, it will then hold the sail out almost flat. This often creates stowage problems, so a telescopic unit is worth considering, but nothing under the heavens comes for free and extending poles bring issues of their own. Some work beautifully, but I've sailed with others that have driven me to distraction, so don't spare the pennies and make sure that the whole caboodle works easily. It's tough enough dancing round on a rolling foredeck rigging a pole without having to fight the gear as well.

On the subject of poles and their stowage, a carbon spar is around half the weight of its aluminium equivalent. If your budget can stretch to one of these wonders, do not hesitate. The difference is remarkable.

A pole that stows with the heel permanently rigged to a sliding mast fitting is a winner, because at no time is it totally detached. When a pole runs amok on the foredeck it is dangerous as well as potentially expensive, so I'd go with this every time and live with the extra weight aloft.

The leeward side

The bigger headsail is flown free on this side, unless the boat has two poles. As long as you are not on a dead run, there is every chance it will draw beautifully. If it flops around, try running the main boom out and sheeting the genoa through a snatch block attached to its end. When more area is needed in light going, roll it up and deploy a cruising chute if you have one.

A chute should not be as big as you think for trade-wind work and it needs 1½ ounce cloth for a typical 40-footer. Don't be tempted by ¾ oz, whatever the sailmaker says. So often, the balmy breezes of one's dreams turn out to be steady force 6. Force 7 and even more is not uncommon. You certainly don't want to be caught out with the chute up when the wind starts to mean business, so a good rule of thumb for taking it in is to watch for the whitecaps that start to kick in when force 4 nudges up towards 5. Use a snuffer system, run off to hide the sail behind the mainsail for hoisting, and particularly for dropping, and you won't go far wrong.

Both sides

Some authorities, including Don Street, have advocated running with two headsails and the main set as well. Grand if you're in a hurry and can pull it off, but don't worry if you're only making 120 miles a day. It isn't usually a race and the important thing is to enjoy the trip and feel comfortable. Time was when people were content with 120 miles and I even knew a couple who used to heave to every night for a sleep in their handsome 38-footer. Crossing from the Canaries to Barbados took them five weeks.

One way of looking at speed on passage is to say: '¼ knot saved is an hour a day on an average boat.' So it is, and that's a whole day extra in port after a three-week passage. Not everyone cares, though. Some people actually like it out there. And why not?

The author's Code Zero headsail. Another way of loading up sail area that's surprisingly easy to handle and offers further options for downwind sailing.

14 SYSTEM MANAGEMENT

Skippering a modern yacht on an ocean passage demands a full understanding of the power requirements of on-board systems in the context of available electrical potential and the means of charging it. It also involves managing water supplies and engine fuel.

Electrical management

We've seen in Chapter 5 on systems that a basic knowledge of electricity is vital, not only for specifying what systems a boat can carry and how much battery capacity she needs to run them, but also for setting up how these batteries are to be charged. On passage, this now gets down to the nitty-gritty. I've often asked Ocean Yachtmaster candidates how they calculate what power their boats are using daily and how long this takes to maintain with whatever generators they are using. Some don't have a clue. They fail their tickets, and so they should.

The ultimate in power saving. A well-trimmed oil anchor light with a powerful dioptric lens is almost as bright as an LED. Lighting it and hoisting it when you bring in the colours at sunset, becomes part of the daily ritual.

In fact, using the watts = volts × amps formula, it is simple to arrive at an approximate power demand for a typical 24-hour day. For a 12V system, all you have to do is read the manuals to find out the wattage for the various items guzzling your power, divide this by 12 and that's how many amps they are drawing. Multiply this by the number of hours they run and that's the answer you want, expressed in amp hours. Some manuals sidestep the whole issue of watts, preferring instead to give us the data directly as a likely draw of amps. This saves us doing a simple division sum, so let's rejoice. Let's look at a few examples:

POWER CONSUMPTION ON BOARD

REFRIGERATION
These systems don't always specify wattage directly. Since the motors come on and off as required, it's really more important to estimate how many amp hours you can expect to draw in a day. The spec may well tell you this for varying circumstances. Let's say it's 50 amp hours on passage with a half-full fridge in moderate ambient temperature.

AUTOPILOT
Here's another tricky one. It works its little heart out in a quartering sea and takes its ease close-hauled. Estimate 3 amps average for a 40-footer sailing downwind. That's 75 amp hours. Ugh. Time to fit a windvane?

NAVIGATION
Plotters can be power-hungry if left on with the backlight turned up. Turn the dazzler right down and watch the amps collapse. If visibility is good and you've no requirement for radar, why not turn the system off altogether? After all, you don't need to know where you are. You are safe, far out in mid-ocean. Pop it on once a day at noon to plot your position and save a lot of amps. Or, if you can't cope with this, just turn it on at the change of watch to enter the log. If it needs to be on to run an autopilot, have it rewired or specify a different make next time. You might feel you must have the plotter running in order to be able to hit the man overboard button immediately were you to lose someone. If that's your priority, keep it on, but understand that it is nibbling away at those batteries to the tune of anything up to 40W, or 75 amp hours per day.

LIGHTS
On a modern ocean sailing yacht, these just have to be LED. Their power draw is then minimal. If you still have incandescent bulbs, a few hours of accommodation lighting plus an all-night session with a 25W masthead tricolour can easily run up 30 or 40 amp hours over a day and a night.

The bottom line

You'll be seeing by now how quickly power usage adds up in today's yachts. If charging relies on a generator, the skipper must know how many litres of diesel this burns in an hour, multiply that by the number of hours the generator has to run to make good the daily power draw, then multiply again by the number of days to go, add a hefty contingency allowance and subtract the result from what's left in the tanks. That's how much the boat has left for motoring through calms, after making sure that she doesn't arrive with the crew cleaning her filters while the genset or engine sucks the last pint or two from the gruesome debris lurking at the bottom of the tank.

Some sort of renewable energy power source is clearly to be preferred. Wind generators are useful at anchor, although many find the noise stress-creating. Solar power is improving all the time, but perhaps the best way forward is a combined wind and water generator. At 6 knots' boat speed, the water function on some of these can produce all the needs of a modest yacht. To be sure, though, you have to know the wattage or the amp flow in order to line it up against what the yacht is helping herself to on a regular basis.

For a yacht with big fuel tanks, there is still much to be said for running such things as water makers and refrigeration from mains power. Topping these up will then come more or less for free during the daily generator run to charge the batteries. It's all a matter of management.

Motoring and fuel management

I'm always interested in talking with voyagers about how much or little they are prepared to motor. Back in the days of tiny fuel tanks and no weather forecasting beyond the barometer, the sea and the sky, what fuel we had tended to be saved for charging batteries and for emergencies. Thus, when the wind dropped, we sat it out, sometimes for days on end, waiting for a breeze.

The result of this was that a 32-footer usually planned passages on the basis of 100 miles in 24 hours. 'Pathetic,' today's sailors would bleat, but that was the reality for many of us. Today, with bigger tanks and reliable, economical engines, all that has changed.

One thing stays the same, however. There's no fun to be had sitting in a rolling sea waiting for wind with everything nagging its life out and the crew planning which of the skipper's limbs to tear off first. With a range of a thousand miles or so under power, many just start the engine if the speed falls below some level they find unacceptable and trundle off at 6 knots with the main pinned in.

A rather more intelligent option, given access to good weather info, is to check the met. If it seems likely that wind will show up within a period you can live with – say 24 hours – sheet in the main, drop the headsails and take the opportunity to read a good book until a cat's-paw on the oily calm tells you it's time to get going again.

Keep the speed down to less than √LWL and fuel consumption falls dramatically.

A further advantage conferred by instant weather forecasting is that, should you see that a fine northeast trade wind is blowing a hundred miles southward of your position, it will often make sense to flash up the donkey and cruise away from your miserable dead air towards the action.

On certain passages you can be pretty sure there will be spells with no wind. The horse latitudes in the North Atlantic are a case in point. If you intend to traverse such an area, either you should have plenty of fuel or take a different route. Sailing ships did and they usually arrived sooner or later.

Miles per gallon

This is often the real crunch about motoring on passage. What follows are the sort of mental arithmetic calculations that all skippers should have done before setting out.

Hull speed is the maximum at which a displacement hull can sensibly be driven. It is calculated by multiplying some constant (C) by the square root of her length on the waterline (LWL): $C \times \sqrt{LWL}$.

Take my boat, for example. *Constance*'s LWL at rest is about 37ft. Call it 38 or so when she's sailing and the quarter wave tucks up under her rather elegant counter stern. For convenience, therefore, let's call $\sqrt{LWL}$ 'around 6'.

For a long-keeled yacht like *Constance*, the constant is likely to be in the order of 1.35. This makes my theoretical maximum hull speed 1.35 × 6, or a little over 8 knots.

Fuel gauges are helpful, so long as they keep working, but in the end you can't beat a dipstick.

My 55HP Yanmar diesel will give me well over 7 knots. It might even manage the full 8, but I've never tried. However, if I keep water speed down to the square root of my waterline length, the fuel consumption drops dramatically. At 6 knots in flat water with a clean bottom, I burn a bit less than 2.7 litres in an hour. Rather than consulting tables of theoretical performance, I know this as an established fact because I have calculated actual fuel burned between 'pressed-up tank' fills while keeping my speed pretty much to that limit. Put another way, that's 2.2 miles per litre.

This is really working data and immediately I can see that my useful range at 6 knots in calm water is at least 1,100 miles on my 150 (US) gallon tanks (570 litres – call it 500 to allow a sensible safety margin).

Root waterline speed is a cut-off point. Above it, fuel burn climbs, sometimes through the roof. Incidentally, it has similar effects on speed under sail. If I'm making 6 knots close-hauled, I'm well pleased and am unlikely to beat this. Off the wind, when my rig is developing more forward push and less heeling moment, I can do better without breaking my neck, but if I can live with that magic 6 knots, my life will be serene, stress free and I'll still knock off that magic 150 miles per day.

Six knots is achieved by 2,100 rpm out of an available 3,000 with my present propeller. If I cut speed to 5 knots, the revs drop remarkably, to something like 1,500 rpm. That represents a massive fuel saving and still gives me a respectable 120 miles per day. Down at 4 knots the Yanmar is literally sipping the stuff. I haven't worked out my range at 100 miles a day, but it is going to be huge. On an ocean passage, especially if my rig were to be disabled, this knowledge can be life-saving.

■ Dipsticks

One of the more disappointing discoveries about modern yachts is that their fuel gauges seem to have a mortality rate somewhat less attractive than that endured by the Arctic lemming. Try, therefore, to make some arrangement for dipsticks. Given a sensible approach to fuel slopping around in the tank at sea, a dipstick is probably the most reliable measure you'll get. In harbour, it is bomb-proof. And you can calibrate it yourself by filling a near-empty tank slowly and marking it every so often as you go. Nobody did that for your boat's fuel gauges and if they are anything like the one on my car, you think you've got hundreds of miles left until the thing suddenly falls off a cliff and tells you to fill up in the next 50 miles or take the consequences.

Fresh water

My first cruising boat had a tank capacity of 35 gallons and I carried a further ten in cans. I never arrived with less than 15 gallons, even after 40-day passages. It should go without saying that all yachts on passages far from assistance should carry enough water in tanks for drinking and cooking, with emergency backup in bottles. Half a gallon (imperial) or, if you are of the metric persuasion, a couple of litres per person per day is adequate. Anything beyond this is a bonus.

On passage, big tanks or a water maker can take up the slack and allow for luxuries such as fresh-water washing up and showers, but it is while cruising once you arrive somewhere that the water maker really comes into its own. Filling water tanks in many areas is no problem and, if you plan to sail in such waters, don't bother with the trouble and expense of a water maker, but remote venues can be a major nuisance. Topping up a 500-litre tank via jerry cans from a stream behind a palm-fringed beach may suit some people's idea of true romance, but I have to say that I have found it something of an incubus. To be freed from this, and all those dodgy taps you are never quite sure about, a water maker really makes a big difference to life's options.

If you don't care to have a water maker and are concerned about water capacity, one workable alternative is to place the tank deck filler caps adjacent to the scupper holes and the lowest point of the sheer. Tropical downpours can be dramatic, and once the decks have rinsed themselves clean, all you need to do to fill up is stopper up the scuppers with the bungs you have prepared previously and remove the filler caps. A friend does this on a boat he designed and built himself and has now circumnavigated four times. He rarely has to come alongside for water.

I used to fill my small tanks by hanging a bucket under the main gooseneck in heavy squalls. The bucket filled in seconds and all I had to do was tip it into the tank and start again. Not so elegant as my chum and undoubtedly less efficient, but it kept me drinking the right stuff in profusion through many a long passage.

When I commissioned a new custom cruising boat, I specified one ton of drinking water. This lived in two tanks deep beneath the cabin sole of a heavy displacement hull. It was 'fill and forget'. I didn't even think about a water maker because I was never so far from a tap that a ton wasn't enough. My present boat carries around 100 gallons (Imperial) or 450 litres. I could certainly cross the Atlantic two-up with that and not give the matter a second thought, but if I were going into the Pacific, I'd probably look into a modern, low-draw water maker.

Cooking gas

Managing this shouldn't be a challenge. Just take lots and make sure before you leave that you can refill bottles where you plan to cruise. Propane is pretty worldwide, but the fittings do not always interchange. A little research into gas arrangements where you plan to arrive, and some time spent pre-planning for fittings to cope, will repay your effort.

One thing is sure: the Mickey Mouse gas arrangements and the tiny, expensive bottles usually supplied with standard production boats are useless on the ocean. If you plan

Fresh bread is terrific for morale, but you need a good supply of cooking fuel.

SAVING WATER

When water is an issue, it pays to consider the following:

- Use a hand or foot pump for drinking and cooking water. The electric pump always uses more than you think. I keep a simple in-line charcoal filter on this pump, so that no matter how vile the water in the tanks, I can always get a decent cup of tea.
- Rinse the pots and plates using a squeezy spray bottle filled with fresh water, rather than giving them the running tap treatment.
- Find out how many pump actions it takes to fill a mug and only use this amount for a round of tea or coffee. This not only saves water, it also saves cooking gas because you never heat more than you need.

- Fit a sea-water pump in the galley and use it for washing up and for cooking where you'd normally salt the water. Rice, pasta or spuds can be 50/50 fresh and sea. Perfect condiment level and you save litres a day.
- In fair weather, shower off on deck with a bucket of God's free sea water every other day if you feel the need. Rinse with a maximum of half a gallon of precious fresh. Try it. It works surprisingly well.
- If you've got loads of water, you can afford to back off on much of the above, but if you don't blench when you see people rinsing plates or cleaning their teeth under a running tap, you haven't yet made the transition from land to the reality of the sea.

to bake bread and live properly, you'll need to beef it up. I carry two 13kg propane tanks for two-up cruising. They last us four months easily and are relatively inexpensive to fill/swap. My previous boat carried three. US bottles are slightly smaller so will drop into a UK locker. With either, we could feed a crew of six for three months – three meals a day plus bread and general bakery – without flinching. One final word. If you plan changing your bottle types mid-cruise, bear in mind that in some cases you may need to fit a local regulator as well. These are not expensive and can be bought over the counter in most places that sell LPG.

The important thing is not to run out on passage. This can only be ensured by monitoring gas usage before you leave and doing the necessary sums.

15 DEALING WITH HEAVY WEATHER

The proximity of land changes everything in heavy weather. Land lying close to leeward can be a deadly danger unless pierced with all-weather harbours, which it rarely seems to be. Land to windward, on the other hand, promises shelter by definition and thus, one hopes, salvation – but only if the boat is powerful enough to beat up to it. Much has been written about these situations and can readily be found elsewhere, but because this is a book about ocean sailing, this chapter will concentrate largely on heavy weather in open water.

Heavy weather can be simply too much wind and waves for comfort while on passage. This is an all-too-normal situation that falls into the 'if you can't take a joke you shouldn't have signed on' category. As an ocean sailor, your boat will already be stowed, with batteries, cookers, deck hamper and the rest well secured, on the assumption that she may at least take a full knockdown.

People have sometimes enquired of me how anyone knows they're in a survival storm. The answer is: 'When you stop asking', because you stop worrying about keeping the course and there's no doubt in your mind that your sole priority is to come through without major damage to ship or crew. Much of this chapter is devoted to dealing with this ultimate challenge.

General considerations

The techniques of storm survival at sea for sailing boats are dealt with later, but there is much that can be done to help a boat perform while still on passage.

Weatherliness

More or less anything that floats can sail downwind. The issues start to arise when the sea boot is on the other foot. A boat that can work to windward in hard going is often called 'weatherly' and, where all other factors are equal, it's generally safe to say that the bigger the boat, the more weatherly she will be. Longer waterlines are a lot happier in a rough jumble of sea, while the additional displacement generally confers sail-carrying power. Whatever the builder's propaganda may say, however, every boat that ever sailed has a frontier beyond which she just can't beat upwind. This is the crunch point when land lies to leeward, so while the data is never published, we all should take a realistic note of where this limit might be.

For prolonged cruising in areas of strong wind, such as the Caribbean, a full hoist jib with no overlap set on an inner forestay is a godsend.

Upwind sailing and different rigs

A 45-footer sporting a poorly set-up rig, a slack forestay and a reefing 150 per cent genoa with a dozen rolls in it won't perform nearly as well as a tautly prepared smaller boat with serious headsails. The roller-reefing compromise that is so attractive in moderate conditions becomes a disaster when the cards are on the table.

■ The double-headed rig

One popular solution is to rig two permanently hoisted headsails. One might be a big genoa that sets adequately with some rolls in up to force 5. The second is a flat-cut 'yankee' – a full-hoist jib with a high-cut clew, no overlap and less than 100 per cent of the area of the foretriangle. If it has a foam luff, so much the better, because all these factors help it to reef better than the monster genoa favoured by production boats. These sails are great for short-tacking into anchorages and generally see a permanent use for cruising in breezy places like the Windward and Leeward Islands of the Caribbean. At near-gale and beyond, even the jib will struggle, and it should then be replaced by a storm jib (see page 198).

■ The cutter

A second solution is to rig the boat with a semi-permanent inner forestay setting a staysail, making her technically a cutter. The cutter's genoa should be cut with a high clew and a foam luff for roller reefing. Better smaller than bigger. The inner stay carries running backstays for heavier going. There's a lot to be said for keeping this sail on a roller as well, because setting it is then dead easy. When it blows up hard, just roll away the genoa and unroll the staysail, which should drive to windward in force 6 winds and above. At such a velocity, it will start out unreefed and therefore setting perfectly, only beginning to be compromised by reefs in full gale conditions.

A cheaper answer is to keep a hanked staysail bagged on deck and hoist it when required. If this is the choice, a conventional reef in it will pay off when things really go to the bad. My pilot cutter had two reefs in the staysail and I can recall a number of filthy nights when I was glad of them both.

In less extreme conditions, the staysail can be set inside the reefed genoa to power up the foretriangle. The boat probably won't point quite so high with both sails drawing, but she will smash through heavy seas more powerfully. Since no yacht points at her highest in such circumstances and the genoa is already down in efficiency through rolling, little is lost and much can be gained. In survival extremes, a cutter retains the option to substitute the reefed staysail for a storm jib and, like any other yacht, she can set a trysail.

■ The unadorned sloop

The reality is that there are single-voyage cruisers out there that do not have sail wardrobes like these and are stuck with the wretched roller genoa. For such a boat working upwind towards safety in severe conditions, the only viable solution is to reef the mainsail as deeply as possible, haul it out flat, sheet it hard in, roll away the headsail altogether and motor to windward at between 30 and 45 degrees as the seas dictate.

Storm canvas
■ Storm jibs

A storm jib is a small, flat-cut jib, high-clewed and just about bulletproof. Time was when these were deployed simply by dropping the working headsail and hanking the storm sail in its place. Unfortunately, with the exception of a cutter with a hanked-on staysail, the forestays of most modern yachts are taken up with permanently rigged roller-reefing headsails.

For a storm jib to be useful, it must be easy to rig. On a sloop, the best method of achieving this is an additional headstay inboard of the existing forestay. Usually, these removable stays are permanently attached aloft and stored at the shrouds to be brought forward and attached to the deck when it matters. One sees all sorts of clever systems for setting them up, but the best is a 6:1 tackle, rigged so the user is pulling up with his back and thighs, secured by a jamming cleat on the bottom block. Foolproof, safe and it works a treat. The storm stay may require running backstays to triangulate its loads, but these can also wait out of the way until their moment of glory.

Care is needed over the sheeting arrangements, always bearing in mind that the boat is not going to point very high under this rig because of shorter luff lengths and the plain fact that if it's this windy she will be suffering a battering from the seas. You won't want to be pointing at 45 degrees, even if the boat can still do it.

For any yacht with a single roller headsail going far from land, some arrangement for an easily rigged storm jib has to be mandatory.

Dedicated heavy weather headsails and a well-organised slab-reefing main are infinitely better than a roller genoa and an in-mast main. I watched helplessly as this little cruising boat ate the wind out of the 55ft charter yacht I was sailing under 'standard' canvas in 30 knots.

■ Trysails

The storm trysail has three advantages over the deep-reefed mainsail:

- Because it rarely sees the light of day, it is unlikely ever to blow out.
- It sets without a boom, so if the main boom or gooseneck have been damaged, it doesn't mind one bit.
- Its tack is well up the mast, so any waves sweeping the deck aren't going to trouble it.

A trysail luff is attached to the mast, ideally on a dedicated secondary track. If there isn't one, it must be slid into the mainsail track through a gate above the stowed main. The higher the stowed main is off the deck, the more important a second track becomes. Clambering around on those little steps that hinge off the mast is not what you want when the seas are house-high and there's more wind than you can stand up in. The sail is tacked down to some convenient point and hoisted by the main halyard. The two sheets are led via turning blocks on the quarters to spare cockpit winches. It should never be sheeted to the end of the main boom.

Trysails set well close-hauled or reaching, but they aren't great on a run because in the absence of a stabilising boom, they tend to flop about. The hammering this gives the gear in 50 knots of wind is not recommended.

Issues arising from apparent wind

Anyone who has come far enough to be reading this book will be more than aware of the bald fact that a boat running fast in an apparent wind speed of 30 knots is experiencing gale-force conditions. The fact that the loads on a boat are so much diminished by running downwind often makes this the option of choice at times of maximum stress in open water.

However, if some unexpected issue arises – perhaps jammed roller-reefing headsail gear, a chafing reef pennant, or simply a big headsail that is proving a struggle to roll away – the natural tendency of anyone trained in dinghies is to turn into the wind, let the sails shake and enjoy the respite as the boat comes upright. The trouble is, in a bigger boat, they don't flap, they flog. In a gale of wind, an innocent bowline on a maniac headsail clew can measure up to a well-hefted pickaxe handle in the anti-personnel-weapon stakes. Such frantic flogging also lays ghastly loads on the rig.

One way and another then, luffing up can make a crisis out of an inconvenience. Assuming that lack of sea room is not a factor, the better choice of tactic is usually to run off. This knocks back the apparent wind and eases the motion, while the squared-away mainsail provides a useful lee for anyone working on the foredeck.

Steering in big seas

We all hope that our self-steering arrangements will continue to function long after human crew have lost interest in being on deck. Unfortunately, they don't always oblige. I have had problems with windvanes struggling in the trough of a big, steep sea, then whipping into vibrant life on the crests. Not good. Unless a boat is notably well balanced, many an electronic autopilot meets its nemesis when the waves pile up, especially if the course is downwind. Put bluntly, there are times when we have to get out there and drive the boat ourselves.

Upwind

■ Long-keeled, heavy craft

A typical long-keeler is steady on the helm with delayed action between rudder movement and alteration in heading. This means that reacting to every wave is unrealistic and largely unnecessary. The time comes, however, where one wave slows the boat and the second knocks her dead. She then ends up 'going up and down in the same hole', as we say. The next thing is that her bow falls off the wind, the sails fill and she

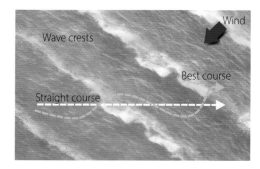

Fig 15.1 *Sailing a flat-floored boat upwind in heavy conditions, see opposite.*

After the gale. This yacht has unfurled a full genoa to keep her moving, but has not yet handed her storm trisail and re-hoisted the main.

stalls, beam-on to wind and sea, slip-sliding 'downhill' until she has gathered enough way for her keel to grip again.

This is downright depressing, but it rarely happens with experienced helms because they have sensed the first wave and borne away 10 or 20 degrees as the boat passes over the top of it. This 'slacker' heading is maintained as she rushes down into the trough to face the stopper. The extra way she has gathered and the fact that she is not meeting the wave so near to head-on allow her to sail over the top of it without being checked. Once clear of the rough patch, she is brought back on to the wind and away she goes again. Pounding in these boats is never an issue.

■ Shorter-keeled, lighter craft

These yachts react more sharply to helm movements, making it viable to steer rapidly off the wind as the boat comes to the crest of each wave. This saves her from plunging straight over the top, dropping like a brick and setting the crew's teeth on edge as she hammers her flat floor on to the concrete-like trough. Pounding not only increases risk of structural damage, it also slows the boat badly. If sailing powerfully, such a boat can be luffed slightly above her best course without losing too much way as she climbs the back of the next wave. This process gives a mean course of close-hauled, or a touch below. Effective, but tiring.

Sailing on autopilot, of course, no such sophistication will be available. If you are still trying to do this, set it up so as not to point too high and try to reduce pounding.

When it's blowing this hard, don't forget to look behind you.

Beam seas

These are the seas that capsize boats. If it is steep enough and breaking, a wave doesn't have to be a lot more than the beam of the yacht to roll her over. In a beam sea, therefore, if things start to look ugly, a human helmsman is a prudent precaution. Only a person can assess the next wave, by sight in daylight or by feel at night, and opt to do something about it. The best autopilot will press on regardless, even to the gates of doom.

When a beam sea looks dangerous, two choices present themselves. Either luff up to it or bear away, so as to present either the shoulder or quarter of the boat to the sea, rather than her vulnerable beam. Which you choose will depend on the strategic situation. In general, however, bearing away is more comfortable as long as it doesn't induce surfing. It has the bonus benefit for a well-balanced boat that, since the alteration will only last a few seconds, there should be no need to attend to the sheets.

Downwind

Safe downwind progress in moderately heavy weather is a matter of controlling speed so that the boat steers easily. For most cruisers this usually means not being over-canvassed, although lighter craft, especially those with flat sections aft, might opt to pick up their skirts and start surfing (see page 204) for a while at least.

Back in the day of huge square riggers running round the world in the Southern Ocean, their crews' greatest fear was to broach. It's just the same for us. Although the results can sometimes be less catastrophic, the broach is still the bogeyman waiting to pounce.

■ Anatomy of a standard broach

Some boats are more broach-prone than others. Generalising is never completely satisfactory and there will be exceptions, but, all factors being equal, anything with a flat underbody, a wide stern, a spade rudder and a sharp bow is potentially a broach waiting to happen. Such yachts usually have large accommodation space and, like all things at sea, this must be paid for.

I've sailed otherwise plausible boats that start to round up at 20 degrees of heel. With the helm already working hard to keep them on track, if they then take a gust that whacks them down to 30 degrees or more, it's all over. The extra immersed buoyancy of the aft cabins lifts the stern, the bow digs in, the rudder root rises out of the water, the rig, which is hanging well out on the downhill side, tries to swivel the boat into the wind and away we jolly well go. Unless we let fly the main to keep her on her feet, the next thing we know is we're head-to-wind with the sails flapping. The boat may even have tacked herself. Twin rudders help this problem, because the leeward rudder is always fully immersed.

At the other end of the scale, my 32ft 1903-built Colin Archer had such perfectly balanced lines, despite her generous midships beam, that she could heel until the water lapped up to the cockpit coamings and still she steered like an old shoe. My more modern Mason 44 with 12ft beam and a deep hull body is not dissimilar.

A deep reef and a storm jib.

■ The gybe broach

A running boat always rolls to some extent. On a heavy lurch to windward, the hull imbalance starts its mischief. The rig is displaced to windward by the roll and contributes to the hull's natural tendency to swerve the boat round. The rudder now stalls, the swerve takes charge and the boat broaches to leeward – towards the boom – gybing all-standing as she goes.

PREVENTION AGAINST THE BROACH

In a fast, light, modern yacht, broaching must be seen in the context of surfing (see below), but there are two things any skipper can do to minimise the likelihood:

- **Keep speed under control**. Unless you intend to go surfing, the ideal speed is about that magical rate of knots your boat can sail to windward in calm water. This is around the square root of her waterline length in feet and at this velocity she isn't generating much in the way of waves. As hull speed is approached, the wave-making increases exponentially and the strains on the rudder rise heavily. Unless surfing is contemplated, check her enthusiasm by shortening sail.

- **Keep her on her feet**. If the heading is allowed to wander, any tendency to roll increases because the yawing adds centrifugal force into the pudding-mix of factors already present. A good helmsman develops a feel for an incipient broach and checks the tendency to swing one way or the other almost before it has begun. Proactive steering will keep the yacht 'on her feet'. Steering reactively to yawing that is already well under way isn't good enough. This is where all but the finest autopilots fall short. Even a sensitive windvane struggles to second-guess what a competent human helm can deal with long before it happens.

Left: A classic broach with the rudder well out of the water and the boat beyond control.

■ Surfing

Any sailing boat except the heaviest can surf down the face of a wave at speeds well in excess of her theoretical maximum. Once surfing, she absolutely must be kept on her feet because, at such speeds, there's no arguing with the forces if she's allowed to take charge. Some race boats designed for long periods of downwind work in heavy weather are exceptionally light, wide and flat aft to encourage stable surfing. The extreme beam renders their rudders liable to lift out of the water when they heel heavily, so deep spade rudders are standard. Twin rudders ensure that the leeward one is kept in the water.

Surfing not only diminishes passage times, it is also a load of fun, but it makes demands on anyone at the helm and even greater ones of an autopilot. Whatever the boat, the key to safety lies in the driver's pocket. Anticipation is everything if the yacht is not to run out of control and broach. The initial tweaking of the helm as the yacht takes off down the wave is similar to helping a dinghy to lift on to a plane. A firm touch of weather helm to start with as the wind grabs her and she tries to round up to weather, then a readiness to steer hard the other way as she accelerates and thinks about broaching to leeward.

Only feel can tell you what to do, and confidence comes with practice, but a skilled helm with dinghy experience will soon be managing fine, as long as the boat isn't driven beyond the edge. The extra miles made good are free of charge, a bit of adrenaline is beneficial for your system and the competitions to see which watch holds the yacht's speed record are terrific for morale.

Survival options for sailing craft in open water

Sailing boats caught out in survival conditions have two sets of options: passive or active. Generally speaking, unless using storm-survival gear, lighter vessels with flat-floored hulls must be actively sailed. Heavier craft with longer keels, particularly those based on traditional working craft, are better placed to look after themselves. Developments since the 1990s with drogues and para anchors have, to some extent, mitigated this situation.

Unless your destination lies far to leeward and you decide to run as a tactic to keep your boat end-on to the waves, to continue steering towards your goal is unlikely to be an option in survival conditions. The highest probability for being knocked down or even capsized is to be caught beam-on by a steep or breaking wave. It follows that all survival tactics should aim to avoid this situation. Unless she is pitchpoled – a rare contingency indeed – a boat that is end-on or taking seas on her shoulder is well placed to survive. The exception is lying ahull which, as we shall see, is only an option for heavy displacement vessels in something short of ultimate conditions. What follows is a list of well-accepted techniques for achieving the right result.

Active tactics
■ **Running off**

Running before a gale has two great advantages: it keeps the boat stern-on to the waves and it dampens down the apparent wind and wave force. As we have noted, unless actively using the gale to add free extra miles, the secret of running safely is to maintain a sensible speed. As the wind rises and you've 'run out of reefs', sooner or later a decision has to be made about dropping all but one sail. The obvious assumption is that the last canvas standing should be the storm jib, but some boats run more stably with a triple-reefed mainsail so long as the boom is heavily vanged and a preventer employed to keep it steady. Trysails are not so good because of the likelihood of gybing in the absence of a steadying boom. Only experimenting can decide what will be best for a specific boat.

■ Extreme running

Bare poles

As the wind rises and speed continues to increase under steadily reduced canvas, the last rag is eventually stowed so that the boat is running under nothing more than the windage of her mast, her spray dodgers and any other likely flat surfaces. In fact, a typical modern cruiser will steer downwind under bare poles in calm water in force 6. In a whole gale, most heavier boats will be making their merry way alongside her at a respectable speed.

There are well-documented instances of boats successfully surviving storms in huge seas by running free under bare poles. Two of these were Bernard Moitessier in *Joshua*, and Conor O'Brien in *Saoirse*. Both were Southern Ocean circumnavigators, their boats were of heavy displacement, both had long keels and both were short-handed or solo.

An unfortunate element of running free under bare poles is that if the boat broaches, or otherwise loses control for a few seconds, she may refuse to bear away back on to a run unless the wind is well abaft the beam. This leaves her potentially at risk, with the choice of starting the engine or unrolling a few square feet of jib to return her to the run. Either is a nuisance, to say the least.

If loss of control or broaching becomes systemic, something else has to be done to keep her stern up to the weather. A further complication is that as the boat runs faster with increasing wind she may burst out of her comfort zone and start surfing. If this isn't part of your plan, you'll be obliged to stream something from astern to keep way down to an acceptable level. Should pitchpoling appear to be a growing possibility, different tactics altogether must be adopted, as there is no known cure for this spectacular ending when a boat is running.

Trailing warps

The best-explored answer to going too fast downwind is to stream heavy warps off the stern. The drag takes off way and keeps the stern up to the weather, assisting the helm or even rendering it wholly or partially redundant. Depending on the shape of the boat, warps are generally best streamed in a bight from either quarter. The pull is substantial, so make appropriate arrangements for securing them and, equally importantly, for retrieval. This technique has been promoted by no less a seaman than Sir Robin Knox-Johnston in *Suhaili*, another circumnavigator with a boat of heavy displacement.

His conclusions are thus different from those of Moitessier and O'Brien. All are men of unimpeachable reputation. The clear message for the rest of us is that there is rarely one single answer. An ocean skipper must be aware of and prepared for all options, then find out what is best for the actual boat on the day when it really happens.

Drogues

If warps are not delivering the goods, or you don't have any that are long enough and heavy enough, even more drag can be achieved by streaming a drogue. A number of commercial drogues are available and the effect on a sailing boat can be dramatic. Drag is considerable, loads are correspondingly high, and chafe on the warp is a real danger. Some users complain that while the drogue certainly reduces way and holds the stern up to the waves, it also weighs down on the stern so powerfully that the boat is pooped. This was the experience of Charles Watson in *Saecwen*, a 35ft long-keeled yacht, in a North Atlantic storm who deployed an Attenborough drogue after broaching and being knocked down under bare poles. The boat took such a beating when held back by the drogue that in the end Watson gave up on it and lay ahull. A series drogue (see right) could have been less harsh in its effects, but these were not available in 1990 when *Saecwen* had her experience.

The *series drogue* is a development of the single drogue that is finding favour among multihull skippers. It has also been used successfully by many monohulls. I have not experienced it, but it sounds like a lot of sense to me. It consists of 100 or more small cones on a tapering rope measuring anything from 240ft (73 metres) to 370ft (113 metres). The ultimate

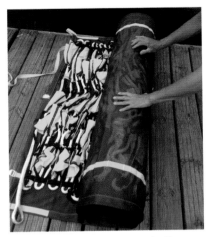

A series drogue has proved effective in many boats. For more info go to www.oceanbrake.com.

specification is decided by the boat's displacement and will be advised by the manufacturers (www.oceanbrake.com). The outboard extremity carries a weight – often a bight of chain – but conventional anchors have also been used. The pull is surprisingly steady, because the length means that at least some of the cones are always loaded up, despite the pulsing of the waves.

The whole drogue is streamed from a bridle secured to the quarters of the boat, with about 70–100ft of line between the bridle and the first cone. So long as it has been stowed in a seamanlike manner, this type of drogue is relatively easy to set and can be retrieved without a winch or a trip line.

Don't forget, if a drogue seems to be holding the boat back too hard, but you need its pull to maintain an end-on attitude, there is nothing to stop you using one with a storm jib set. The strains will rise substantially, but it won't pull the yacht in half and may well be worth trying.

■ Motorsailing to windward

Another method for keeping a boat more end-on than beam-on to the waves is to sail to windward. This might sound insane for storm conditions, and some boats just won't be powerful enough to do it, but it was a conclusion drawn by the official committee considering lessons learned from the infamous and tragic 1979 Fastnet Race. Clearly, this option will depend on weatherliness, but it can certainly work for the right craft in a moderate gale.

The problem, apart from loading up the apparent wind and smashing into the seas, is that many of today's cruisers either do not have a storm jib, or perform erratically under deep-reefed main and headsail because of their hull characteristics. It is well known that plenty of boats with poorly balanced hull lines experience sudden weather-helm problems as they heel. On a day-sail, or in a fully crewed race boat, this wretched state of affairs is usually dealt with by dumping the mainsheet traveller car down to leeward, but this is just not on in a short-handed cruiser with the crew increasingly exhausted.

In something less than monumental storm-force heavy weather, and given a blow not expected to last beyond the range of fuel you are prepared to burn, a better survival option for such yachts can be to motorsail very slowly upwind with no headsail set. The main is deep-reefed, sheeted hard in and flattened as much as possible. If you have a mizzen, that's even better.

The technique is very similar to what fishing boat skippers call 'dodging'. Speed is controlled so that the yacht can just steer and no more. That way, no issues arise about leaping off the wave-tops and thundering down into the troughs with banging, crashing and potential damage.

Passive techniques

■ Heaving to

In my days with pilot cutters on the oceans, this was my preferred method of dealing with conditions I didn't like. Given the right boat, it takes off most of the way and sets her up so she lies stably with her shoulder to the waves and wind. The technique has fallen out of general use. Indeed, I have sailed with Yachtmaster instructors who do not know how to do it because many of today's yachts have a cut-away forefoot.

A traditional gaff cutter heaves to phenomenally well because of her deep forefoot and her gaff rig, whose centre of effort moves forward very little as she reefs. Such a boat can heave to in remarkable comfort and survive any gale in which it is possible for her to carry canvas. Traditional Bermudan yachts, like my own, can also heave to reasonably effectively. Yachts with flat underbodies and salient keels may be able to balance up their hove-to rig to maintain a stable state in flat water, but the first wave will throw the forefoot to leeward and destroy the equilibrium. Sadly, heaving to just doesn't work for them, although in easier conditions it can allow them to lie-to without a helmsman.

The mechanics of heaving to

A boat heaves to with one sail trying to shove the bow downwind while the other counteracts it. The rudder assists the weaker cause to create an equilibrium.

Backing the jib keeps the bow off the wind. The yacht is now stalled. Sheeting in the main encourages her to luff up against the backed jib as she drifts against the lateral resistance of her keel. This all leaves the boat beam-on to the weather and drifting to leeward. Steering hard to windward with either tiller or wheel causes her to point up towards the wind. A suitable craft will now achieve a stable equilibrium at between 30 and 50 degrees from the wind, the helm is then locked or lashed and the helmsman can go below to brew a pot of tea.

Evidence exists that certain yachts can heave to under mainsail alone. If she has a shallow forefoot and thus no grip on the water forward once her keel stalls at low, heaving-to speeds, a boat's bow will fall off the wind rapidly in any sort of a seaway without the need for a backed jib to help it. Under mainsail alone with her helm lashed down, she will come up looking for the wind. As her mainsail starts to spill, the windage of her rolled genoa, coupled with almost zero resistance from the forefoot, is enough to hold her off the wind and prevent her from tacking herself.

The amount by which any headsail is backed has a marked effect on how the boat lies. So does the trim of her mainsail. On modern yachts, the main is often too powerful, leaving them continually trying to luff almost head to wind. If this happens, experiment with easing the kicker/vang a few inches to let the leech depower, rather than easing the sheet too soon. The possibilities for achieving balance are many, even for a sloop. For ketches and yawls, they can seem endless.

Heaving to in practice

Heaving to in a modern yacht rather than a gaff cutter, chafe is going to be a major factor where your jib sheets cross the shrouds. On my current masthead cutter, I heave to under staysail and get rid of the genoa altogether. If I'm going to be hove-to for long, I re-lead the staysail sheet inside the lower shrouds to clear everything. It's a nuisance, but it's worth the trouble in the end. Yachts with smaller headsails, big mains and aft-swept spreaders do unexpectedly well in the chafe stakes. The real culprits are the older masthead rigs like my own which lack a staysail. Genoa sheets on a masthead rig seem inevitably to foul something. If you don't re-lead, it's no good sitting out a storm and imagining you won't need a new set of sheets afterwards.

As to technique, while it's perfectly possible to heave a yacht to by hauling the jib across to weather and waiting for her to slow down, it's a lot easier to tack and leave the old working headsail sheet made up on the winch, instead of letting it fly. The boat will lurch nastily as she comes about on to the backed headsail, but she'll soon sort herself out. Steer high to help her lose way, then, when she finally stops answering the helm, secure it so it is trying to steer hard to weather, and kiss your troubles goodbye.

■ The para anchor

Anyone who has hove to through a storm in a suitable yacht knows how desirable it is. Sadly, as we have seen, many modern yachts are compromised, usually by a lack of forefoot, which allows their bows to blow off the wind. The situation is exacerbated by the way the centre of effort of a Bermudan mainsail and headsail move forward as they are reefed. Smaller yachts that have inherently more suitable characteristics may also suffer from having their bows knocked to leeward by each successive sea, but any of them can be talked into heaving to and pointing as high as her skipper wishes by deploying a para anchor.

The para anchor is like an airman's parachute in the water. It works as a drogue, except that it is generally streamed from the bow. If its warp is led directly from the bow roller, it will leave the boat lying head to wind, which is not recommended by some experts because it may compromise the rudder if the boat falls back on it. In any case, the shoulder-first attitude of the truly hove-to yacht is hard to beat. By leading a springline, via a snatch block, from the quarter and rolling-hitching it to the warp some distance forward of the bow, the boat's angle to the action can be adjusted to find the optimum. Although she can lie thus with sail set as though she were hove-to, she may well be better off under bare poles. Boats vary. Only experiment can show what's best for the boat on the day.

The slick left by the para anchor as the yacht drifts to leeward is said to assist in calming the worst of the seas. Lin and the late Larry Pardey, short-handed sailors of vast experience in small yachts, have written extensively in praise of this technique, which goes a long way towards making up the shortfall in the modern yacht's options. It should pass without saying that attention to chafe is a vital consideration.

■ Lying ahull

Lying ahull was once an established survival method. If one was dealing with workboat types with heavy displacement or yachts developed from them, it made at least some degree of sense and I have personally used it successfully to ride out two protracted North Atlantic storms of at least force 10 with appropriate open-ocean seas. Before considering lying ahull, however, it is vital to understand the boat's stability and capsize resistance characteristics. These are not necessarily the same thing (see Chapter 1).

A boat left completely to her own devices usually lies around beam-on or a little downwind of this. If she doesn't have proven characteristics for looking after herself, this is exactly what you do not want, so a prudent skipper shouldn't even contemplate it. However, suitable craft can lie ahull with reasonable safety, as long as the waves are not so steep and high that capsize is inevitable for any vessel at all. Many have done so without coming to harm. Given enough wind on the mast to steady the boat, things are less uncomfortable than you might imagine. For a long-keeled yacht of substantial displacement and moderate beam, leeway may not prove so shocking either.

Although lying ahull can provide a viable answer for the right vessels suffering too much wind to carry canvas and heave to, the inevitable beam-on aspect renders them more vulnerable than other techniques. As soon as the weather moderates sufficiently for something to be done to bring the boat away from beam-on, action should be taken.

Helm position

Lying ahull, it's always tempting to lash the tiller to leeward (wheel to weather) to encourage the boat to lie with her head closer to the wind. Unless the steering arrangements are completely invulnerable, this is not necessarily a good idea. I can verify that when a boat's head is knocked away to leeward by a wave, she begins sailing under bare poles and, as she gathers way, the rudder causes her to round up on the face of the next wave. She now stalls near the top almost head-to-wind, to be thrown backwards on to her steering gear.

The best outcome is that linkages or tillers are broken. The worst is loss of the rudder itself. Risk to the rudder must be weighed against spending more time beam-on, but my study wall is adorned with a fine ash tiller snapped like a carrot by making this mistake on a nasty night. I have since secured the helm amidships and found it a safer option.

Further reading

A general book like this can only go so far on any subject. This chapter represents a digest of modern thinking assessed in light of my own experience. If you feel a need of further commentary on serious weather, I recommend that you read Peter Bruce's *Heavy Weather Sailing*, Steve and Linda Dashew's *Surviving the Storm* and Lin and Larry Pardey's *Storm Tactics* and *Heavy Weather Cruising* by the author of this book. You will then be thoroughly educated and in a strong position to make a sound decision based on solid material.

For a boat that will do it in any conditions, heaving to is the best way of defusing a nasty situation. Here, the author's Mason 44 heaves to on a breezy day under reefed main and staysail, pointing around 45° to the wind.

16 IN HARBOUR

Anchoring and mooring

The bower anchor

Techniques for berthing alongside vary with the conventions and docking arrangements of the country you are visiting. Anchoring and mooring are, so to speak, the same the whole world over. Anchoring, in particular, is the ocean sailor's speciality. After all, who wants to pay to lie in a hot, public, airless marina when they could be a hundred or two yards offshore, free of charge with a good dinghy alongside, total privacy and the trade wind keeping them cool?

Magazines publish learned articles from time to time on the scientifically tested relative merits and downsides of numerous anchor types. It isn't for me to cast doubt on their findings, but the real-life fact is that once you're out there, what matters is a decent anchor of some sort, well dug into good holding ground on a long scope of heavy chain or an even longer one of springy nylon. Chain is probably better in most circumstances. It doesn't chafe and a relatively modest length confers equivalent holding to a far longer scope of rope. For some boats, however, it is too heavy, so they will opt for some chain to attach to the anchor, then lots of beefy nylon.

The nature of the human condition is that we all love what we have, so these sailors will preach that nothing holds like a nylon rode. The chain gang will shake their heads sadly and lay out another five fathoms of scope. The man with a CQR anchor, developed before the Second World War for flying boats, will swear it has never been bettered, while the recent purchaser of a Spade will assure you that since he bought it he's never looked back.

Readers might be shocked to learn that when I acquired my 1911 pilot cutter *Hirta* displacing 35 tons, she came equipped with 45 fathoms (that's about 85 metres to you) of half-inch (12½mm) chain and a 1cwt (50kg) fisherman dated 1891. Any empirical test from recent years will assure you that the man who anchors with a fisherman is doomed to drag, but in 15 years that wonderful hook never budged. I almost never had to lay out a second anchor and I sat out some nasty

> ## THE BOTTOM LINE IS THIS:
>
> - Ship the biggest hook you can manage as your bower.
> - If you are going with chain, don't be tempted by anything lightweight, such as manufacturers may try to supply.
> - Kit out with the longest length you can stow with the weight you can bear, then buy a powerful windlass to handle it.

nights in all sorts of holding. It set as well in tropical white sand as it did in muddy old clay back home. So impressed was I with this ground tackle that when I commissioned *Westernman*, another pilot cutter, but smaller at 22 tons, I ordered a hand-made 85lb (40kg) fisherman to the same design and backed it up with a similar length of $^7/_{16}$ inch (11mm) chain. The results were gratifying. In 12 years it never, ever dragged.

Now I'm not recommending that yachts should all be equipped with monster fisherman anchors, which can be the devil to handle and stow, plus a weight of chain that trims them down by the head. I mention this to make the point that it doesn't pay to listen to too much prejudice.

My current 44-footer *Constance* has 45 fathoms of $^3/_8$ inch (9.5mm) chain, a 65lb (30kg) Bruce anchor on the stemhead and a reliable, but modestly powered, Maxwell Nilsson electric windlass on a vertical shaft. It all works wonderfully.

Ground tackle is the most important item of safety equipment on board by a country mile. Seen in that perspective, it's not expensive either. If I were down to my last thousand pounds, I'd rather spend it on ground tackle than a liferaft.

Additional anchors

■ Hurricane hooks

Back in the days of unreliable engines, offshore yachts would often carry four anchors. For most of us today, this is over the top, unless you choose to stow a monster 'hurricane hook' down in the bilge. There's nothing wrong with this. In fact, it's a good plan, as long as you remember the advice of Uffa Fox, who observed that the only place to stow weight on a boat is below the centre of gravity. You'll probably never use this hook and to be any use on, say, a 40-footer, it is bound to weigh at least 100lb, so it really must be down in the bilge somewhere, ideally amidships. If the boat has no usable bilge, that knocks the hurricane anchor on the head.

■ Kedge anchors

All serious boats must have at least one secondary anchor, which, on a sensible scope of rope or, ideally, further chain, will hold them in a gale of wind. Should the bower be lost, this one provides immediate on-board backup. It also serves as an extra when conditions are so bad that laying out a second pick seems like a good idea. It makes sense for this one to be a different type from the bower. It also is a 'must' that it can be lowered into the dinghy with a long length of chain, or rope, for distant deployment. If the yacht runs aground in a tideless area and can't be motored off, the next course of action is to lay out the kedge as far away as practicable, lead the rode to the windlass and heave her off, ideally the same way she went on.

A third, smaller anchor is useful for heaving the stern up to a swell running into an anchorage, for example, to ease rolling. It's also useful as a kedge for bow-to anchoring in easy conditions in places like the Baltic. A favourite for this job is a lightweight, high holding-power Fortress with wide flat flukes that can be stowed in a cockpit locker.

Anchoring technique

■ Scope

With suitably heavy chain in secure holding, a scope of 4:1 measured from the bow roller to the seabed is adequate for most boats in most weather, especially in deeper water. Three to one can work fine for heavier boats that lie quietly due to a deep forefoot. Boats with no appreciable forefoot that skitter around on gusty days will be better off with longer scopes and anyone anchoring mainly on rope must reckon on 7:1 or more. When things start to cut up rough, just lay more and more scope. After all, the cable isn't doing much good in the locker and, as long as you have a windlass, retrieval presents no issues. Unless the roadstead is crowded and the guy downwind of you has an ugly mien and doesn't look like letting go another foot of his chain, why not lay out the lot and sleep easy?

■ Setting the bower anchor

Having settled on a suitable spot in the anchorage, the next job is to make absolutely sure that the anchor is set. To be certain of this, I typically stop the yacht under power at the point I want the hook to be. I then begin laying out cable as the boat blows away. Soon she's lying beam-on and trundling downwind merrily as she lays her chain in a nice straight line. If there's no wind, I motor slowly astern.

Once I have laid the scope I've decided on, the windlass is snubbed and we watch her slowly round up head to wind as the anchor takes a tentative nibble at the bottom. As soon as the situation stabilises, I put the engine slow astern and watch a transit abeam of me. She will start out by moving downwind. As the hook takes a better grip, she loses all way and actually starts to spring back up to windward by virtue of the weight of the cable. At this point, I tickle her astern once more until she has taken up the chain, before applying considerably more power astern. Nine times out of ten, she moves a little, then sticks tight.

If she can stand all that power, it's going to take an awful lot of wind or wave to shift her, so I pour myself a well-earned sundowner and settle down to watch for the elusive green flash.

■ Anchor weights

When you're short of scope because of a crowded anchorage, or are expecting a serious blow and have already laid out all your cable, a heavy weight lowered down towards the seabed improves the catenary, damps snubbing, and generally helps out. Such things can be bought from good chandleries. If the chandler has never heard of one, don't darken his doors again. Mine is called a 'Chum'. I've had it for years and every now and again it has assured me a sound sleep. For a practical demonstration see the author's YouTube video at https://youtu.be/ZPskVtblrfg. A modern brand is the New Zealand 'Anchor Buddy'.

If you don't want to spring for a 'bought one', you can knock one up for yourself by using a giant shackle, a length of rope and some suitable weight; 50kg is useful for a 45ft boat. There is, of course, the unpleasantness of having to handle such a brute. The wonder of the real 'Chum' is that the weight comes in the form of four or five lead 'biscuits', which are slipped on to the device one by one. What a joy.

■ Storm anchoring

The huge benefit of most ocean anchorages when set against the places many of us must anchor in tide-swept northern Europe is that tidal stream is rarely an issue. This simplifies storm anchoring wonderfully.

I hear people talking about rigging two anchors on the same length of chain in tandem and, like most matters appertaining to anchoring, I don't doubt it works for them. To me, it always sounds fraught with potential problems. An easier way of deploying an extra pick is to bring the dinghy round to the bow and lower in the second anchor. If this comes with a fair length of chain, lower that in too, because you'll never drag it across the seabed. Now row or motor away upwind on a course approximately 40 degrees from the angle of the main bower cable, easing out the chain as you go.

If this anchor is on rope only, or rope with a short length of chain to assist setting and protect against seabed chafe, you can safely have a hand on the bow pay out the rope as you move away. Go as far from the boat as the cable allows, then dump the hook over the side, making sure it doesn't foul your clothing and drag you down with it to Davey Jones. You'll have sailed too far by this time to end your days like that.

All that remains is to set the anchor from on board. The scope should be so huge that a strong hold should go without saying. With two anchors set like this, I generally heave on the rope cable until the catenary of the chain on the bower drops a little. Both anchors are now holding and taking their own share of the load. As long as the wind doesn't shift too far, you are now as near bulletproof as you can be.

■ Steep-to anchorages

All over the world there are anchorages deeper than we'd like. The problem is often that we can get a hook in near the shore in 40–50ft, but if we swing with the stern to the ocean rather than the beach, we just don't have enough scope. This is because the bottom is now running 'downhill', and an anchor needs a lot more scope on a downhill slope than it does the other way round. It stands to reason really, doesn't it?

The answer is often to drop the hook close in, so that you end up with a safe scope of 4:1 or 5:1, then run a line ashore to a handy rock or a tree. Heave this in over the stern and the yacht is safely moored. She won't blow out to sea, that's for sure, and the anchor is well set on a secure, uphill slope with a reliable scope of chain.

■ Snubbing

Chain, wonderful as it is, carries two inherent problems. It snubs up tight under snatch load, which can pull out even a well-set anchor, and it is noisy in a bow roller as the boat swings around. Both issues are dealt with by a snubber. A snubber is a length of nylon rope with a chain hook on the end that can be snatched on to the bight of the cable. Failing a hook, a rolling hitch will do, but a hook is so much neater.

A snubber should be long enough to let more scope out and allow the snubber to run with it. Otherwise, when more cable is needed in a hardening wind, the first thing you'll have to do is shorten it in order to retrieve the snubber. Ideally, 40–50ft works well.

An anchor-snubber working well.

Once the anchor is set, hook the snubber to the chain outboard of the stem head and lower away another 10ft or so. This carries the hook below the surface. The snubber can then be hove up so that the chain lies in a bight and the snubber is taking all the load. It is led in through a fairlead or the other-side bow roller and cleated off.

Where the load on the anchor is such that heaving up the snubber is an unattractive option, pre-measure it, secure it inboard and lower it away with the cable. When the snubber comes up short, keep surging chain until there's a loop under the snubber. Job done.

Long lines

Every deep-sea voyaging yacht should carry one or two extra-long lines of serious dimension. Nylon is favoured. These have obvious uses in extreme weather when you may opt to trail warps. That apart, you may not use them for years, then one day, something unforeseen happens and nothing else will do. They can be deployed to lengthen an anchor cable, if the boat has to be anchored in exceptionally deep water, or in conditions so extreme that all the scope you have is demanded, and then a load more.

I once used mine in Arctic Norway when a gale-force katabatic wind off a mountain glacier started to rip the pontoon to which I was lying away from its moorings. I could barely stand in the wind, but managed to battle my way ashore with my monster rope. I tied it round a tree, which didn't pull out by the roots, and brought my end back to my Samson post. The rope saved the pontoon and with it my boat, plus one or two others as well.

Mooring

While anchoring remains the essence of free ocean cruising, mooring buoys are appearing more and more frequently in anchorages, where once we could all lie at peace, secure on our own ground tackle. I cannot speak of the Pacific in recent years, but the Caribbean is certainly becoming infested by this menace. Moorings always seem to spring up in the best places, leaving the anchoring yacht to fend for herself way out in the open. However, what can't be cured must be endured, so here, for what they are worth, are a few thoughts.

▪ Reliability

Moorings in far-flung places are often not serviced in the way the visitors' buoys are in a professional harbour in Europe, North America or Australia/New Zealand. The first assumption

Securing the stern to the shore while anchored off. Note the chafing arrangements rigged in an area where this sort of thing happens a lot.

must be that, unless you can see numerous well-run yachts lying to them on a windy day, they are poorly maintained and cannot be relied upon. If the water is shallow and warm enough, of course, you can always pick one up, then dive to check it out. Otherwise, treat them at least with a degree of suspicion.

■ Coral seabeds

Sometimes moorings will be laid that enable yachts to visit areas in which anchoring is discouraged or even banned in order to protect vulnerable habitats. You can expect to pay for these, as you can for most others, although the seabed is sometimes merely a pretext for finding another way to milk the cash cow.

■ Securing to moorings

As with most things, methods of securing to mooring buoys vary with buoy and place. Occasionally, a long mooring pennant will be left floating for passers-by to pick up. Very nice too, if it's clean. Often, however, a buoy will just have a steel ring to which you are expected to secure. Sometimes, this can be a wire loop with some sort of plastic protection against chafing. Typically, people secure to these by passing a mooring line through them and bringing it back on board, then lying to the bight. If they are worried about their safety, they pass a second line the same way as the first.

You've probably gathered by now that I don't like shouting the odds about how to do things, but here I make an exception. To lie moored to a slip rope, or even two slip ropes, is rank bad seamanship. The bearing surface where they pass through the eye on the buoy is minimal and they will saw away all night long under cover of darkness, chafing their expensive little hearts out. I've seen an 18mm line chafed through in a single night.

To prevent this happening, there's no need to unshackle the anchor and lie to chain, unless really serious weather is around the headland. All you need do is pass the slip rope, then heave it up very short so you can reach the buoy from the bow. Now pass a second line through the eye and round again to form a full round turn. Bring the end back over the bow and tie a very long bowline. Ease away on this and the slip rope to fall back from the buoy and lie to the bowline, which has triple the bearing area. The eye end, because it is secure, will not chafe at all. Let the slip rope go slack, but keep it on as a catch-all.

When you leave, heave up on the catch-all slip rope, taking the load off the bowline to untie it. Because the loop is so long, you won't hurt your back reaching down to it. This leaves you lying to the slip rope, which you can let go neatly at your leisure.

Tenders

Many cruising yachts spend longer at anchor than they do at sea. The tender and its means of propulsion is therefore a critical part of the path to happiness. Notice that both are mentioned in the same sentence. That's because, like chips, salt and vinegar, you really can't consider one without the other.

Hard dinghies

Time was when everyone rowed or sailed their tenders, but that was in the days when inflatables hadn't been thought of and cruisers were traditional boats. Traditional boats usually had enough clear deck space to stow a hard dinghy, and hard dinghies can be rowed or sailed properly. Modern yachts like mine, with their decks cluttered with ropes led aft, skylights, hatches, powerful vangs and the rest, simply cannot ship a solid boat. There isn't room.

Having tried both ways extensively, I'd say this is a pity. On my pilot cutters I had stem dinghies that could be launched in a minute or two from a standing start, ready to take me ashore or lay out a kedge in an emergency. A sailor gets ashore with a dry bottom in a hard dinghy, which is a massive plus. One designed for load carrying can hump a lot of groceries. If it's not too smart it's unlikely to be stolen and you don't have to worry about it against a rough dock. Above all, it can be rowed, which frees the owner of the wretchedness that can be the outboard. Outboards will get an airing in a few paragraphs, but remember, if you have a suitable dinghy the whole question never arises. And don't think I am a hopeless reactionary living on Planet Zorb. I cruised for 30 years with no outboard, using a series of good dinghies. My 40-footer had a superb clinker-built pram designed by none other than Nathaniel Herreshoff. The 50-footer used a fibreglass boat with a sharp stem. The 32-footer carried a nutshell clinker punt. Any of them could have been fitted with a simple tie-on leeboard and a lug sail, but we never bothered.

Rowing takes time and has some limitations on range, but it is totally reliable and, unless the rower dies on the job, it never breaks down. It also keeps you fit. No explosive outboard fuel need be carried, and no back-breaking outboard humping takes place. Launching and recovery are simply contrived using a halyard of some sort, but hard dinghies can be fairly heavy, so dragging them up beaches can be an issue.

GENERAL POINTS

- A yacht's tender should, ideally, be able to carry all her crew, plus a few cases of rum, a sack of potatoes and a hand of bananas.
- It must be readily hoisted aboard and lowered to the sea, which means it must have good strong lifting points, together with strops where necessary.
- Unless small and readily flipped, it needs a drain to let the water out.
- A robust outboard attachment point is a must, unless you intend to row.
- If the latter, it has to have serious oars and rowlocks and, in any case, all dinghies have to be equipped with alternative means of movement if they rely on outboard power. This often consists of Mickey Mouse paddles masquerading as oars in Toytown rowlocks on the sides of an inflatable. Make sure yours work before relying on the motor in a stiff trade wind.
- Towing dinghies around in cruising grounds is common practice, so the little boat must tug along easily. It needs a strong point to secure a long painter and another to attach to a wire strop by which you will secure it, complete with padlock, to the boat or the dock in areas of known banditry. Having the yacht's name indelibly marked on it isn't a bad scheme either.
- Another technique for securing the dinghy against thieves and keeping it generally safe is to hoist it alongside the yacht overnight. A spare halyard does the lifting and the boat is secured fore and aft to stop it banging around.

Hoisting the dinghy on a spare halyard is good for security and keeps the bottom clean.

Given the deck space, I'd go for a hard dinghy every time. Now that I'm not the youngest man in the anchorage, I might even add an electric motor to my inventory, but for me those days are done. The decks on my Mason 44 just can't accommodate a dinghy big enough and I'm not about to sully her lovely counter with davits, so it's a blow-up job from now on. There's a surprise benefit, though. Occasionally, one has no choice but to land through surf. In a hard dinghy of any weight, this is potentially dangerous. An inflatable that is not a RIB is less likely to deal you a shrewd blow on the head if you are seriously upset. It may also be lighter, so that as you jump out thigh deep and grab it, it's a lot easier to pull to the beach.

Inflatable dinghies and RIBs

Look at a crowded dinghy dock in a mainstream tropical anchorage and you'll see far more inflatables than anything else. Big yachts and charter boats will probably have rigid inflatable boats (RIBs) with a hard bottom and inflatable tubes for stability, comfort and to keep the spray out. RIBs are wonderful things. Given a suitable outboard they can plane, so they get you there fast and can have long range. A good one can also handle at least some degree of rough water. They can carry plenty of cargo and are, in many ways, the perfect solution in the modern world.

Unfortunately, they have a number of disadvantages. The greatest of these is just the same as the hard dinghy. They demand space on deck to stow. Davits might seem a likely option, but people who have experienced a big wave breaking clean over a boat tend to form other conclusions. Davits are great on the cruising ground. They are less suitable in the North Atlantic. Notwithstanding this factor, a surprising number of modest-sized yachts manage to stow a small RIB somehow, with the foredeck as a common option.

The great thing about a hard dinghy is that anybody can row it. This chap's dad can cover a mile or two without breaking a sweat or troubling the outboard.

If you can't cope with a RIB and a hard boat is out of the question, you are stuck with some sort of straight inflatable. Soft, flat floors are hopeless and while slatted wooden floors have their attractions, they do not offer any lateral stability in crosswinds, so tend to blow around. The most common solution is a 'high-pressure inflatable floor' (HPIF) type with a blow-up keel to give a deep vee-shaped entry. Like a RIB, these are only realistically driven by a motor, but this is true of most of today's tenders. HPIF boats are popular and I have one myself. It's lighter than a RIB to drag up a beach or lift aboard and it can be rolled away and bagged at sea, but of course it is more vulnerable to damage, so users need to be dab hands with the puncture repair kit. All in all, a solid, sensible compromise.

Outboards

Unless you are lucky enough to be able to ship a proper hard dinghy, you are going to need an outboard motor. Power, and hence weight, will depend on your dinghy, but also on your own aspirations. Do you intend to race around the planet at 20 knots or are you content to shuffle along at walking pace? Most of us settle for something in between and outboards reflect this.

A big outboard is fine, once it's on the dinghy, and even a 40HP two-stroke – if you can still find one – can be started by a fit person using only the pull-cord. The trouble is that two-strokes are outlawed in many countries these days and a big four-stroke may well need a battery to start it. Hmmm. So that's question 1: Can I start the outboard I fancy I'd like? Perhaps more importantly, can my partner start it too?

Any outboard that cannot be operated by both members of a two-person team condemns one of them to an intolerable state of subservience. 'Could you run me ashore, darling?' does not sit comfortably with the sort of independent spirit that goes cruising, so the motor absolutely must be easy to start. This cuts size and power down, but it also reduces fuel consumption. This is good news and not only because of the money saved. No sane person wants petrol, or gasoline, on a yacht at all. If you are stuck with it, you might as well carry as little as possible in, it should go without saying, a sealed, self-draining locker similar to that set aside for cooking gas.

A smaller outboard is also a lot easier to lower to the dinghy and to retrieve on board. A small crane or derrick with a tackle to assist in this potentially expensive task is a big help. Many a back has been 'put out' wrestling with outboards.

■ The electric option

I have now done away with fossil fuel outboards altogether and re-equipped my 10ft HPIF boat with an electric outboard made by the German firm Torqeedo. This will run at slower speeds for several hours, or at higher speeds for shorter times. There's plenty of power to handle strong winds or foul tidal streams and no nasty surprises because it keeps me clearly informed of the state of its power unit. It has a panel with readouts that show how fast the boat is going (via GPS), how long it can continue at this speed and how far this will take it.

The unit strips down easily (no bolts) into three main parts, any of which can be carried by a ten-year-old, then reassembles on the dinghy transom. The battery, which is integral, rather than a separate, heavy item, charges on board without pulling too much from the main bank. My wife can lift it on and off the dinghy singlehandedly and can start it every time. All she has to do is turn the twist grip and off she goes. No dangerous, smelly petrol to buy and store, no grease, no servicing, no heavy lifting, no grief at all. The battery should last for a number of years before replacement.

The motor isn't cheap and it has to be said that its range is not so great as the theoretically infinite distance a conventional outboard can manage as long as you keep feeding it, but I save on fuel and I have a happy time not having to put up with all the 'downers' of the alternatives. And it's quiet, which is a jewel of inestimable price. For me, it is the prefect solution.

If you aren't in a tearing hurry – which an ocean cruiser should not be – a quality electric outboard such as a Torqeedo is the way to go. If you need extra-long range, an additional battery will keep it running at 3½ knots to Christmas and back – and it's so light a child can handle it.

EXTREME EMERGENCIES

17

Extreme emergencies is a subject on which we all hope never to become practical experts. Storm survival, catastrophic gear or hull failure, sudden flooding, mid-ocean collision, fire, piracy and the rest give rise to major stress. Some of these, such as man overboard, are best dealt with by training and, in the modern world, electronic equipment, but you can't train up for all the possibilities of things going badly wrong.

In lieu of a systematic, pre-planned set of actions, the best substitute is general preparation or, at the very least, a sensible knowledge of what the options may be. The five minutes after the mast goes over the side are critical to what befalls a crew over the coming days or weeks. They are not to be squandered scratching heads and wondering what's best to do next. This chapter cannot possibly offer answers for all emergencies. What it can do is mention a few common specifics and attempt to inculcate an attitude of self-help based on a well-prepared, fully equipped boat that has had the misfortune to suffer a major trauma. It's up to every skipper to know the boat and stow enough tools and spares to be able to cope.

Man overboard

The mechanics of this subject for coastal situations are well covered elsewhere, including my own book *The Complete Yachtmaster*. However, out in deep water far from realistic assistance, things are different in a number of respects.

High latitudes

In high latitudes, especially anywhere near ice, a casualty in the cold water has a foreshortened lifespan. As with first aid, informed opinion about how to deal with such matters moves on from year to year, but at the time of writing, US authorities were promoting the '1:10:1 principle'. This concurs with ideas put out by others, including the Canadians, who know a thing or two about cold water. The principle concentrates on the actions to be taken, or not, by the casualty in the water, rather than telling those on board how to get the boat back to him or her.

■ Do not let it happen

Thinking back to one or two hairy moments in my own life, I can testify to the absolute necessity of using a harness when the chips are down. Had someone gone over the wall one dark twilight off Cape Brewster in northeast Greenland with a gale howling off the icecap, growlers and bergs close by, bergy bits tossing around in a 15ft sea and two men wrestling with a tricky reef out in the fog, it would have been down to me to recover them. I didn't fancy the job and was heartily relieved to see them back in the wheelhouse. On a night like that, even with a personal AIS transponder, you probably only get one chance. Much better to make it a good one by clipping on.

1:10:1 PRINCIPLE

1 – *one minute to gain control of your breathing*
When you are precipitated into cold water, the first automatic reaction is to catch your breath. If your face is under water when this happens, you drown, so get a grip and don't open your mouth. After a minute, the tendency to gasp and even hyperventilate usually subsides.

10 – *ten minutes of meaningful movement*
Unless the water is down near freezing point, ten minutes is around what you get to sort yourself out. If your life jacket needs adjusting, your EPIRB has to be triggered, a hood pulled over your face etc., do it straightaway because in ten minutes' time you will very likely have lost sensation in your fingers and will be starting to experience hypothermia. Don't try to swim. Go into the best sort of foetal huddle you can manage in order to maintain what body heat you have.

1 – *you may now have up to one hour before becoming hypothermic and losing consciousness*
Exactly how long depends on age, fitness, water temperature and probably other factors as well, but unless the water is near freezing, it's probably longer than you think. It's important to realise this, because imagining that death is only five minutes away can actually cause people to lose hope and physically give up. Once consciousness is lost, unless you are wearing a life jacket that keeps your head up, you are, to all intents and purposes, a goner.

Downwind passage making

Having taught and examined man overboard techniques for 40 years, I've seen more fudges over the issue of running downwind than I can shake a winch handle at. 'MOB' exercises are usually done from a beat or a reach, only rarely with a booming-out pole set up and a preventer on the mainsail. As for a spinnaker, instructors who tackle that one are worthy of military medals, yet these are the situations that confront the real-life ocean sailor.

Boats making passages with spinnakers set usually have a full crew and can drop the kite in short order. As long as they haven't lost touch with the casualty, their situation is now no different from the student on a Day Skipper course in the Solent. The short-handed yacht under downwind rig with poled-out genoa and perhaps another headsail on her nominal lee side has bigger problems.

The priority, after taking steps to keep an eye on the head in the water, is to get rid of the headsails. Roll them up or drop them straightaway, then put the boat close-hauled under main and start the engine, after first taking a careful look round to make sure no ropes have been kicked over the side. A rope in the prop now could mean a fatality. As with the spinnaker boat, this one is now back on her Day Skipper course, except that she has probably run a lot further downwind of her missing crew than anyone would like.

In a two-up boat, keeping a permanent watch on the casualty with all the other

The author and his shipmates about to steer due north from Iceland trying their survival suits for size.

jobs that must be tackled is unrealistic, so by far the greatest danger lies in losing the person altogether. There is also the nightmare possibility that a lone watch-keeper has somehow fallen overboard and nothing is known until his or her partner comes on deck, bleary-eyed, wondering why they weren't called earlier.

In what are home waters for many of us, a call to the local SAR team on Channel 16 will have a helicopter overhead in no time, but this is not going to happen in mid-ocean. In the past, the only hope was to sail or steam back on a reciprocal course and look out. Today, with equipment available such as a personal AIS SART (search and rescue transponder), which will fix the casualty on the chart plotter as accurately as if they were a navigation buoy, there is every chance of a safe recovery. One of these is really enough for a cruising boat if the budget is already stretched – and which one isn't? It can be passed from watch to watch like a baton. Far out in the tropic night, alone under the stars, its reassuring lump in the pocket will seem the best money you ever spent.

Steering failure
Rudder failure

Every year, a number of yachts on transatlantic passages suffer rudder failure or loss. Not all are able to cope and some have been abandoned. I was once in mid-Atlantic on a 60-footer with a variable-draught rudder whose lower half parted company with us and went to the mermaids. What remained wasn't up to much, but as long as we kept our speed well down and shortened sail we were able to limp the last thousand miles or so. Had we lost the whole

A broken rudder is a big problem, but it doesn't necessarily mean abandoning ship.

thing, I was confident we would manage, because the switched-on owner, recognising the essential weakness in his rudder, had prepared a rudderless steering system that I now know had every chance of working. It didn't attempt to use a spinnaker pole over the stern or, indeed, any sort of jury rudder. Instead, it relied on a drogue, winched from one side of the stern to the other, as required, to provide balance.

If you have a modest-sized boat and the windvane steering has a rudder of its own, such as a Hydrovane or a Windpilot Pacific Plus, you should have no problem reaching port as long as you balance the rig and are prepared to slow down.

Otherwise, especially if you have a spade rudder, it is vital to pre-plan a system and to try it out beforehand. The boat will steer a lot better with the rudder intact and lashed amidships than she will without one at all, but you will at least get the idea and iron out any hopeless features that only trial and error can reveal. Most of today's authorities agree that the drogue system is most likely to succeed, although I once took the lines of a race-boat crew who sailed up to the dock in the US having lost their rudder 500 miles out past the Gulf Stream. These skilled mariners brought her home simply by balancing the rig, but it must be said that she was a thoroughbred.

Wheel-system failure
■ Emergency tillers

Most boats with wheel steering now come with one of these as standard. Experience shows, however, that while the thing may be sitting proudly in a locker awaiting its moment of glory, when it is offered up to do its job, it may prove less than effective. Some literally cannot be turned. One I heard of did not fit its socket. Several slotted in OK, but the shaft was so long and unsupported that when anyone tried to use it, the thing buckled out of line. In this last case, what was needed was a removable bracket to support the shaft – yet another job for something you hope never to use. The others really weren't much good at all.

Some emergency tillers work well, but nearly all require power assistance of some sort. One of my boats was of 22 tons displacement and was tiller steered. She needed tiller lines and a tackle to keep her on the straight and narrow in any sort of a breeze using her main steering system and this was standard on larger yachts back in the day when most used tillers for preference. Operating them wasn't too arduous. You just had to know how.

Tiller lines are usually the answer for emergency units. Some people rig a tackle, in which case it's a job best done before you leave rather than trying to lash it up from the block and string bag in a mid-ocean gale. Others use single lines led to winches. Either way, if all that's gone wrong is a wire off a pulley, your best bet is to heave to, use the emergency tiller to secure the quadrant so you don't lose your fingers trying to put the wire back on, and fix it.

■ Autopilot backup

One of the most charming features of a below-decks autopilot is that, unless it's a lightweight one that drives the wheel in the cockpit, it has a ram acting directly on to the steering quadrant. This means it is independent of the wheel and all its mechanism. If the steering linkages or even the wheel itself are damaged, the autopilot will still steer the boat, as long as everything can move freely. This can be a bonus without price.

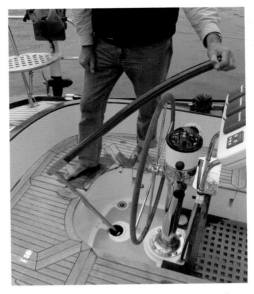

It's by no means rare for an emergency tiller to be unworkable. This one, on a Mason 44, has been well thought out.

Mast loss

The first thing to say about this is that, unless you are on a really long passage such as Panama to the Marquesas, and you manage to get halfway, a cruiser with a useful range under power will be able to motor in, bearing in mind that a range of 1,000 miles at 6 knots could well grow to 1,500 or more at 4½. As with 'man overboard', the first thing to think of before starting the engine after a dismasting is: Are there any ropes over the side?

Even if you have enough fuel to make it to somewhere useful, the motion of a mastless sailing yacht is so awful that rigging some sort of jury sailing rig will be a must, even if it's just to steady her down. If fuel is short, the rig will have to drive the boat, so a downwind destination becomes more than attractive. Obviously, this doesn't have to be the one you set out for originally, which is partly why sailing ship skippers never wrote 'Liverpool to Sydney' in their log books. It was always 'Liverpool towards Sydney'. We can learn much about attitude from these men.

It is beyond the scope of this book even to begin recommending means of setting up jury rigs. Suffice it to say that thinking outside the box always seems to be the answer. A mainsail set on a spinnaker pole mast with its foot as a luff has worked more than once. Trysails suddenly come out of their bags to perform sterling service. Crazy forestays set up from the surviving mizzens on ketches have set low-aspect genoas with their heads tied in a knot to make them fit. The list goes on, but it only works if the yacht has plenty of bulldog wire clips, Dyneema for standing rigging, spare blocks, a box of duct tape rolls, one or two extra bottle screws in the rigging bag, a decent store of shackles and so on. In short, plenty of spares and a skipper or a mate whose mind can move beyond the perfections of the London Boat Show.

Flooding

It has to be said that when the high-water alarm suddenly shrieks its dire message in mid-ocean, it can sap your morale dreadfully. Unless the boat has automatic bilge pumps, the first action is get pumping and see if you are winning or losing. If you're winning – and you usually are – you can now put in some quality time discovering where the water is coming in, after tasting it for salt or fresh, of course. If it's fresh, you are pumping the water tanks over the side. This is good news, because you aren't sinking, but you'll be glad you stowed those extra gallon containers of emergency drinking water. If it's salt, and you aren't aware of any collision, it's down into the bilge to work systematically through the possibilities.

On a fully crewed boat there is much to be said for having a 'flooding plan'. Here, each crew member is encouraged to become expert at one area of the boat. Three people who know the location of the seacocks, the pipes, the plumbing unions and everything else that might fail are far better than one.

Having found the point of ingress, do you have suitable bungs and hammers to hand to deal with it? A bag of assorted softwood bungs is really almost as good as taking the time and trouble to hang the right one by every skin fitting. More to the point, what about the really big holes that can be planned for? Specifically, the rudder stock and the propeller shaft. Stern gland failure can generally be managed by repacking (do you have spare packing if yours is not a drip-free seal?) or, at worst, by caulking it up with some sort of packing string. Wooden boats have oakum or caulking cotton on board, which is ideal. If the shaft falls out altogether, you have a big problem. Stuffing greasy rags down the tube with screwdrivers may get you home, but nothing stops a leak like a softwood bung hammered in hard, then left to swell up as it soaks in moisture.

The rudder-stock gland is another huge hole that can appear just when you don't want it. To lose the rudder is bad enough. To sink because the hole left by the stock could not be bunged for lack of forethought could be described as carelessness. Rudder-stock glands are often above the waterline. Every skipper should know whether this is the case or not and, if not, what sort of head will exist if the shaft is gone. These glands are often tricky to access. A plan of some sort, in the mind at least, could save the ship, leaving her crew free to sort out a jury steering system.

As for major breaches left by collision with debris or, worst of all, a half-sunk container, watertight bulkheads are the best answer by far, but many yachts do not come with these as standard. If you are flooding badly through a gash on one side, tack if need be to get it on the high side, then stuff it with all you can find – sleeping bags or duvets are a favourite. The old trick of 'fothering' with a spare sail or some other collision mat passed under and round the boat may give short-term relief, allowing you to formalise matters to some extent inside. Underwater epoxy, pieces of plywood, self-tapping screws and bolts may help. In particular, shoring up any repair with poles, such as oars stretching across to the other side of the ship and banged into place with the heavy hammer, may staunch the flow sufficiently for the pumps to cope and give the crew a chance of saving themselves. In the end, it will be a matter of taking an iron grip on the natural tendency we all feel to panic when water is coming in under pressure, then digging deep and using all the initiative in the box.

Abandoning ship

Abandon ship anywhere along a civilised coast, or even 200 miles offshore, having given an effective shout on the VHF, DSC or EPIRB you're going to be rescued within 12 hours – probably a lot less. Things may prove different in mid-ocean. Helicopters are out of range, jurisdictions become vague, ships may have to be diverted, there is even the grim possibility that nobody may know you are there.

With this in mind, it pays to understand exactly what you'll find in the liferaft. Whatever it is, it won't be enough, so the next job is to decide on any extras and pack them in a floating grab bag. Now select some water carriers and stow them somewhere that you can't fail to find them in a hurry. Empty a quarter of their contents out to leave a good air gap so that they will float.

The priority is still to maximise chances of rescue, so the number one item in or near the bag is the EPIRB. If you have individual units, keep one in the bag. Grab the hand-held VHF as you step off and make sure it's always been kept charged up. If there's a hand-held Iridium phone on board, take that too. Flares and a powerful LED strobe light can still save the day if the watch on a passing freighter isn't listening to the VHF – and, believe me, under some flags this does happen.

It should go without saying that remaining with the yacht until she disappears below the waves is even more important out here than it is in the English Channel. If sinking seems a probability, launch the raft in good time and, if conditions permit, have someone start to load it up while others try to save the ship until the last minute. A laminated 'grab list' kept in the chart table with the Mayday script is a really sensible precaution, because unless you're infinitely wealthy, a lot of what you're going to need would have to be doubled up to stow it permanently in the bag. The hand-held VHF and the main EPIRB are cases in point. Such a list will make sure that, if you have a few minutes while abandoning, these will be used profitably. The chances of surviving in the raft and of being picked up will then be a lot better.

Because emergencies tend to freeze the brain, everyone should have a job in the abandoning procedure and they should all know what it is before the time comes. If there are more than two in the crew, one can send out the Mayday messages, one could be in charge of the grab bag, another attends to sorting the water cans, while two strong ones deploy the raft and bring it alongside for boarding.

Preparation is everything when it comes to abandoning ship. 'Lifeboat drills' are not generally popular, but on an ocean passage they make a lot of sense. Tackled with a slice of humour, they can even be a useful diversion in fair weather during the first dogwatch when all hands are awake and waiting for their sundowner. If you run a dry ship I suppose you could offer them a nice cup of tea as reward, but how you maintain morale is up to you...

Sea survival course

In the UK, the RYA run courses in sea survival. These cover the use of liferafts and associated safety and distress equipment. Survival techniques both in the raft and free-floating in the

Helicopters have been known to attend rescues several hundred miles offshore. You'll hope never to meet them, but you'll welcome this person with open arms if ever the time comes.

water are studied and practised in a pool. Search and rescue operations are demystified. Absolutely anyone planning on crossing an ocean who wants to live should sign on for this one-day enlightenment, or the equivalent in other countries.

Piracy

If you are determined that a small, on-board arsenal is going to be the best protection against pirates, read the closing section of Chapter 20 for further guidance.

Piracy has been an issue for long-distance sailors as long as I have been out on the ocean. Back in the 1970s, the word was not to go anywhere near Colombia, where drug-runners were coming aboard armed to the teeth, tossing the crew over the side, then using the yacht for a run. Historically, the China Sea has sometimes had areas off-limits, passed by undefended small craft at their peril. At the time of writing, the northwestern part of the Indian Ocean has become a no-go zone with hostage-taking a prime source of income. Even parts of the Eastern Caribbean are well-known for small-time bandits boarding yachts, demanding money and valuables with armed menaces, and occasionally carrying these out with fatal results.

Wherever you sail, there is always the chance you may be unlucky, but, barring the remote contingency of being boarded in a relatively safe place, the only real answer is to give established regions of pirate infestation as wide a berth as possible. Rather than chancing one's luck anywhere near the Horn of Africa en route for Europe or the Americas from the East Indies, for example, it makes sense to round the Cape and head up into the South Atlantic, rather than hack up the Red Sea and traverse the Mediterranean. I've known owners avoid that area by the dire means of putting the yacht on a ship, rather than approach the Gulf of Aden and the aptly named 'Gate of Tears'. Better a hole in the wallet than a hole in the head, you might think.

PART 3 · LIFE ON BOARD

18 CREW

Much of my ocean sailing has been two-handed with my wife as crew. During the 15 years I had my big pilot cutter we generally had at least one extra man on board in addition to me, Roz and my daughter Hannah, who began her voyaging life experiencing pack ice off Cape Farewell at the age of four. On that passage we shipped a crew of four men, all of whom have become lifelong friends, while Hannah is still sailing in her own boat to this day.

In my earlier days I sailed with some larger crews on disparate vessels with varying degrees of happiness, or lack of it, so my own experience of crewing issues, viewed from before and abaft the mast, is fairly comprehensive. I've also watched different boats and seen some crews roistering ashore together after a passage, while others stand like statues with arms folded and suitcases lined up on deck, ready to jump ship as soon as she touches the dock.

Don't discount a powerful sailing boat because you can't do everything singlehanded. If there's crew, it's no bad thing to have work to do.

Compatibility

Couples

If you're a couple you have probably sorted this one out by now. If not, you soon will, one way or the other. Happily, statistics seem to indicate that more couples find their relationship strengthened after a long voyage together than the other way around. Perhaps I'm lucky, but I never had to persuade my wife to go cruising. She was all for it from 'day one'. If one half of a pair is hanging back when it comes to commitment to the project, sort it out before you leave. It may get better on passage, but it may not, and if it doesn't the whole thing will be a bust.

It isn't for me to advise others how to convince their partner to do something they may not initially fancy, but there is often mileage in finding a common cause that involves the boat. My wife hadn't sailed much before we left on our first voyage, but she was a mustard-keen traveller. The boat offered her a means of arriving in far-off places at an affordable rate, and to turn up feeling that, having crossed the ocean blue, and not-so-blue, to be there, she had a right to step ashore with confidence. In due course, she found she really enjoyed making a home on board and finally started to like the sailing too. Now she is the world's best crew and I can't imagine sailing far without her.

Larger crews

I'd say try to sail with people you know well, whenever you can. Drinking mates who sound plausible in the pub can prove an unexpected disappointment when the going turns nasty. Folks with whom you have some history, even if it's only digging a tough hole in the road, have a track record that goes beyond talking, which, as we all know, comes cheap at any price.

Strangers are best avoided unless there's no option, in which case it's down to interview. If things reach this pass, my own experience indicates that it's best to go with gut feeling rather than be swayed by intellectual arguments, even ones that come from yourself. I've seen it time and again. You meet Joe Soap. There's something about him you don't quite like, but the feeling soon passes when you begin talking. Soon, all seems weighted in his favour, so you sign him on. It's only halfway across the ocean when he goes quiet and shifty that you know you've made a mistake. And then you're stuck with the guy for another fortnight, or maybe much longer, because the one thing neither of you can do on a boat, if you don't like it, is step off.

Mankind developed some degree of second sight millennia ago. It's in our cell nuclei. Very likely it happened before our ancestors could articulate more than a few grunts, so we're never going to be able to rationalise it. But those forebears of ours survived against all odds, so they weren't stupid. We ignore the lessons they have left us at our peril. If you aren't sure at first meeting, leave him out!

Commitment to the cause

Perhaps the single most common cause of friction in a yacht is when not everyone on board wants the same outcome for a voyage or a passage. If all hands (or even both hands) are rooting for the same thing, they have the perfect foundation for working naturally together. If one is disaffected, it will show and morale will suffer. In any case, that person will not be having a good time and since he or she is putting up with the same deprivations as everyone else, it doesn't seem fair. If one half of a couple wants to try his luck in Greenland while the other half would rather be sailing the tropic seas, someone will be frustrated and it's not going to be a happy ship. It's vital, therefore, that everyone makes their positions clear at the outset so that the situation can be resolved by negotiation. If that fails, it's probably better if the boat goes somewhere else altogether or one party hops off and leaves the other to it.

A place of their own

Unless the crew is a contented couple, on a protracted passage everyone needs some sort of space they can call their own. Of course, in an ideal world this will be a private cabin, but for many of us in small yachts such luxury must always remain a pipe dream. It's not asking too much, however, that everyone has a locker to stow their gear and a bunk; somewhere they can go off watch and, nominally at least, be private. If they don't have this, people feel cast adrift.

When I had five or six crew on my biggest boat, this was a real problem. Men had to sleep as best they could on saloon berths, others had to try to give them space, a degree of hot-bunking was inevitable, even in good weather, with one man coming off watch and stepping into a space just vacated by his shipmate. It worked, just, but only because the chaps went out of their way to look after one another. They were held together by a strong common purpose and a shared determination in the face of constant bad weather. That, and a lot of 'in jokes'.

Berthing forward of the mast is fine in harbour, but it doesn't generally work at sea, unless the yacht is sailing downwind in moderate conditions. It's just too uncomfortable, especially in a flat-floored yacht that pounds with the wind forward of the beam. This needs to be borne in mind when planning accommodation and how it is to be shared out.

Above: The toys have a place to call their own. Every crew member needs one too.
Below: Get the children thoroughly involved and you'll have crew for life.

Family crews

I've heard it said that the ideal age for children on board is between six and twelve years of age. Having been there as a parent, I can see a lot of sense in this. Of course, younger and older can work well too, but a six-year-old can foster a lively interest in the proceedings, while a committed, switched-on twelve-year-old can learn to take a watch in the right circumstances. Within this age group, most parents with the initiative to set out on such a venture are able to deliver decent on-board formal education, perhaps with the help of a correspondence course.

Find the jobs that suit you best and don't feel constrained to be good at everything. When anchoring, the author works the foredeck and the heavy gear, while his wife drives the boat.

I know that when my daughter first went to school at the age of eight she was well in advance of her peers in all the educational essentials and my wife had managed the whole thing at sea using no more than the sense she was born with and a liberal supply of carefully selected books and visual aids. In areas such as interacting with adults and other children, enjoying the world around her and taking a lively interest in what was going on beyond her own fantasy world, she was streets ahead. Once teenage years approach, examinations loom and further education starts to beckon.

Long-range cruising usually seems to pull families closer together. Inspirations abound, but I have been particularly taken with a short, very non-professional video (youtube.com/watch?v=WEbeefEkcx8) posted by my friend Leon Schulz from Sweden, who took a one-year sabbatical with his wife and two children and wrote a book about it called *The Missing Centimetre.*

Men and women

Here's an area that a writer considers at his peril. So much politics and misinformation has arisen since I first went to sea that what some would call sexual stereotyping has become the truth that dare not speak its name. I promise you, I am not a sexist. I know and respect many women who are as good as or better skippers than their male counterparts. If you're a lady and that's what you want, good luck to you. You have my full support and I'd be happy to serve under your leadership, but let's have no nonsense either.

My wife Roz and I worked out how we operate best many years ago by trial and error and we have never had cause to doubt our judgement. I run the deck most of the time, I tend to look after the machinery and to navigate. Roz does most of the cooking, victualling and any teaching that may be required. She also makes most of the decisions about changes to the accommodation, lighting, décor and all those areas that create a home rather than a machine from a boat. Strategic decisions are taken together.

That being said, her helming and general performance on deck are terrific, her forbearance when things go badly is far better than my own and, if I drop dead, she is more than capable of bringing the ship to a safe haven. As for me, I can sweep out and clean the heads with the best of them, my bacon sandwiches are much admired and some brave hearts have sailed many miles to share one of my 'force ten' curries.

In other words, Roz and I are, to some extent at least, interchangeable, but in times of plain sailing we concentrate on what each does best and enjoys doing the most.

We brook no nonsense about trying to boil it down into one and the same creature, because we aren't. I'm stronger than Roz; she has more stamina. She cooks better than me; I'm a professional navigator. I love handling a boat from the helm; she'd rather work the lines, which is a good thing because she's a lot more agile than I am when it comes to hopping ashore, and the way we operate a boat in harbour, nobody has to pull a mooring rope much at all.

But we switch roles when it makes sense. For as long as I can remember, I have worked the foredeck when anchoring. Roz drives the boat. This dates back to the days when we had no windlass and someone had to manhandle a 35lb CQR and an awful lot of heavy chain on a boat with no engine. That had to be me and the job stuck. Today, we have a windlass and a self-stowing anchor. We never have to touch the hook at all. In normal use, Roz could deal with the sharp end just as well as me now, but we have settled into jobs with which we are comfortable and we work really well as a team.

The bottom line of this rant is: Do what you really want to do, not what some politically correct idiot is trying to force you into. Suit yourself. You're the boss, after all.

Watch systems

I don't want to write too much about this subject because, to be frank, there is any amount of informed opinion out there about the best way to tackle it. I have crossed oceans with full crews working the ancient system of sail – 'four hours on, four off' and two two-hour dogwatches between 1600 and 2000 so that the watch rotates each day. This works as long as the watches sort out their own timetable, perhaps with one on deck, while his watch-mate takes a nap or reads down below, ready for the call should it come. Others with a full crew like to work 'three on, six off' to get a longer watch below. This makes sense if there are enough of you, and no dogwatches are needed to keep things changing round each day.

Two-up, I favour 'three on, three off' during the 12 hours of nominal darkness, then no system at all for the 12 daylight hours, allowing either sailor to catch up on sleep while the other looks out, according to need and conscience. Three-up, this works even better, because you can lower the hours on watch to two. 'Two on, four off' sees the night out with miraculous ease, as anyone will agree who has stood the torture of the sort of solo five-hour watches I once suffered in charge of a 500-ton coasting ship while the skipper slept out his watch below. By contrast, two hours passes so fast you are calling the next watch almost before you have achieved any night vision.

For this reason, in bad weather, Roz and I sometimes cut our watches to two hours on and two off. If it's awful, there have been times when an hour has been all we can take, but catnapping for every other hour can lead rapidly to exhaustion. Fortunately, really shocking

Any watch-keeper on my boat who doesn't wake the next crowd with a mug of tea doesn't get asked again.

weather doesn't often last long enough for that to happen. When it does, we have been hove-to long since and we're back to three-hour watches once more.

Passing the time

I don't know if it's a factor of advancing age, but these days I rarely find time dragging its heels on my three-hour watches. I navigate, I sail the ship, I think about the passage, I contemplate the stars and I write up long screeds in the log book. I brew coffee, I lash up a bit of a meal from dinner's leftovers, and I watch out for ships if there are any, which generally there aren't. The time flies by, and the last 15 minutes are taken up with making tea for my mate so that it's ready to drink when she gets the call. Failure to offer a brew as you hand over and brief the new watch is a hanging offence on my boats.

Of course, there will always be finger-waggers saying 'he loses his night vision every time he switches on the light to read his book', but we live in an imperfect world. On balance, it's better to be awake and lively with vision to a small extent impaired than it is to be half-asleep with perfect eyesight. I shut my eyes tightly for a minute or so before going on deck after I've had lights on down below. This helps a lot.

Years ago, time crept by more slowly. In those days I'd read for five minutes, shut off the light to get used to the dark, then pop out on deck for a really careful look around and to sniff the air. Then I'd go below again, and so on. It worked well and kept me awake. I once read *War and Peace* crossing the Atlantic. I used to write, too.

The main thing is to work out something that suits you and your crew. Not all metabolisms are the same, but I reckon if I get six good hours' sleep in 24 at sea, that's generally enough.

Night orders

The key to proper rest for the skipper is to have confidence that, no matter how much or how little they know, those on watch are in no doubt about when you are to be called. In a boat without radar, or if you're feeling mean with the ampères, the cause will be a vessel on a steady bearing. In any boat it will be a material change in weather or the sky going black to windward. The important thing is that you've made clear those things that concern you and that the message is understood. Finally, of course, there's the catch-all: 'If in doubt, give a shout.'

Your orders can be a simple understanding for a crew of two or even three, but once the numbers start racking up, they ought to be written down so there can be no ambiguity.

However tired you are when you're called out for what ends up to be nothing at all, never be anything but positive. As soon as crew begin to doubt how their call will be received, they'll hesitate – and next time it might be the *Queen Mary* showing red and green dead ahead.

Keeping them happy

With larger crews than a couple, I make a point of everyone delivering log book entries. Some of the ones that have turned up on my boats over the years are hilarious. Making a joke out of discomfort is the best way of dealing with it. When crossing the North Atlantic west-about via the Subarctic, the old boat was leaking so badly going to windward that our theme song became Edward Lear's *The Jumblies*, who, you will doubtless recall, went to sea in a sieve:

> *In spite of all their friends could say*
> *On a winter's morn, on a stormy day*
> *In a sieve they went to sea.*

I turned to one morning at 0400 to find that somebody had entered a verse from further down the text in the 'remarks' column at midnight:

> *When everyone cried, You'll all be drowned!*
> *They called aloud, 'Our Sieve ain't big*
> *But we don't care a button! We don't care a fig!*
> *In a Sieve we'll go to sea!'*

Lying awake later, listening to the clanking of the pumps, I had to laugh. We might be in dire straits, but crew morale was sky high. It carried us through and we arrived in Newfoundland in good order.

If a happy crew needs the sort of team spirit fostered by good humour, regular meals that come up on time every time are equally important. Meals are the punctuation marks of life. If they show up late or are unappetising, people lose the sense of order and morale slides rapidly.

The bad apple

One disaffected crew member can poison things for everyone, so it is critical that the skipper keeps a sensitive eye open for anyone 'going on the blink'. Rather than open mutiny and answering back, the first signs are often becoming uncharacteristically quiet and not joining in the general banter. Most people have an ego of some sort and skippers need to bear this in mind. We aren't running military or merchant ships. There is no establishment to back up a skipper, so Captain Blighs don't get far in yachts.

Discipline isn't about subordination, it's self-imposed and is centred on co-ordination and team effort. When someone seems to be sliding out of the team it will soon affect all hands, so if you can't work out what the problem may be, you really have to take him or her on one side and ask. When you receive the answer 'nothing's wrong', as you probably will, your powers of polite interrogation will be tested to the full, but you have to get to the bottom of it before you can help.

It's natural to assume that the problem lies with you, but it may not be anything to do with the ship at all. Often, it's something on shore. Perhaps a married man is worried about his wife. Maybe he feels guilty about leaving her while he goes off to have fun, or perhaps it's simpler than that and he can't stand the way the cook whistles at his work. OK. Fine. Tell the cook to stop whistling. It's bad anyway and likely to conjure up a gale. Anyone knows that!

Keep a tight ship

There's not much space in a yacht at sea. Once people start dumping gear in the saloon, or leaving stuff lying around in the cockpit, others will begin to feel that 'if we all did that we'd soon be living in a slum'. And they'd be right. Tidiness is vital on a crewed yacht. If you're a couple you'll make up your own minds and far be it from me to interfere with how you live, but where others are concerned, the only way is to keep the lid on.

Try to sweep out every day, have the heads kept like a new pin and so on. Do it and you'll never know how important it is. Leave it out and it's another reason for people to become alienated. Give the devil no opportunities. Use rotas if need be, but maintain a tight ship and be proud of her.

Articles

An old friend of mine from Dublin circumnavigated from South Africa in the 1950s on an ancient Norwegian rescue ship. Before they sailed, her crew of several young men sat round the saloon table and agreed articles. These stated who was responsible for what, who would pay what and when, who was to be skipper, and so on. All this was written down and everyone signed. When signs of friction showed themselves from time to time, as they often will, the friends produced their articles and accepted what they had signed on for. They were all reasonable men and the problems went away.

Serve the ship

I once went to sea with a TV star who couldn't understand that all our lives didn't revolve around serving her needs. It was then that one of the simplest truths about being happy together on board dawned upon me. Here it is. Live by it and you won't go far wrong:

> Our first duty is to serve the ship. If we do that, she will look after us, and because none of us is thinking first about himself or herself, but only about the greater good, we share our main motivation and will live in harmony.

19 HEALTH AT SEA

My first on-board medical kit was supplied in 1974 by a sailor chum who was a veterinary surgeon in his day job. Its contents would have frightened any but the stoutest heart into getting well soon. The laxatives would have moved horses and the antibiotic wound powder recommended for coral cuts came straight from the barn where unfortunate ram lambs had surrendered their tupping tackle in an irreversible session under the knife. A one-litre bottle of udder cream was prescribed for sunburn – it worked a treat – and the final addition was a two-yard red ensign, which, our medical advisor affirmed, would come in useful for covering the bodies of our failures before committal to the safe keeping of Davey Jones.

Primary healthcare at sea is all about eating and sleeping properly, maintaining personal cleanliness, avoiding extremes of exposure to sun and cold, following safe practices on deck and generally employing common sense. It seems fair to assume that anyone in charge of a yacht sailing across oceans can take care of these basics without advice from the likes of me. It's when things go wrong that we all need help.

The very least any skipper should do is undertake a serious first-aid course. This should be followed up by a chat with the local GP or a doctor friend about any preventive immunisations required for the proposed voyage plan. Advice should also be sought over what sort of medicines beyond the usual painkillers and bandages might usefully be shipped. When I sailed away with my vet's medical kit, few of us did more, but things have changed for the better.

Before writing this chapter and bearing in mind my eccentric personal experience of medical issues afloat, I spent time with Dr Spike Briggs. Spike has raced round the world, and now runs MSOS, Medical Support Offshore Ltd. This company delivers training, medical kits and 'telemedical support' for sailors far at sea as well as within wi-fi range of the coast. The whole operation is so thoroughly modern that I was amazed at what can be achieved in a world where total communication is rapidly approaching. Most of this chapter is based on their advice. It would be pointless for me to try to write a potted *Ship's Captain's Medical Guide* in these pages. Instead, I propose to point skippers in the right sort of direction to seek proper professional guidance.

Coming to terms with risk

A yacht with a young adult crew in good health has a fair chance of completing a simple oceanic voyage, such as an Atlantic circuit, without requiring any medical attention beyond what they can manage themselves. If the crew are, say, a couple, who have decided to keep medicines to a bare minimum for reasons of budget (there cannot be any other reason, setting aside the very occasional religious objector), they will have assessed their chances and opted to take the risk.

As soon as crew are signed on from outside the core unit – children, perhaps, or non-family adults – everything changes. I bought my first liferaft in the early 1980s to give my own child and my friends a second chance. I couldn't really afford one and until then my wife and I had sailed without, having come to terms with what this actually meant. In the absence of any radio communication, we weren't going to put anyone else at risk if the ship went down, so we made our choice to take what came, prepared our boat as well as we knew how, and were lucky. As soon as others were involved, this approach became morally untenable. We owed it to our crew to do the best we could within our means.

'The best one can' is, of course, a hard thing to define. When it comes to selecting and equipping boats, none of them are perfect, but with a good tool kit there is much that a creative human can do to fix up problems that arise, so we all must make our own peace with our selection. Our bodies as machines are somewhat different. Many are not young, healthy adults. Even if we are, each of us carries a quantifiable risk of traumatic damage or some malfunction that spirals out of our control.

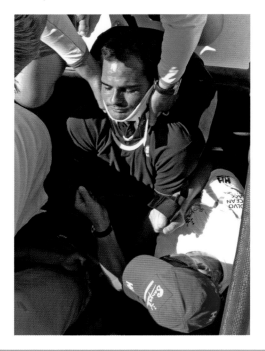

Specific risk management

MSOS advise that in quantifying risk, it's important to understand that on a typical yacht, the chances of needing help are equally split between trauma and illness. This includes hard-driven race boats. On a cruising yacht avoiding extremes of latitude and predictable heavy weather, the balance is likely to move away from trauma, but things can still go wrong when we least expect them.

At age 28, I was thrown against a projection on the mast of my gaff cutter in a squall somewhere north of Cuba. I felt my ribs go. Fortunately, I had just hove in the deep reef and bent on the small jib, so my wife could sail the boat alone without fuss. She sent me below and read the medical book.

In those days, this suggested strapping up the chest and taking complete rest. Strapping proved painful, so I opted for rest alone. I was allowed out only to take sights and set a course for South Carolina, where we eventually arrived in good shape. I reported to a doctor who declared me 'on the mend'; and that was pretty much the end of the matter. The point is that it was a minor medical emergency with two young people. It could have been so much worse.

I suppose that cruise was around 15,000 miles in duration. With two on board, this makes 30,000 crew miles. In addition to the usual cuts, bruises and occasional nasty infections, we had suffered one potentially serious trauma. Based on observational data from professionals, it seems reasonably safe to say that some notable medical incident is likely to occur once in every 10,000 crew miles. An incident demanding external advice will crop up every 100,000. Crew miles, remember, not miles sailed. The need for immediate evacuation is rarer, but it is still quantifiable.

Even if you find these risks acceptable – and plenty still do – setting out without the best medical arrangements you can find leaves you and your crew vulnerable to the chance incident – the fingers dragged into a winch on a black night and mashed, the sudden shooting pain deep inside that says something is seriously wrong, when the boat is a fortnight from the nearest port and so on.

The ship's 'medic'

Just as one person is usually in charge of victualling the ship while another specialises in machinery, every yacht should have a 'ship's medic'. If this is someone with previous experience in first aid or even medicine, this is good news. If not, steps must be taken to train them up. The skipper, too, must have equivalent training, so that if the medic or the skipper is knocked down, there is still somebody who knows what to do when the cook has suffered serious burns and the cabin boy is bleeding to death.

The job of medic is not to everyone's taste and, if possible, a volunteer should be sought from among the cooler-headed crew members. If the crew is only two, both should be trained up.

Options for assistance

At the time of writing, there are two firms specialising in supplying a complete medical package for far-ranging yachts. MedAire (www.medaire.com/yachts) is a US-based company that began with aircraft and has moved into yachting. They are highly professional and are a large organisation. MSOS (www.msos.org.uk) have already been mentioned. Although growing steadily to meet demand, they remain a small, personal group. If you call them up from mid-Pacific, it is not unlikely you will actually know the doctor you are speaking with. Both companies offer a complete range of medical kits, which can be tailored to suit special needs. Both also deliver training courses and telemedical support on a

24/7 basis. Because I have first-hand experience of MSOS I shall describe the way they operate. I don't doubt that for those preferring a big outfit or one that is primarily US-based, MedAire are equally effective.

Commercial requirements and medical kits

Since the 1980s, a yacht operating commercially in any way at all must carry certain medical equipment and her crew are obliged to have passed a course in using it. Kit and course vary between basic first aid and a five-day course in emergency medicine, depending upon distance. A so-called 'Category A' kit is good for worldwide operation beyond 150 miles from a safe haven. 'Cat B' lies between 150 and 60 miles, while 'Cat C' is required for any commercial vessel up to 60 miles out.

If you are taking money from crew beyond a genuine sharing of immediate expenses, it's up to you to contact the MCA, the US Coastguard, or whatever your national authority may be, to find out where you stand. Whatever the situation, MSOS can sort out what you must have to comply with the law.

If you are non-commercial, what you do is up to you. Many people, particularly on larger yachts, opt for the 'MCA' packs on the basis that they provide the same sort of useful guide to best practice as the 'Code of Practice of Small Commercial Vessels' does for the boat and her equipment.

A worldwide medical kit from MSOS, plus a telephone hookup, is about as reassuring as it gets.

Non-commercial kits

MSOS divide their 'amateur' kits into 'Distant Ocean', effectively for yachts going transatlantic or otherwise worldwide, and 'Near Ocean', recommended for voyages to closer areas that remain remote, such as, for Europeans, Spitsbergen, western North Africa or the North Atlantic islands. They also produce a lighter-weight kit for short-handers and singlehanders called an OSR kit. They produce specific options for fully crewed race boats or adventure yachts. Specialist requirements are taken care of by add-ons such as paediatric kits and additional equipment for divers, which might typically include an oxygen kit.

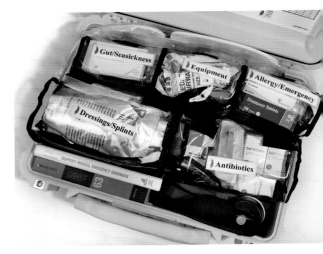

An MSOS medical kit thought out by doctors with real deep-sea experience.

■ Make-up of a medical kit

All MSOS kits are packed in yellow, airtight, watertight Pelicase boxes. These are so effective that kits coming in late for service at three years old often still smell like a well-run hospital when opened. Kits in zip-up bags have invariably fared a good deal worse.

The contents of a kit from MSOS or MedAire are arranged on a modular system based on body organs or specific areas such as skin repair. The MSOS system is founded on feedback from crews who've had to use it for real. It has proved intuitive. Kits are not cheap, but neither are medicines, and in order to maintain the stocks needed, providers are legally obliged to use expensive, climate-controlled storage facilities.

In an ideal world, the 'medical chest' should be serviced annually, but this obviously doesn't always happen. The doctors are aware of some level of inevitability and do their best to plan accordingly. Taken as part of the big picture, the cost of service is by no means high.

The system

The MSOS recommendations for total medical care involve a three-stage operation: training, medical kit and telemedical support.

Training

Assuming you are opting for something more than the minimum first aid course in your village hall, which probably concentrates more on road traffic accidents than near-drowning and hypothermia, the professionals offer brilliant courses for our specific needs. If you plan to

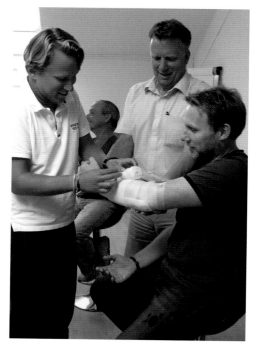

Doctors at MSOS show how it's done.

sign up with, say, MSOS, it makes total sense for skipper and medic to go on one of their courses. The minimum is one day, but three- or five-day versions are more useful if you plan to be far from assistance. Courses are organised so that where possible a dozen or so sailors can get together. If you have a big-enough crew, they'll come to you.

Medical kit

Training with the gear you will be using is an obvious benefit. You can take the kit without the training, but, given the gravity of looking after the human machines, you can see that course and kit go together like fish and chips.

Telemedical support

This is where today's sailors are in a different place altogether from yesterday's. I've been out on an evening with Dr Spike when his phone has rung. If the caller's number starts with 88, it's Iridium and it's going to be a client. He's on the case there and then. Ideally, if it's not a dire emergency, the doctors like an email and, if possible, a picture or two as well. That gives the patient or his shipmates time to gather thoughts about symptoms and it gives the doctors time to reflect on likely outcomes. Satphone is by far the most common way of speaking with a doctor today. It is still possible to patch through via SSB, but this hardly ever happens. Non-speech comms via basic email can also work.

Having a real doctor when you need one, even if he or she is 10,000 miles away and is just a calm voice on the phone, is worth every penny the call costs. The price of the telemedical service itself is a reasonable weekly charge.

Medical and disaster insurance issues

This can be a tricky one for far-ranging cruisers and is particularly sticky if, like me from time to time, you are a paid professional skipper. As we all know, basic, non-professional health insurance often comes with bank accounts and the like, but it can pay to do better. The most important area to be sure to look into is that of rescue and repatriation. Some countries have a charming way of making you pay to be rescued once you are safely back on *terra firma*. If this figures high on your risk assessment list, ask your yacht insurance broker how you are fixed because the cost can be ruinous. Not all cheap health insurances cover repatriation, so make sure yours does.

If you're a professional skipper, Fastnet Marine Insurance in Southampton, UK, can help. While you're there, ask about personal indemnity insurance as well. Both are hard to come by elsewhere.

Written guidance

If, in spite of the advice given here, you decide to go it alone on matters medical, I strongly recommend that you buy a copy of Spike Briggs' book written with his colleague Dr Campbell Mackenzie. The *On-board Medical Emergency Handbook* is streets ahead of anything else I have seen. It tackles this unpopular subject in a clear, graphic manner with flow diagrams for many common situations. Traumas and illnesses are both covered, all drawn from practical experience of being at sea, as well as years of putting broken bodies back together. Buy it and read it from cover to cover more than once. You owe it to yourself and your crew.

A nasty injury doesn't always spell the end of a cruise. The author once completed a two-handed ocean passage with broken ribs and here is seen nursing a damaged ankle.

20 BUREAUCRACY

Bureaucracy is a fact of life. It can be a major nuisance, but there's no avoiding it. It's another case of 'groan you may, but go you must'.

Ship's papers

Essentially, the rule is: If it looks like a document that someone might one day ask for, take it. The following are certainly files that must go into the briefcase. They should be originals, not copies, and they must be in date:

DOCUMENTS

- Registration
  The nature of this will vary with nationality. In the UK it is either a laminated copy of the boat's entry in the Small Ships Registry (SSR) or the so-called 'Blue Book' that comes with 'Part 1' registration. Note that SSR certificates go out of date after five years and must be renewed.
- Bill of sale/proof of ownership
- VAT-paid evidence
- Radio licence, ship and personal, with EPIRB etc. all accounted for.
- Passports and visas
  Note that some zones such as French Polynesia may want these to have at least six months of life left in them, so keep them well in date.
- Certificates of competence
  Often not technically required, but some sort of certificate is well worth carrying. The EU 'International Certificate of Competence', which is very easy to acquire, is often more

useful than my RYA/MCA Ocean Yachtmaster Examiner's ticket. Of such is the mind of the bureaucrat.

- Crew lists
  Most authorities ask for a crew list. Make one up in columns with a box for 'skipper' or 'crew'. Add more columns for date of birth, place of birth, passport numbers, and have numerous copies to hand. It saves a lot of time.

- Insurance documents, for boat and crew
  As to the latter, you might imagine that what you do about health is between you and your God, but some authorities disagree. See opposite page for further comments on boat insurance.

- An up-to-date log book of your voyage
  There is no need to invest in a 'bought one'. An exercise book properly filled in with times, positions, crew aboard, etc. is fine, but do keep this up to the minute. It may be asked for at any time.

When a RIB-full of officials arrives alongside, it's reassuring to be confident of your paperwork.

Note also the following:

If you carry a liferaft, some countries, including those attached to France, may demand that your service certificate is up to date.

The same can go for flares. Believe it or not, France has declared out-of-date flares to be illegal, so the old philosophy saying 'flares that are in good physical condition but a year or two out of date always work so you might as well carry twice as many' is now no more. Carry them by all means, but be aware that some chap with a clipboard may not like it.

A recent printout of a bank statement can be useful for convincing officials that you can buy a ticket home. It may also help prove you are who you say you are for acquiring visas.

> Nothing impresses a certain type of official more than a flamboyant ship's stamp, so if you are of the extrovert tendency, get one made up and stamp such things as crew lists. It goes down well in some quarters.

Insurance

Depending on deductibles and other details, full hull insurance for worldwide cruising could set you back with a big hit. This can be so heavy that sailing uninsured is still considered an option by a surprising number of committed voyagers.

The uninsured boat

If funds are tight, you may be considering going off uninsured. I have done this in my young days on the logic that if the ship were lost, I would probably be lost also and wouldn't care if I saw my money again. Anything less than total loss, I would deal with myself. This was bolstered up by the fact that I was broke and was either going to sail uninsured or I wouldn't be able to sail at all. So, no case to meet. Off I went, and if certain places demanded an insurance certificate, I would just go somewhere else.

After a number of years without troubling the insurance companies, things turned sour when I fell foul of a set of circumstances through no fault of my own that left me with a huge yard bill in the United Sates. The person who ran into my anchored boat had assured me he would pay this, but changed his mind when the work was completed. Had the offer to repair not been made, I'd have managed somehow myself, but now I was faced with an account I had no chance of settling and was in direct danger of having to sell my boat to clear my debts. Insurance would have paid straightaway, then chased the malefactor, leaving me free to carry on with my life. As it was, I lost a year hammering through a court case, which, I am happy to say, I won. All was ultimately resolved favourably, but the outcome could have been a lot less attractive. Since that day, I have always carried insurance.

Third-party cover

Boats can sometimes be big, heavy lumps that can do a lot of damage if things don't work out as we'd have liked with the other boats close by. For many, the ideal scenario would be third-party cover only. Sadly, few if any insurers are prepared to offer this to long-term voyagers. Before setting off uninsured, therefore, we must ask ourselves how we'd feel if we were to do so much damage to someone else that we couldn't pay for it.

Awkward insurance conditions
■ Mandatory insurance

Some places demand insurance before visas are granted, including, at the time of writing, Australia and New Zealand. This is to ensure that the country is not saddled with destitute sailors who have lost their boats and now have nothing. Elsewhere, it may be enough to prove access to sufficient funds to repatriate all on board. In certain countries, nobody cares a fig. It's up to you to find out.

■ Limitations

Some insurance companies suspend cover if a couple opt to undertake an ocean passage two-up, demanding an extra crew person or two to validate cover. You may find this incomprehensible. I do, but that is sometimes the way it is. Find out in good time who you are insuring with and check carefully what conditions may be tucked away in the small print.

The United States

The US is a litigious nation. Healthcare is extremely expensive and third-party incidents can run up horrific bills. If you intend sailing anywhere that falls under US jurisdiction, examine your insurance carefully, then ask your broker if you are covered. Some companies suspend cover in the US.

Clearing customs

The one thing officials in small countries love is to find that all your pieces of paper are in order. This happy state of affairs begins with a clean customs clearance from the previous port. If you don't have the right form, your portion will not be enviable, so you absolutely must get one. Clearance bureaucracy can take a long time in some countries, it can be expensive and inconvenient, but it's their land, not yours, and if you want to stay there you've no choice but to accept it with the best grace you can muster.

On a whistle-stop cruise in the West Indies it can drive strong men to drink, but there's no help for it. Allow half a day, stand by to wear out some shoe leather trudging between offices in the heat, don't forget your crew list, plus all the passports, and hope to be pleasantly surprised.

The backhander

Bribery is an issue that Westerners can find difficult to come to terms with. When I arrived in Brazil in 1975 I was asked to hand over US$50 – a lot of money there in those days – to a man known as a *despachante*. The term translates more or less as 'facilitator', but he was, in effect, a bribe broker who dispensed the loot to those officials entitled to it. I refused to pay, being young and naïve. As days went by, things mysteriously stopped working out for me and I ended up with a short spell in a jail down the coast, from which my wife sprang me by finding the right man and handing over the money.

I learned from my foolishness. When my boat needed hauling and I was told 'tomorrow' on five consecutive days, I bought a bottle of whisky and handed it over to the crane man. He became my new best friend. We were hauled at sunrise the following morning and benefited from true Rolls-Royce treatment.

Of course, with my background as an honest boy from the North of England I don't condone all this, but the fact is that in some countries certain people are hardly paid a living wage and they have to make it up somehow. Everyone understands how things work and it pans out better for everyone if you don't rock the boat. These days, there is less of it around than there was, but it still exists. A $10 bill tucked into a driving licence can save a lot of trouble, and popping one into the passport on a border notorious for corruption may assist progress. The beauty of it is that nobody can accuse you of trying to bribe anyone, because the money could easily have been shoved in there by accident.

The important thing is not to try to bribe a non-corrupt official and the best way to find out how the wind blows is to ask around the waterfront. The cruising community will know how matters stand.

Firearms

Beth Leonard, the American writer, tells us that in her wide experience, around one third of voyaging crews carry firearms. To arm or not is highly contentious and in the end may well depend on how you view the world, your place in it and your fellow men.

If guns make you feel safer, there's nothing I will ever say that will change your mind. It might help to know, however, that I once carried a gun, but experience showed it to be a waste of time and an incubus that could work against me in the very situations where it was most needed. Here's the scoop:

You can't have it when you most want it

Every time you clear into a country you will be asked if you have any firearms. If the answer is 'yes', they will be confiscated and returned when you clear out. If you answer 'no' and hide them away somewhere, you are breaking a serious law and must be prepared to take the consequences if caught. Discovery is unlikely, but should you be boarded and found out, it is likely that you will be thrown in jail and your yacht impounded. If you're lucky, you'll escape with a swingeing fine and a reprimand, but cases are on record of sailors serving six months' hard labour and losing their boats. I have even heard of death sentences being threatened in certain out-of-the-way places.

The irony is that the very time you may feel you need the gun's protection – in a remote anchorage when you are boarded by someone with malice in his heart – you won't have it, unless you are prepared to take some shocking risks. Out at sea, clear of customs and immigration, it will offer cold comfort, but you won't need it a thousand miles from land, unless you are foolish enough to sail pirate-infested waters.

The backfire

It seems more than likely from anecdotal evidence that as many people are killed or wounded by their own firearms as are saved from harm by loosing off a few rounds in the right direction. Examples abound, some famous, of decent people appearing with guns, only to be dispatched by the superior armament of the boarders. More than enough cases exist where boarders who came on to the yacht without firearms have managed to grab the gun and turn it against its owner. If you are unlucky enough to be boarded by any but the worst of desperadoes, give them what they want. It's bad for a man's ego, I know, and it sets a poor precedent, but if you submit there is every likelihood that you will still be alive to get on with your life in the morning.

The mistake

A nervous person with a gun can be a serious danger to others who may mean him no harm. I have been boarded by villainous-looking characters whose language I did not speak and felt serious concern, only to be clapped on the back and handed a pair of lobsters. If I'd had a gun at the time and had been feeling gung-ho, I dread to think of the orphaned children I might have left in my panic-stricken wake.

21 FOOD AND WATER

Fresh water

Many of today's sailors take a lot of bottled water on passages. Whether you do or not, a generous supply of water in bottles outside of the tanks is a sensible precaution. Tanks have been known to let us down through leaks, contamination or just from being drunk dry. If a water maker malfunctions it may dish up half-salty, undrinkable water, so it's vital to be covered. Obviously, if it comes to keeping up your liquid content entirely from bottles you won't be living on the generous supply you'd like, but you won't die or be reduced to drinking beer and whisky all day.

Planning

In the days when small tanks made water a serious consideration on our boats, my wife and I planned on drinking two pints each per day. We filled a half-gallon can in the morning and that was our 24-hour drinking ration. In her book *The Happy Ship*, which concentrates on such matters and is recommended if you can find a copy, Kitty Hampton says the same.

My present yacht carries so much water I can't believe I ever lived like this, but I did. You may well opt for far more, and no doubt other authorities will demand it, but if ever things get tricky, it may be of comfort to know that two pints per day is absolutely fine for healthy young adults, even in the trade winds.

I might add that it's important to label the half-gallon can. We used a similar one for the day-to-day paraffin in our lamps. One morning after a tough night my wife, half-asleep no doubt, filled the kettle from the paraffin can, boiled it and made the tea. There was no explosion and often I think I am only here as a living manifestation of the mercy of Almighty God.

Whatever you decide as the daily allowance, unless you have a water maker and very accurate dials or, better still, sight gauges, measuring out each day's supply is a good idea.

Quality

Water from the tap is fine to drink in northern Europe, most of North America, Australia and other Western-style countries. In some places it is less reliable. Where there are any doubts, slip in the required amount of water purifying tablets and, as a final backstop, boil it thoroughly before drinking. Watch out for ice bought off the beaten track as well. It is highly doubtful it was frozen down from any source other than the kitchen tap. Even bottled water may be suspect. Many years ago in Brazil, a local TV programme ran a feature on some well-known brands and discovered that one contained a minute, but measurable, quantity of human faeces.

Using sea water
■ Washing up

I'm sometimes horrified watching a non-sailor washing up on a boat. The amount of water consumed is a real shock. If you must have copious supplies of water to feel you are doing the job, the only answer is to install a sea-water pump in the galley and wash up in that. It's not ideal, but it saves the real McCoy and, with plenty of good-quality detergent, you can manage. Also, for rinsing, don't forget the squeezy bottle described in Chapter 14.

■ Showering

The same goes for showering. Although my last boat carried a ton of fresh water, just to be sure we only showered on passage a couple of times a week, following the seamanlike system of wetting down, turning off the spray, soaping all over, then firing it up again to rinse off. That way, a man can shower using well under a gallon of water. In cold weather, such a régime will take care of cleanliness.

To maintain good health, of course, a daily minor strip wash for the tricky bits isn't a bad plan. Once the ambient temperature climbs to reasonable levels, the whole business can often be carried out on the foredeck using a bucket of sea water, perhaps with a cup or two of fresh to rinse the hair. Highly refreshing.

In really heavy weather, baby wipes are great for keeping fresh at no cost to the ship.

■ Cooking

Why shake bought salt into clean fresh water when the yacht is surrounded by brine? When salty water is the order of the day for rice, spuds, pasta and the rest, cut the tank water with 50 per cent sea to save water and salt too.

Planning food for a passage

Contemplating a plan for feeding the troops on a long passage is daunting. The answer to an impending feeling of helplessness is to take one step at a time and to think initially in terms of no more than a single day's food.

Breakfast and lunch

We always have something different for breakfast at sea. It's an important meal, coming as it does after a long night with nothing much else to look forward to. We go with porridge, omelettes stuffed with leftovers, bacon as long as it lasts, our own yoghurt with muesli and so on. My wife cooks drop scones when bread runs low.

Lunch also varies. Sandwiches are the staple, cheese on toast in bad weather, salads made from white cabbage, pulses, pasta etc. The choice is endless and it should always be fun.

Dinner

This is the main event on most boats. As a general proposition, simplicity pays. You may decide to cook a roast for a celebration, but the best day-to-day policy is to keep the main course down to a couple of pans if you can. What sort of things can you always fancy? On my boats, evening meals tend to be staples like curry, chilli, pasta, Chinese stir-fry, stew and other favourites that can be knocked up in one pan. The rice, spuds or whatever fills it out, uses another, and that's dinner. Very good it is too, as a rule.

Now make up one week's menu using these dishes. Next, multiply it by the number of crew and the number of days you expect to be at sea. Now add a further 50 per cent factor in case something goes wrong, go out and buy it all. It's as simple as that.

You might like to feed the crew a proper pudding in the evening. In higher latitudes, the likes of treacle sponge go down very well. Buy puddings in cans and buy canned custard too. It tastes great and is no trouble at all for the cook, who is doing his best in difficult circumstances.

Work the same sums with breakfast and lunch, and you've cracked it. The supermarket trolleys will be lined up at the checkout and you may have to find a van to transport it all back to the ship, but it will disappear in the end, even the backup stores.

Extras

All that's left is to think about what my crew refer to as 'greedies'. These are treats, naughty bars, biscuits and the like, which the night watch might want to rip into when boredom sets in. 'Blotters' to nibble with a sundowner in fair weather are important – crisps, nuts etc. So are 'Sick Bics'. These are simple biscuits (cookies) such as old-fashioned 'Rich Tea'. Most people can stomach one or two of these where a chocolate digestive might have them running for the side to throw up yet again. The seasickness will pass, but in the meantime...

Take lots of sandwich material, and if any of these, such as peanut butter (American citizens only), or Marmite for the Brits, or any other strange national necessary, are going to be unobtainable, buy in bulk before you leave. I cannot imagine a day without Marmite and handing over a spare jar can make you the new best friend of some poor ex-pat with a strong sense of nostalgia.

Bread

My wife always bakes bread on passage. She uses dried yeast and a mix of white flour and stoneground brown wholemeal. She enjoys bashing the dough and we have always found a warm place to help it rise when it's cold on deck. On a modern yacht full of systems, something is always munching away at the batteries and getting warm in the process. One of my yachts had a calorifier under the quarter berth. We ran the engine once a day to charge batteries etc., and that locker was always warm enough to kick-start the yeast.

There's little that boosts morale like the smell of fresh bread. I'd just hand out this warning. Never let the hands get hold of a loaf until it is well cooled down. The only way to cut warm bread is to hack off great doorsteps and your lovely loaf won't last a watch if you let them near it. Home-made bread is often good and dense. Once cool, it can be sliced lovely and thin so it keeps going until the next baking day.

Keeping food fresh

It's great having a big freezer, but not everyone does, and if you rely on one you may end up disappointed. Some of the best free meals I have ever eaten have come about when a cruising yacht in an anchorage has suffered a fridge meltdown and has to give away the fillet steaks the skipper has brought all the way from Timbuktu.

It's hard, but the best thing is to plan your food on the assumption that the freezer will pack up. If it doesn't, that will be a happy conclusion.

Before refrigeration, everyone used cans for meat and for many vegetables too. None of us use cans much in our homes these days, but they are still there on the shelves, so go and check them out. Try them before you leave, because some brands of steak make fabulous stews and curries, while others are a tin of weak gravy with chunks of gristle floating around in it. Don't buy on price. It rarely pays. I have suffered horribly on ships whose owners saved a few pounds on victuals and spent fortunes on radio equipment, demonstrating an odd sense of priorities.

Hard vegetables such as cabbages (take leaves off the outside, don't cut) and squashes keep pretty well on the whole, especially if they are slung in netting. Not everyone likes this. My pal Rod Heikell hates it and packs his carefully in plastic containers with plenty of air circulating. Air is the general answer. That, and not too much light.

Don't take the outer skins off onions until you get to the tropics. They keep better with them on. Potatoes should come in a sack with the earth on them. Avoid the clinically clean ones from supermarkets. Green tomatoes last well, as do green bananas. The trouble with the hand of bananas, by which we are all tempted in tropical islands, is that you can't eat them for ages, then suddenly one day they all ripen at once and there's a glut. Still, they look good and as long as they have been checked for cockroaches, they make an amusing diversion.

Eggs should, wherever possible, be bought straight from the hen. A fresh egg keeps an amazingly long time. A couple of months is common. If you are really up

CANS

One final word on cans: In the days of wooden ships and iron men, we used to remove the labels because they always ended up soaking wet and falling off anyway. They would then clog the bilge pumps and be a general nuisance. An unlabelled can, of course, is a passport to a cornucopia of surprise meals, so the lids were labelled with a permanent marker clarifying what the contents might be. 'Mush' stood for mushrooms, 'Rat' for ratatouille, and so on. Since cans are usually stored on end and packed in tightly, it pays to keep up the tradition even if you aren't planning for an inundation in the food locker because, with labels, you can find at a glance the one you seek.

against it for a long passage, roll them in Vaseline when they are still warm from the chicken and they will keep for ages, but it helps to turn them frequently.

If your departure port is in a civilised neighbourhood, load up on vacuum-packed bacon and other meats. A decent butcher will often do this for you if you ask nicely, and it lasts for so much longer, even without refrigeration.

Hard cheese will keep, especially if vacuum packed or, better still, encased in a wax cocoon. Have nothing to do with tempting soft cheese on passage. I have known Camemberts served up to hungry men, which had all hands staggering from the festive board clutching their foreheads, save only the late Robert St John Riddle. And really, there was nothing I ever saw that beat that mighty warrior of the trencher.

Grow your own

On one long voyage, my wife and I fell into the way of making our own yoghurt. We started by buying a pot of natural live yoghurt, popped some of it into a thermos flask and topped it up with milk. In due course, the milk turned in a nice sort of way, the deed was done and we had yoghurt for ever more for the price of some old UHT milk. It was delicious and that culture just kept on trucking.

We never went so far as to grow mung beans or cress, but I've met folks who do. I don't suppose it makes much difference to the ship's economy, but it's fun if you're far from home and are missing the vegetable patch. What we still do is grow herbs in containers, trying to remember to take them below at sea. Little saps morale so much as the carefully nurtured basil being washed out.

Use all leftovers

Because food is a finite resource on board, much can be saved by developing a culture of using leftovers. Some of the breakfasts served on my boats have been interesting, to say the least. Instead of a frugal bowl of health-giving muesli, the lads have been served curry omelette with cucumber raita on the side, followed by toast (home-made bread getting near the end of its tether) and

> **5-DAY STEW**
>
> In really heavy weather, resurrect the five-day stew. Eat what you can, leave the pan on the go and top it up from another can of steak, beans, a chopped onion, or whatever else you can find and fancy. This speciality dish of the sea has the benefit for the gourmet of never being the same twice!

marmalade. You can't beat it. Spanish omelettes go down well too, and anything can be stirred into those.

Midnight feasts for the watch on whatever's left from dinner are so much better than chucking it to the fishes. Don't wash the pans. Leave them for morning and let the nodding denizens of the graveyard watch fortify themselves instead.

Beware of the pests

Cockroaches

There's no wretchedness in the tropics like a cockroach infestation. A full-on supermarket cockroach from latitude 15°N can have a body length equal to the average man's thumb, with antennae stretching this out by a further 200 per cent. Boat 'roaches rarely achieve such noble proportions, but even a modest specimen can run to well over an inch.

Unless ruthless vigilance and a zero tolerance policy are adopted, they will take over your life. It isn't squeamish to find it disturbing when a platoon of cockroaches attempt to board your soup bowl as you dine aboard an infested yacht. You might be discreetly flicking them on to the cabin sole when the skipper finally joins you from his galley. Expecting him to wave some sort of wand that will put an end to this horror, you are dumbfounded when he ignores the livestock and digs into his meal as though only you and he were present. That's what happens to people. They accept defeat. All I can say is: Remember Churchill!

Unlike the rat, there seems little hard evidence that the cockroach does mankind serious harm, yet there is something primevally repugnant about the beast.

They have a good life on board. Judging from their population growth rate they enjoy regular sex, yet politically they are so far to the left that Karl Marx would have envied their devotion to the cause. Setting their personal value at nothing, they think only of the good of the community, which doesn't include you, by the way. Individually, they have an underdeveloped sense of survival, submitting meekly to the size 12 deck shoe in the certain knowledge that, collectively, they will have the last laugh. Because many people living in infested yachts choose apathy over fumigation, the creatures end up being so well tolerated that one wonders who the yacht is really being run for.

The answer to avoiding life membership of the Cockroach Cruising Club is simple: Keep them out.

Cockroaches board us by three main methods: stealth, infiltration and direct assault. They can be found almost anywhere, but they love downtown supermarkets, home-grown vegetables, pre-packed foodstuffs (I once caught two mature samples coupling inside a

TO DEAL WITH MOST ENEMY INFILTRATORS:

- Load up on quality bug spray.
- All packaging material from shopping expeditions is best kept on deck while the produce is transferred to your own containers.
- Cardboard boxes should be returned to the shore as soon as possible. Use your own containers for dry goods.

- Each and every fruit or vegetable must be inspected, washed on deck where appropriate and kept in string bags.
- Books from any source at all should be treated as suspect, spraying insecticide inside their spines to neutralize eggs sown like tiny land mines.

sealed cereal packet) and the spines of books swapped from infested yachts. Best of all, they enjoy the underside of old wooden docks.

The stealth boarder can arrive on our own clothes from pestilential yachts. After a jolly evening carousing with the neighbours while dodging the scuttling forces of darkness, be sure to strip off on deck when you return to your boat, shake out your gear, then slosh the planking with lots of water, just in case. You'll have swatted any big hitchhikers before you leave the party, of course, but it's easy to miss a lively youngster or two in the dark. And remember, two is all it takes...

The direct assault brigade either march up the dock lines or they fly aboard. Never, therefore, anchor close to leeward of a yacht you know to carry a full complement, and don't lie alongside a dock overnight in the tropics unless you are truly confident of your berth.

The final advice in this war zone briefing is that, like all warriors, we must turn our backs on our civilised dislike of taking life. Killing a big cockroach eye-to-eye in unarmed combat is unpleasant because, when you tread on one, it makes a noise like crushing a matchbox and they are fat enough to leave a nasty mess. Banging one with your fist demands a high level of moral fibre, but you can at least be reassured that they don't mind dying. Their race has remained unchanged since the time of the dinosaurs and they can live through nuclear fallout. As their personal lights go out, your victims know their offspring will be around long after we have either blown ourselves to glory or been traded in by evolution for a newer, racier model. So don't feel bad.

Don't let them on board in the first place and if ever you see one in your saloon, it is immediately your number one priority. Hunt it to the death before you do anything else at all.

Weevils

Time was when the only places you expected bugs in the dry goods were deep in the tropics. You could always be confident of anything bought in a higher-latitude shop. Well, not any more! I've copped a family in a pack of spaghetti from an upmarket superstore in an English country town. Their offspring had punched their way out of a neighbouring pack and established a bridgehead in the boat's flour, the pasta shells and, for all anyone knew, the ship's biscuits as well.

If they're in the rice – a common favourite – wait till you're going to cook it, then dump it into a flat dish of cold water. The weevils float up and you can scoop them off, but you must be quick. Once they drown, they sink again and you've missed your chance!

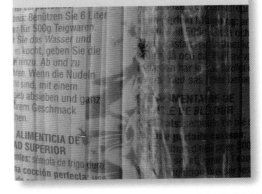

WEEVILS

Unwrap all dry goods when you're stocking for a long trip, take a peep, then stow them in sealed containers. That way, if you do get unlucky, at least the damage will be limited.

Winter in a foreign yard. Note the rat guard on the stern line.

Rats

Rats are everywhere. I've had them scuttling round my decks in the snow in New York City and I've beaten them off with a winch handle in Portugal. If they're around, it's best not to go alongside. If you must, try to lie off the berth and rig rat guards on your lines. A gallon plastic container with a hole in and the top cut off will do. Set the guards open-side to the shore and the little horrors can't get over them. It sounds crude, but it worked for me.

Booze

Booze is totally subjective. Some won't have it on board, like the US Navy. Others follow the lead of the Royal Navy in the days before electronics finally brought a noble tradition to its knees, and start every day with a tot of rum that would stun a horse. Most of us fall somewhere between these extremes.

Common sense dictates where and when we stock up the drinks locker, but it certainly pays to look around. In the West Indies, for example, the poor sailor can satisfy a thirst readily with rum, which is available everywhere at remarkably popular prices. Wine, on the other hand, frequently disappoints. I would advise the tropical sailor to buy wine only in screw-top bottles as corks so often infect the contents. I once purchased two fine-looking bottles of claret in St Kitts for my Christmas dinner. As it happened, it was blowing so hard on Christmas Day that rowing ashore in my 10ft stem dinghy was not an option, so we settled down to enjoy the vintages. Both were corked beyond drinkability so we were obliged to drink rum with our suckling pig. Tough, eh?

As for the issue of drinking at sea, I would say this: I don't like hard and fast rules on boats because the ocean so often throws up a wild card that makes nonsense of all our ideas. The idea of being tipsy on passage is, to me, unthinkable, but I have a strong head for liquor and so, on a lovely evening with the boat dipping along sweetly and supper simmering on the hob, my shipmates and I will gather in the cockpit and share a beer or a whisky as the sun elongates from a ball into a hot-air balloon and finally sinks from sight. It's a magic moment. For me, a drink makes it even more memorable, but we all must make our own peace with this one.

Fishing

Nobody can bank on it, but in certain latitudes, fishing on passage can supply a bountiful extra source of fresh food as well as being a lot of fun.

The trade-wind belts abound in flying fish. These will come aboard at night and many's the morning the scuppers will be studded with finned aviators whose luck ran out during the hours of darkness. Boarders are usually relatively small, and small flying fish are a washout on the breakfast table. They are all bones. A skilled person with a sharp knife can fillet the larger ones that come in at the tonnage of a moderate mackerel, but it isn't easy, so this source of free food doesn't usually come up to scratch. However, flying fish are a crucial link in the ocean food chain. They are lunch and dinner too for big pelagic predators such as dorado (called 'dolphin' by sailors of old), wahoo, sailfish, tuna and the rest. In the right mood, these guys will take just about any lure you drag in front of them, so where there are flying fish, there is food for the sailor who takes the trouble to hook it.

Close inshore, some reef fish, or predators who have been eating them, are poisonous. It pays to ask locally about this, but out at sea anything that bites is edible, and usually delicious.

Victualling via your own hunt satisfies a primitive need and saves a lot of money.

Fishing tackle

This can be as fancy as you care to make it. I have done very well using an old wooden frame with a hundred yards of heavy shark line wound up on it. The end of this is knotted to a swivel on to which is secured 10ft or so of piano wire with a swivel and a serious cod hook on the end of that. The lure would be a length of colourful teased-out rope, perhaps with a bit of an old baked bean tin lid worked into it to catch the sun. Even better lures can be bought almost anywhere in the form of rubber squid-like creations with goggly eyes. This setup is simply trailed in the wake of the boat until a fish hits it.

The shock of the strike can be ameliorated by making a loop in the line near the cleat, and holding this in place with a length of motorcycle inner tube knotted across it. When a fish hits, the rubber stretches out, helping the hook to set without too much violence and advising the watch on deck that action is taking place. There's no sport in what follows. The line is plenty strong enough, so all you do is haul the fish in hand over hand. If it's huge you may lose it, but with gear like this you are unlikely to hook any monsters of the deep.

A gaff hook may help to lift your victims on board, but the hook generally holds well enough. Once landed, a bash on the head with a winch handle often suffices to stun the fish.

Other boats often carry highly sophisticated fishing gear with rods and expensive variable-drag reels. Anyone setting out on this route will take advice from fishermen of experience, so I have nothing extra to offer. Certainly, the rattle of a reel with some drag on alerts the crew to a bite more effectively than the silent but deadly inner tube and, with lighter line, more excitement can be had playing the catch. I have sailed on boats with such serious kit that we have hooked six-foot marlin, then let them go, of course. Butchering so beautiful a creature would be beyond me, but I have no problem slicing up a two-foot tuna for fillets or steaks. One pal of mine had a freezer permanently stuffed with fish and rarely ate anything else.

COMPUTERS, THE INTERNET AND RADIO COMMUNICATION

Computers

There will always be free spirits who will not have computers on their yachts. I admire this and wish them well. For most of us, the on-board computer is now a fact of life. It has revolutionised many things. The same small box takes care of much of our navigation, entertainment and communication, while among its other varied attributes it is a primary source of weather information. So pivotal to our safety and happiness has it become that even those of us who have seen it arrive from nothing find ourselves asking: What did we ever do without it? The truth is that we managed very well, but nobody can argue with the proposition that things were a whole lot less convenient.

Computers and the whole subject of IT are moving on so rapidly that anything written here will be out of date by the time the book goes to press, so I will stick to making general points for consideration.

PC or Mac?

Back in the shady past of the cyber world there was little doubt that, despite the groans of the Macintosh aficionados, the PC was the way to go. The reason for this was that just about every reputable navigation program used a PC platform. That has moved on. Now, as in life generally, you can 'pay your money and take your choice'. Whichever you opt for, make sure the chosen unit can run all the applications you might ever want.

Inbuilt computer or laptop?
■ **Inbuilt**

The benefits of an inbuilt computer are power and security, in that it is tucked away somewhere safe and dry so it can't tumble off the chart table. Its only enemy in this respect is creeping damp, and a proper marine unit should be proof against this common menace. An inbuilt computer can also have a bank of USB ports to plug in a DVD player for installing software and watching movies on a remote screen, for hooking up to a GPS dongle, a phone and a hundred other useful items. It will also feature a proper keyboard and a mouse. Roll-away keyboards are great and use no space at all.

The downsides are that they are relatively expensive, you can't pop them in a briefcase and take them to the cyber café, and they will, in time, become outdated and require replacement. The middle objection is usually spurious because most people who now have an inbuilt computer also ship a laptop and probably a tablet as well.

■ Laptop

Surprisingly cheap, a laptop can be pensioned off when it becomes last year's technology, perhaps to become a dedicated navigation unit. Modern hard drives are more than big enough for all you could ask, the keyboards aren't bad and a neat little USB mouse costs pennies. My laptop lives on the chart table where it runs a software raster-chart plotter from Meridian. It handles weather, comms and the rest when I can arrange a wi-fi connection. When I want to watch a movie, I put the unit on the saloon table, but I could connect it to a big screen if I was so inclined. I am not, because I don't like screens staring at me when I'm not watching them and I sold the one on my main bulkhead as soon as I bought my yacht. I replaced it with an original oil painting.

The main downside of a laptop is always said to be vulnerability to soakings, general damp or going flying. I can see that this is a strong argument, but speaking as I find, I have been running one for fifteen years with no special arrangements and without mishap. If things get seriously active I do occasionally tuck it away somewhere safe, just as I do my sextant. Were I unwise enough to deploy it during a 180 degree knockdown and it zoomed past my ear, I suspect that, unless it cracked my skull as it went on its way, its loss would be the least of my problems.

Both forms of computer draw power, either by an inverter or directly from the batteries. In either case, the draw is not big enough to weigh heavily in the balance of which route one takes.

Navigating by computer

This is dealt with in depth in Chapter 9. As for the hardware, navigation programs, even relatively sophisticated ones, don't ask much of today's computers, which are well capable of running modern games. Any halfway reasonable unit will do the job. If you favour the laptop approach, there's a lot going for the idea of using an old one, with its hard drive wiped clean of all superfluous material, for running the navigation. It will cope easily and can serve as a backup for the main unit that runs everything else. With modest second-hand PCs changing hands for £200, you might even consider carrying a third, pre-loading it with the software and packing it away safely, just in case the main navigation takes an unplanned dive to the cabin sole.

Hooking up to the sky

This is the crunch. Until it is hooked up to the internet, a computer is severely limited. It can manage navigation and movies, but to use email, weather forecasting and all the rest of the wonders of the cyber world, we must somehow connect with the main body of humanity. The options vary in direct proportion to financial resources. It is fervently to be hoped that this situation will ease, but at present it remains a major issue.

Shore-based internet

■ Wi-fi

For many, this is still the only realistic answer. It's relatively cheap if not free, but it's a nuisance having to paddle ashore to find a cyber café. Some marinas purport to offer wi-fi to their customers. Occasionally this works, but in my experience it is rarely much use. Cyber cafés have served me well in many parts of the world. If we take our own laptops or tablets, we are usually safe enough from internet crime.

Wi-fi booster aerials

Wi-fi booster aerials that hook up to the laptop via an ethernet cable can be purchased for all sorts of prices and deliver a wide variety of results. They can be portable, 'stick-on-when-in-use' USB-connected units bought for less than the price of a decent meal out, or permanently mounted, high-end antennae, but they all rely on a shore-based signal in the end. Only satellite communication or SSB can deliver a true offshore connection.

■ Mobile (cell) phone-based hookups

These, of course, depend entirely on finding a reliable mobile phone network. The task can be a tough one in the UK, notably in Scotland, but improving nets throughout much of the civilised world mean that 4G and 5G signals are now readily available, at least when secure alongside or in an anchorage. I recall sailing into the mighty fjord of Scoresby Sound in northeast Greenland and being delighted to find four bars on my phone with only an Inuit settlement between me and the North Pole. One cannot say the same for a berth in some Solent marinas.

Smartphone hot spot

With decent reception at 4G-plus levels, a smartphone can create a wireless or bluetooth hotspot for the boat to which tablets or other equipment can connect. This works well, especially if you have an advantageous contract. Without one, the SIM may be subject to ruinous roaming charges for data. The usual trick of buying a pay-as-you-go SIM dedicated to a particular country can make a big difference.

Mi-fi routers

These are a sort of super-dongle that work like a mobile phone. They can be remarkably powerful at a sensibly low cost. Cheaper ones operate inside the boat, so the antenna is low down for reception purposes, but for £200 or so one can acquire a quality weatherproof unit with a far more serious antennae that will out-perform a phone, with download speeds good enough to stream movies.

VHF is a must, but many of today's sailors demand more.

Comms – an ever-expanding world.

Deep-sea computer hookups and radio communication

VHF

Although VHF with its line-of-sight limitations may seem almost irrelevant to oceanic communications, it remains the unique ship-to-ship tool of contact. If you want or need to speak to a ship, this is what you will use, attracting attention either via DSC or Channel 16.

SSB vs satphone

High-frequency Single Side-Band radio (SSB) was, until the second decade of the millennium, the only realistically available communication stream for most deep-water cruisers. Falling costs and rising technology are making inroads into this with improving satellite communications. Satphones are relatively easy to set up, require no special user licence and the hardware can be (depending on how much data you expect to pass) relatively inexpensive. SSB costs more to install and needs more technology in the way of antennae. It demands more from its operator and, if it is to drive emails and weather data, must be backed up with a Pactor 4 modem (cost not far short of £1,000). Once up and running, it offers much that the satphone cannot give.

■ The bottom line

Satphones seem to be favoured by sailors on relatively short sabbaticals, rally participants, and so on. A number of satellite systems are currently available with Iridium as a front runner. SSB is not dead or even moribund. It is robustly alive and remains the favoured option for most free-ranging long-term cruisers. As noted, more, better and cheaper satcom will no doubt come on stream, as this is an area of rapidly improving technology. I therefore make no attempt to predict the future or even to cover all available options.

SSB

PLUS POINTS OF SSB
- Long-range distress broadcasting to all ships and shore stations
- Short emails, position reports etc. can be sent with no online charges
- GRIB weather forecasts, weather reports and weather faxes can be received worldwide
- Can be used for joining and participating in broadcast 'nets' set up between cruising boats to share information, gossip, calls for technical assistance and much more
- Scheduled communications with buddy boats

DOWNSIDES OF SSB
- The cost and hassle of assembling the kit, which must have at least a whip aerial or insulated backstay and a ground plate. This must be well installed if reception and transmissions are to be fully effective. No compromise can be accepted.
- User must qualify for a long-range radio certificate, although at the time of writing, this consists of a lifetime restricted radiotelephone operator's permit (VHF DSC) and a ship's radio licence for the SSB, which lasts ten years. This is not to be confused with a ham radio licence, which is rigorously tested.

SATPHONES

PLUS POINTS OF SATPHONES
- Simple installation via 12V charging units and USB connection to laptop
- Relatively inexpensive hardware, but by no means cheap. You will be well served by investing in an external antenna
- As easy to use as a mobile phone
- Short emails, position reports etc. can be sent with no online charges
- GRIB weather forecasts, weather reports and weather faxes can be received worldwide
- Private phone calls worldwide

DOWNSIDES OF SATPHONES
- Can be even slower than SSB for emailing etc.
- All internet time must be paid for either by contract or off-contract payments
- No cruiser net availability, so if you enjoy feeling you are part of a community, this will cut you off
- Faster, more powerful internet connections are available with large dish or dome antennae, but these are a lot more money (can be in excess of £3,000)

Whatever your choice, as with everything to do with self-sufficiency on deep water, it is best if you can manage to install the comms hardware personally, then you will know what course to take in the event of difficulties. Perhaps understandably, many people are disinclined to spend the time to acquire the necessary expertise, but fortunately, specialists exist whose working lives are dedicated to solving installation problems.

The last word on basic internet communication should go to SailMail, a non-profit organisation who, for modest money, will make email and basic GRIB data etc. work for you with your existing kit, be it SSB or satellite. If you are starting from scratch, their comprehensive internet site helps you decide what to buy for your needs and your budget. They can be found via any search engine and many of my friends have used this service with contentment.

CONCLUSION

Joshua Slocum once remarked that the sea is meant for sailing on. How right he was and what a simple world he cruised in. Looking through the pages of this book brings home to me how technical ocean sailing has become. If we aren't careful, maintaining our ever-growing list of systems can take over half our lives, while communicating electronically with others soaks up the rest of the day. On the basic old boats that were my nursery, the biggest jobs at sea were working up the noon position and planning a set of evening star sights. This left long periods with little to do but interact with shipmates, read worthwhile books, stare at the ocean, consider the sky and think. My log books from this period make far better reading than the ones I produce today, probably because my life was so uncluttered.

I think the message is that while few of us are going to turn our backs on the gear which can make our lives easier, we should concentrate on keeping it to a minimum. Less gear, less potential for trouble. Less trouble, more fun.

If you haven't yet crossed an ocean, you'll discover that, for the first half of a passage, your thoughts turn towards the lands left astern, friends you've made and difficulties you have overcome. Somewhere around halfway, your mental screen will start projecting images of the places where you are bound. The past fades and you find yourself suspended in a world of your own where what has been is gone away, and what's to come remains unsure. Shut down the radio and the timelessness of it all becomes acute. You are living in the moment and have become the person you really are. Landsmen find this hard to comprehend, but once you've been out there and done it, you'll know, and you'll never be quite the same again.

All that remains for us is to leave a clean wake in the lands we visit on our voyages. We can't turn back the years to when a cruising yacht was a rarity in the ports and anchorages of the world, but we can sail thoughtfully so that, even as our numbers increase, we sailors still make our planet a better place.

INDEX